Wordsworth
and
the Zen Mind

John G. Rudy

Wordsworth
and
the Zen Mind

The
Poetry of Self-Emptying

STATE UNIVERSITY OF NEW YORK PRESS

Production by Ruth Fisher
Marketing by Nancy Farrell

Published by
State University of New York Press, Albany

© 1996 State University of New York

For information, address the State University of New York Press,
State University Plaza, Albany, NY 11246

Library of Congress Cataloging-in-Publication Data

Rudy, John G., 1943–
    Wordsworth and the Zen mind : the poetry of self-emptying / John
G. Rudy.
        p. cm.
    Includes bibliographical references and index.
    ISBN 0-7914-2903-2 (CH : alk. paper). — ISBN 0-7914-2904-0 (pbk.
: alk. paper)
        1. Wordsworth, William, 1770–1850—Philosophy. 2. Self
(Philosophy) in literature. 3. Spiritual life in literature.
4. Zen Buddhism in literature. I. Title.
PR5892.P5R83 1996
821'.7—dc20   95-19528
                                                                      CIP

To
Maria, Elena, and Daniel

CONTENTS

FOREWORD

The great Whiteheadian scholar, a former teacher of mine at Chicago, Charles Hartshorne, once casually remarked, "I was a Buddhist before I knew it." Such a remarkable statement echoes through the minds of many insightful thinkers of the West, including William Wordsworth. Wordsworth had that rare and keen vision which penetrated the ordinary perception of things. The central thrust of his poetic vision was to realize the universal grounds of existence, always open and intimate, but grounds human beings, unfortunately, tend to obstruct and occlude by their inadequate perception. He lived in the midst of the industrial revolution and disdained London for all it represented: human existence reduced to mere mechanical tasteless endeavors. By contrast, he sought peace and solace in the wide open country by taking trips to the hinterlands and abroad.

In this delightful work, John Rudy has focused on Wordsworth's synoptic perception which he feels is closest to Zen-experience. He has rendered us a service by removing the many obstacles that seemingly plague East-West treatment of the metaphysical and cosmological nature of experiential reality. Accounts by the Asian masters reveal that Zen-experience is very plain and simple. No lofty peaks to scale, no abstract elements to contend with, no phenomenal layers of experience to peel off. The keys are thoroughgoing naturalism and everyday-mindedness. Rudy captures well this spirit of Zen in Wordsworth and strikes the notes of harmony. He maintains the inviolable bond of man and nature as graphically illustrated, for example, in the Hua-yen (Avatamsaka) philosophy of mutual identity and mutual penetration. Popularly rendered, this refers to "all is one, one is all" (identity) and "all in one, one in all" (penetration). This is by far the clearest expression of the interrelated nature of things to which ecologists are attuned. It is the basis on which the Asian mind deftly dealt with the paradoxes in everyday living or activity where, for example, the simple and the complex do not clash but fuse together and define each other in the process. Indeed, in Zen-experience, simplicity is complexity and complexity is simplicity. Such a paradoxical statement can easily be traced back to the early Mahāyāna "wisdom sutras" (prajñāpāramitā) where they profoundly assert: "form (rūpa) is emptiness (śūnyatā) and the very emptiness is form."

Japanese Zen nourished the samurai's quest for mental and spiritual tranquillity but it also contributed, more importantly, toward the making of a unique ethos undergirded by exquisite aesthetic qualities, such as *sabi, wabi, aware,* and *yugen.* Rudy brings these qualities to bear upon Wordsworth's lifelong poetic engagement, thus enticing East-West dialogue to a finer point. Proponents on both sides will now have a most intimate and direct form of discourse in deep and dynamic spirituality.

Kenneth K. Inada
Distinguished Service Professor
State University of New York at Buffalo

PREFACE

This study has a twofold purpose. It seeks to provide a Zen context for understanding the spirituality of the English poet William Wordsworth (1770–1850) and attempts to enrich the East-West dialogue as it has been unfolding since the pioneering work of D. T. Suzuki and Kitarō Nishida. Combining methods of modern literary scholarship with the philosophical initiatives of the Kyoto School, this effort crosses disciplines as well as cultures, requiring that I write to several audiences and in a way that makes modest assumptions about the knowledge of my readers. In deference to the general reader, therefore, I have chosen to avoid the idiom of poststructuralist literary analysis while retaining the contemporary critical emphasis on close textual examination. Similarly, my philosophical discourse, in deference to readers unfamiliar with Buddhism, progresses from introductory-level discussions of Zen thought and art in the early chapters to the more technical idiom of the Kyoto School in the later portions of the study.

As for the structure of this effort, I have attempted to incorporate the dialogical paradigm of the East-West conversation by inverting the rhetorical procedures of the earlier and later sections of the study. Whereas parts 1 and 2 bring Zen thought and art to Wordsworth in order to elucidate his spirituality, part 3 explores and affirms the universality of his spiritual insight and experience by applying his work to the Buddhist context, specifically to illuminate the dominant moods of Zen. If Wordsworth is to take his place as the world-class poet he celebrates in his famous Preface to *Lyrical Ballads* (1800), a figure whom he conceives as binding "together by passion and knowledge the vast empire of human society, as it is spread over the whole earth, and over all time," his work must be understood not only in terms of how it benefits from the application of other cultures but also in terms of what it contributes to those cultures.

The extent to which I have broken new ground in understanding Wordsworth's spirituality, however, would be obscured were I unwilling to discuss the limitations of the extant scholarship on his poetry. On the few occasions when I have undertaken to comment on studies of Wordsworth, I have endeavored to avoid a critique of Western literary scholarship and the philosophical principles on which it is based, preferring instead to adumbrate lines of demarcation that provide opportunities for alternative rather than contending interpretive visions. So far as my critical efforts reflect the inclusiveness of Wordsworth's spirituality, my study will, I hope, contribute to the growing community of intercultural and interreligious communication now occurring on a global scale.

ACKNOWLEDGMENTS

The initial research for this study was made possible by a Faculty Fellowship from Indiana University Kokomo in the summer of 1991. I thank Stuart Green, Dean of the Division of Arts and Sciences at Indiana University Kokomo, for supporting my application for that grant.

I wish to express my deepest gratitude to Masao Abe, present patriarch of the Kyoto School, for his interest in my work; to Donald Mitchell, Professor of Philosophy at Purdue University and author of *Spirituality and Emptiness*, for directing a significant portion of my reading in the East-West dialogue and for offering important suggestions for revising the manuscript; to Kenneth K. Inada, Distinguished Service Professor at State University of New York Buffalo, for undertaking to read and comment on this study; and to my wife, Maria, for her help in proofreading.

I thank the editors of Fordham University Press for permission to employ in chapter 3 portions of my essay "Wordsworth and the Zen Void," which appeared in *Thought: A Review of Culture and Idea* 65 (1990): 127–42. I am grateful, as well, to the following publishers and authors for permission to use quotations from copyrighted works: "Destruction" and "Shell" by Shinkichi Takahashi, from *Triumph of the Sparrow: Zen Poems of Shinkichi Takahashi*, trans. Lucien Stryk and Takashi Ikemoto, copyright © 1986 by the Board of Trustees of the University of Illinois, reprinted by permission of the University of Illinois Press; "Devoid of all thought" by Chao-pien, from *Living Zen* by Robert Linssen, trans. Diana Abrahams-Curiel, copyright ©1958 by George Allen & Unwin Ltd., reprinted by permission of Grove/Atlantic, Inc.; *An Inquiry into the Good* by Kitarō Nishida, trans. Masao Abe and Christopher Ives, copyright © 1990 by Yale

University, reprinted by permission of Yale University Press; *Manual of Zen Buddhism* by Daisetz Teitaro Suzuki, copyright ©1960 by Grove Press, Inc., reprinted by permission of Grove/Atlantic, Inc.; "Nightingale's song" by Issa, from *The Penguin Book of Zen Poetry*, ed. and trans. Lucien Stryk and Takashi Ikemoto, copyright © 1977 by Lucien Stryk and Takashi Ikemoto, reprinted by permission of Lucien Stryk; "November 3rd" by Miyazawa Kenji, trans. Hiroaki Sato and Burton Watson, from *From the Country of the Eight Islands: An Anthology of Japanese Poetry*, copyright © 1981 by Hiroaki Sato and Burton Watson, reprinted by permission of Doubleday, A Division of Bantam, Doubleday, Dell Publishing Group; *Paradise Lost* by John Milton, reprinted with the permission of Simon & Schuster from the Macmillan College text *Complete Poems and Major Prose* by John Milton, edited by Merritt Y. Hughes, copyright © 1985 by Macmillan Publishing Company, Inc.; *The Poetical Works of William Wordsworth*, 2d ed., 5 vols., ed. Ernest de Selincourt and Helen Darbishire, copyright © 1952–59 by Oxford University Press, reprinted by permission of Oxford University Press; *The Poetry of Enlightenment: Poems by Ancient Ch'an Masters*, trans. and ed. Master Sheng-yen, copyright © 1987 by Dharma Drum Publications, reprinted by permission of Dharma Drum Publications; *Religion and Nothingness* by Keiji Nishitani, trans. Jan Van Bragt, copyright © 1982 by Keiji Nishitani, reprinted by permission of The University of California Press; "The Ruined Cottage," MS.D, reprinted from *William Wordsworth: The Ruined Cottage and The Pedlar*, ed. James Butler, copyright © 1978 by Cornell University, used by permission of the publisher, Cornell University Press; "The stream hides itself" and "Leaves falling," from *The Way of Zen* by Alan W. Watts, copyright © 1957 by Pantheon Books, Inc., reprinted by permission of Pantheon Books, a division of Random House, Inc.; *Tao Te Ching* by Lao Tzu, trans. Stephen Addiss and Stanley Lombardo, copyright © 1993 by Hackett Publishing Company, Inc., reprinted by permission of the Hackett Publishing Company, Inc.; "There's something bottomless" by Kitarō Nishida, reprinted by permission of the publisher from *The Still Point: Reflections on Zen and Christian Mysticism* by William Johnston (New York: Fordham University Press), copyright © 1970, 1989; "This slowly drifting cloud is pitiful" by Dogen, from *Encounter with Zen: Writings on Poetry and Zen* by Lucien Stryk, reprinted by permission of The Ohio University Press/Swallow Press, Athens;

poems of Hyobong and Kusan Sunim, from *The Way of Korean Zen* by Kusan Sunim, trans. Martine Fages, ed. Stephen Batchelor, copyright © 1985 by Songgwang Sa Monastery, reprinted by permission of Weatherhill, Inc.; *Zen Comments on the* Mumonkan by Zenkei Shibayama, English language translation copyright © 1974 by Zenkei Shibayama, reprinted by permission of HarperCollins Publishers, Inc.; poems of Dabei, Etsuzan, Bunan, and Honei, from *Zen Poems of China and Japan: The Crane's Bill*, trans. and comp. Lucien Stryk and Takashi Ikemoto, copyright © 1973 by Lucien Stryk, Takashi Ikemoto, and Taigan Takayama, reprinted by permission of Grove/Atlantic, Inc.; poems of Bunan, Daito, Jakushitsu, Manan, Saisho, and Yomyo-Enju, from *Zen: Poems, Prayers, Sermons, Anecdotes, Interviews*, trans. Lucien Stryk and Takashi Ikemoto, copyright © 1963, 1965, 1981 by Lucien Stryk, reprinted by permission of The Ohio University Press/Swallow Press, Athens; poems of Bashō, Chiyo-ni, and Hsiang-yen, from *A Zen Wave: Bashō's Haiku and Zen* by Robert Aitken, copyright © 1978 by John Weatherhill, Inc., reprinted by permission of Weatherhill, Inc.

INTRODUCTION:
THE PURER MIND

I n his Prospectus to *The Recluse* (1814), the work which announces that the chief aim of his poetry is to examine and to celebrate the mind, William Wordsworth writes:

> Not Chaos, not
> The darkest pit of lowest Erebus,
> Nor aught of blinder vacancy, scooped out
> By help of dreams—can breed such fear and awe
> As fall upon us often when we look
> Into our Minds, into the Mind of Man—
> My haunt, and the main region of my song. (35–41)[1]

Though it emerges as a potential nightmare realm, the mind appears here as a distinctively human phenomenon accessible to the poetic self committed to exploring it.

In poignant contrast to the image of mind depicted in the Prospectus is that which the poet offers in his "Lines Composed a Few Miles above Tintern Abbey" (*PW* 2: 259-63), which he wrote and published in 1798. Describing a moment of deep repose along the banks of the Wye, Wordsworth tells of how he owes to the "beauteous forms" of the harmonious landscape, which includes cottages, orchards, and hedgerows as well as such naturally occurring phenomena as woods, sky, and cliffs,

> sensations sweet,
> Felt in the blood, and felt along the heart;
> And passing even into my purer mind,
> With tranquil restoration. . . . (27–30)

1

Wordsworth does not explain what he means by "my purer mind," and he makes no effort to adumbrate its dimensions. He speaks only of its receiving sensations of the "beauteous forms" of the surrounding environment and of his own subsequent restoration in tranquillity. After mentioning how the "unremembered pleasure" of such experiences contributes to "a good man's life . . . acts / Of kindness and of love" (33–35), he returns to the theme of what he owes to the forms of things, proclaiming finally the emergence of a

> blessed mood
> In which the burthen of the mystery,
> In which the heavy and the weary weight
> Of all this unintelligible world,
> Is lightened:—that serene and blessed mood,
> In which the affections gently lead us on,—
> Until, the breath of this corporeal frame
> And even the motion of our human blood
> Almost suspended, we are laid asleep
> In body, and become a living soul:
> While with an eye made quiet by the power
> Of harmony, and the deep power of joy,
> We see into the life of things. (37–49)

Both the Prospectus to *The Recluse* and the lines from "Tintern Abbey" imply that human consciousness must be understood in relation to a deep and abiding spirituality. But the terms of that spirituality are profoundly different in these works and lead to very different perceptions of what Wordsworth means by his reference to the mind of humankind as the "main region" of his "song." The Prospectus depicts the region of mind as a specific place accessible to our understanding through the application of a clearly discernible cultural idiom. The poet's reference to Chaos and Erebus, for example, recalls Milton's portrayal of the fall of Lucifer in the early books of *Paradise Lost*. Though Wordsworth, earlier in the Prospectus, spoke of passing beyond "Jehovah—with his thunder, and the choir / Of shouting Angels, and the empyreal thrones" (33–34), he nevertheless uses Miltonic imagery and the Judeo-Christian culture it evokes to locate himself in relation to the mind he wishes to explore. The effect is twofold. Firstly, we gather the impression that a journey into mind is a troublesome, possibly a forbidden, undertaking. Secondly, we cannot help but recall Satan's famous claim that "The mind is its own place, and in itself / Can make a Heav'n of Hell, a Hell of Heav'n."[2] The Miltonic references contribute a sense of the mind as a separate realm and suggest, further, that Wordsworth's poetic undertaking is grounded in a culturally rich, dramatic confrontation between human consciousness and the individual self.

Even when the poet abandons his allusions to the mind as a place of fear and awe and as a potential danger to the venturing self, he does not move beyond a dualistic perception of mind as one thing, the world as something else. Later in the Prospectus, for example, Wordsworth evokes the prothelamic metaphor of the healthy mind as existing in a state of marriage with the world. Asserting that "Beauty" is "a living Presence of the earth. . . . An hourly neighbour," while questioning why "Paradise, and groves / Elysian" should be viewed as "A history only of departed things, / Or a mere fiction of what never was" (42–51), he declares confidently that

> the discerning intellect of Man,
> When wedded to this goodly universe
> In love and holy passion, shall find these
> A simple produce of the common day. (52–55)

The marriage Wordsworth here celebrates, however holy its occasion and unitary its effect, preserves nevertheless a distinction between the "discerning intellect of Man" and the world that joins it in the mutual creation of a quotidian paradise of Elysian beauty.

The "purer mind" of "Tintern Abbey," however, is much more difficult to locate and describe. Indistinguishable from its surroundings, it is aligned with a spirituality outside or beyond the idiom of a specific cultural tradition. So far as it can be said to exist at all, the mind to which the poet alludes in "Tintern Abbey" is in a state of disappearance. The "beauteous forms" that attract the poet's consciousness serve not to define it, as in the Prospectus, but to produce first a set of "sensations sweet, / Felt in the blood, and felt along the heart," then feelings that contribute a moral climate of "kindness and of love," and finally a "serene and blessed mood" that suspends "even the motion of our human blood," leaving the percipient "a living soul," adrift in a condition of disembodied, centerless spirituality. The movement of thought and image here, though no less powerful in its effect on him than the soaring expectations of the Prospectus, is downward toward a spiritual ground that hides or obliterates the sense of mind as a distinct intellectual realm. To feel sensations "in the blood" and "along the heart" is to be sensation itself, not a separate being experiencing sensation as impulses different from the self. One cannot locate the mind in a still point or stable perspective outside the moving events that constitute it. The "beauteous forms" that produce the sensations and the "purer mind" that receives them occupy an existential priority, a unitary ground of being in which percipient and perceived emerge as variant aspects of each other.

In the "blessed mood" resulting from this configuration of moving sensations, the poet speaks of seeing into the "life of things." But the "life" into which he sees, like the "purer mind" that perceives, is disembodied, unlocated, a state "In which the heavy and the weary weight" of things "Is lightened." So far as the sensations of things form the very being of the perceiver, the things seen and the act of seeing are extensions of each other. The seeing eye, like the "purer mind," is unsituated, or, if situated, then existing in the motion of the poet's bloodstream; it is moved not, as in the Prospectus, by an impulse to discover something separate from itself but by a "power / Of harmony" that makes it quiet, passive, requiring only that it open simply to what is—literally, to the moving dimensions of its own nature. The result is a mode of seeing in which the weight of things, the density and mass that make things separate and distinguishable, disperses or falls away into a spiritual ground upon which all things, including the observer, appear light, disembodied, free of specific location, lacking not form but substance or essence: having been "laid asleep / In body, and become a living soul . . . We see into the life of things." The light of seeing is coextensive with the lightness of being that comes with the sense of the essential emptiness of all things, their essencelessness.

The cognitive process of these lines, so far as we can employ such terminology, involves a steady renunciation of anything that could stand between the observer and the observed. To be a "living soul" in this sense is to be one with a world in which all things, including the human individual, are in motion and interanimate with all other things, hence disembodied, lightened, continuous with a moving environment. To see into the life of things so construed is to *be* the life of the very things one may perceive initially as "unintelligible" to the separate self. Unlike the visionary state marked out in the Prospectus, the spiritual ground Wordsworth apprehends in "Tintern Abbey" enables him to see not a new paradise, a place construed, so to speak, as the result of a creative engagement with that which is perceived initially as external to himself, but a world of "things" uncolored or unadorned by the imaginative application of a cultural overlay of images extracted from a human spiritual or religious tradition. The intelligibility Wordsworth encounters here, a mode of apprehension that lightens in the sense of both illuminating and disburdening, shifts the grounds of knowing from the individual as a separate observer to a perceptual field in which knowing is a condition of the being of all things. Cognition so conceived is not an act of discovery so much as a surrender to being, a yielding of the separate self to a condition of identity with, rather than apprehension of, "the life of things."

In book 2 of *The Prelude*, the massive poem he devoted to the growth and development of his own mind, Wordsworth describes these early visionary states more specifically and at greater length than in "Tintern Abbey":

> How shall I trace the history? where seek
> The origin of what I then have felt?
> Oft in those moments such a holy calm
> Did overspread my soul, that I forgot
> That I had bodily eyes, and what I saw
> Appeared like something in myself, a dream,
> A prospect in my mind. (2.365–71)[3]

The question of origin as Wordsworth presents it here is, of course, unanswerable. If indeed all that one apprehends appears like something in oneself, whether viewed as a dream or as a prospect in the mind, the perceiver is for all practical purposes that which he perceives. Her state of consciousness is prior to the question of source and tends to render nugatory all concern with origin. To seek origin as a cause beyond oneself, that is, to seek it outside the dimensions of the mind, is like trying to see the very eye by which one perceives. At the same time, however, the force behind the question, the generative impulse to know, is both pertinent and necessary, for it impels recognition of a profound spirituality, a "holy calm," as Wordsworth calls it, that eliminates all sense of self and other in a condition of radical oneness with the world. To question the origin of one's feelings in the ambient light of such consciousness is to understand that in moments of high unitary vision, we cannot speak of the human as one thing, the natural as something else. Both the human and the natural share the same absence of origin and essence, the same bodilessness, the same lack of density and mass, the same inaccessibility to conventional logic and intellect.

Occasionally, however, Wordsworth's concern with origin, with the desire to know the source of his feelings, becomes a usurpative energy linked to the needs of an insecure, possibly traumatized, self. In the middle portions of "Tintern Abbey," for example, Wordsworth looks back on the visions of his youth with the discerning eye of a suspicious intellectual. Sensitive to the limitations of his present spiritual life, he tells of how he frequently recalls his early visions for solace in his adulthood, amidst "the fretful stir / Unprofitable, and the fever of the world" (52–53). But he is diffident, moved by a sense of their possible vanity, as he implies in line 50, before going on to say:

> And now, with gleams of half-extinguished thought,
> With many recognitions dim and faint,
> And somewhat of a sad perplexity,
> The picture of the mind revives again. . . .(58–61)

The earlier light is now "dim and faint." What the lines from *The Prelude* offer as a generative question, as an interrogative mood that forwards and enhances the developing sense of mind as a capacious extension of nature, surfaces in "Tintern Abbey" as an admission of limitation. Writing from the perspective of a troubled adulthood, Wordsworth admits that "I cannot paint / What then I was," when nature was "all in all" (75–76). The "picture of the mind" as it emerges for him in the middle portions of "Tintern Abbey" is framed by a "sad perplexity" and distorted by the presence of an alien concern—the compensatory need to derive human lessons from nature and to find for the self a secure, if subdued, place within that which he had earlier experienced as coterminous with his own being:

For I have learned
To look on nature, not as in the hour
Of thoughtless youth; but hearing oftentimes
The still, sad music of humanity,
Nor harsh nor grating, though of ample power
To chasten and subdue. (88–93)

There is a certain peacefulness here, a marked quietude that bespeaks a mind at rest, but it differs radically from the earlier repose in which the abiding harmony of things rose upon the poet as an innate aspect of his being and as a "power of joy." The quietude Wordsworth now experiences results from learned behavior, from the disciplined submission of a chastened and subdued self. What he had experienced earlier through an efflorescent opening to a realm of disembodied, essenceless forms now comes to him as a teacher, as an otherness bringing with it authority and a poignant sense of the human as somehow distinct from the very nature out of which it comes and to which it is joined in obedient submission. The present learning process is focused in the human dimension and culminates not, as earlier, in a dispersal of the self into a decentralized and disembodied consciousness but in the individual apprehension of a separate coadunate force or power indwelling in things, a kind of *elan vital*, as it were, that yields for all things and all beings a cohesion among, rather than an identity with, each other. In the "sad perplexity" of a troubled adulthood, Wordsworth writes:

And I have felt
A presence that disturbs me with the joy
Of elevated thoughts; a sense sublime
Of something far more deeply interfused,
Whose dwelling is the light of setting suns,
And the round ocean and the living air,
And the blue sky, and in the mind of man. . . . (93–99)

The "serene and blessed mood" of lines 37–49 has given way to "a sense sublime / Of something far more deeply interfused." The defining characteristic of the earlier mood is its alignment with spiritual emptiness, with the absence of essence. The later "sense sublime," however, apprehends a "presence," a "something" that is yet separate from the things it inhabits. Moved by this presence, Wordsworth concludes, in lines that parallel the theme of mutual creativity in the Prospectus, that he is yet

> A lover of the meadows and the woods,
> And mountains; and of all that we behold
> From this green earth; of all the mighty world
> Of eye, and ear,—both what they half create,
> And what perceive; well pleased to recognise
> In nature and the language of the sense
> The anchor of my purest thoughts, the nurse,
> The guide, the guardian of my heart, and soul
> Of all my moral being. (103–11)

If the visionary focus of this passage differs from that of lines 37–49, so also does the sense of pleasure and morality Wordsworth acquires from his experiences in nature. The earlier pleasure, together with the "little, nameless, unremembered, acts / Of kindness and of love" it produced, derived from the visible absence of stability, from a process "In which the affections gently lead us on" until the human is suspended. Wordsworth's experience of pleasure, goodness, and spirituality issued earlier from the happy acceptance of motion. Lines 103–11, however, depict a mood grounded in the need for stability. Wordsworth is now "well pleased" rather than joyous in his acceptance of "nature and the language of the sense" as the "anchor" of his thoughts. He looks now to nature for guidance and protection. The earlier process of opening to the world of things, of blossoming to an acceptance of instability as the ground of his being, of his own being as well as that of other things, has given way to a quest for moral and intellectual anchorage.

It is important for us to understand, however, that the later mood, the "sense sublime / Of something far more deeply interfused," does not replace or in any way negate the earlier state of "serene and blessed" dispersal into centerless consciousness. To his credit, Wordsworth does not reject the visions of his youth as false or vain, nor does he lose the impulse to move somehow beyond the present selfhood that obscures his earlier experiences of oneness with nature. He turns, instead, to his sister Dorothy, claiming that

> in thy voice I catch
> The language of my former heart, and read
> My former pleasures in the shooting lights
> Of thy wild eyes. (116–19)

Dorothy retains the "purer mind." Her "wild eyes" have not been dimmed by "the fretful stir / Unprofitable, and the fever of the world." Even in her later years, when the "wild ecstasies" of her youth will have "matured / Into a sober pleasure" (138–39), Dorothy will retain, not a mind that seeks for anything beyond itself, but one that accepts freely, that opens to the impulses of nature—to the shining of the moon, to the play of "misty mountain-winds" (134–36). It is a mind that will persist as a "mansion for all lovely forms" and whose memory will be "as a dwelling-place / For all sweet sounds and harmonies" (140–42). Being the eyes of nature itself, Dorothy reads only what is there and seeks nothing beyond the surface of things.

Structurally, the poem reveals a movement from memories of disembodied spirituality, through a sense of sublimity as inclusive of a chastened but nevertheless persistent selfhood, to a final displacement of the self in the poet's deferral to the spiritual force and authority of his sister. Her acceptance of the mystery of things, her ability to see, hear, and feel without necessarily seeking for an intellectual principle behind things, for a separate logos, as it were, is the measure of her identity with the universe. To the extent that he catches in Dorothy's voice the language of his former heart and in her eyes the quality of his former pleasures, the earlier state is yet alive for the poet. The dimensions of its effect may have altered for him, and the manner of its surfacing may differ from one situation to another, but its power to displace the self is no less persistent. The poem thus celebrates a spirituality grounded in the notion of mind and world as a composite unity manifested through the necessary disappearance of the self as the locus of perception.[4]

But what the poet offers as a vital unity his readers tend for the most part to understand in contexts that emphasize fundamental distinctions among the components of his vision. Influenced more perhaps by the Prospectus to *The Recluse* than by "Tintern Abbey," critical discussions of Wordsworthian unity employ a dualistic idiom that presents mind and nature as complementary, but nevertheless separable, realms. Relying, for example, on the following lines from the Prospectus—

How exquisitely the individual Mind
(And the progressive powers perhaps no less
Of the whole species) to the external World
Is fitted:—and how exquisitely, too—
Theme this but little heard of among men—
The external World is fitted to the Mind (63–68)—

M. H. Abrams claims that the central vision of Wordsworth's poetry is the power of the individual mind "as in itself adequate, by consummating a holy marriage with the external universe, to create out of the world of all of us, in a quotidian and recurrent miracle, a new world which is the equivalent of paradise."[5] Kenneth R. Johnston argues similarly that "Wordsworth's great faith is in Nature, the extrinsic, what is 'out there,' and in the *excursive* power of Imagination to go out to meet it."[6] Frederick Garber, also focusing on the marriage metaphor, asserts that "Wordsworth's was a middle way, giving equivalent weight to each partner in the relationship. The high argument in the Preface to *The Excursion* is an exercise in parity, its main point the creative efficiency that comes from interlocking the powers of mind and world."[7] More recently Barbara Schapiro, invoking the principles of modern quantum physics, maintains that "imagination and Nature, or mind and the material world, are mutually reflecting realms for Wordsworth—the order of mind mirrors the order of Nature."[8]

Other readers find in Wordsworth's poetry a radical opposition between the mind and the external world. David Perkins, for example, argues that what is foremost in Wordsworth is "his sense of the gulf between human nature, with all of its greedy demands, its turbulent assertions, its often chaotic passions, and the rest of nature."[9] For Geoffrey Hartman, the central drama in Wordsworth's poetry is an unresolved opposition between imagination and nature, a tension that culminates in a willed, akedah-like binding of the individual mind with the external world.[10] Charles J. Rzepka, extending the work of Robert Langbaum, Frances Ferguson, and David Simpson, sees Wordsworth as struggling to achieve personal and professional identity in a paradoxical dialectic comprising "on the one hand, a solipsistic self-diffusion and mental appropriation of the perceived world as part of the self within, and on the other, a search for right recognition that will give this indefinite, inner self outward form and definition."[11] And John Jones, underscoring Wordsworth's high regard for solitude and distinctness, condemns the entire critical involvement with questions of unity in romantic poetry: "The large and lazy assumption that the Romantic poets were all striving to express unity has obscured the structure of distinct but related things which is the world of Wordsworth."[12]

Whether viewed as the poet of nature whose work affirms a vital connection between the individual mind and the external world, or as the complex, problematic, often contradictory poet of a suppressed imagination and a divided identity, Wordsworth evokes for many readers a powerful sense of a separate creative self deeply conscious of, sometimes preoccupied with, its own transforming and organizing energies. The recorded confluence of mind and external world, when it occurs in Wordsworth's poetry, produces critical responses grounded in a dualistic idiom that stresses the notion of unity as a partnership or alliance of deeply related but nevertheless separate items.[13]

The source of the critical tendency to employ a dualistic idiom in discussions of Wordsworthian unity can be traced to the intellectual predisposition of Western culture itself. Western thought is "plagued," as Amalie Enns puts it, with a subject-object dichotomy that "begins with Plato who located truth in the intellect, thereby separating man from his world and the entities in it." This separation, according to Enns, "was intensified by Descartes and continues to preoccupy philosophers to our own day."[14] Though "plagued" is perhaps a little strong, the impulse behind the word conforms to the insights of many thinkers who have looked into the cognitive procedures of Western culture. Winston L. King, for example, remarks that the "Cartesian division of reality into immaterial, invisible, subjective consciousness and material, visible objectivity is the epitome of Western thought, the creator of its cultures and civilization. Out of this climate has arisen the Western dichotomous type of logical assertion that A is *not, can*not be B."[15] Criticism tends naturally to reflect the philosophical mileau which helped to produce the texts readers engage. M. H. Abrams, to cite yet another of this important scholar's works, finds Wordsworth's effort to effect a reciprocity of mind and nature representative of "the overall movement of thought in his age." Explaining that Wordsworth represents life "primarily in terms of a transaction between two agencies, his mind and outer nature," Abrams proclaims: "For the great contemporary philosophers in Germany—Fichte, Schelling, Hegel—also represented all human experience as generated by an interaction between two agencies; and what Wordsworth called mind and Nature, they called the self and the other, or subject and object."[16] Readers working within the parameters of Western philosophy, especially as it appears to have influenced romantic poets, employ, imperceptibly perhaps, a critical idiom that reflects such basic dualisms as internal and external, mind and nature, self and not-self. Albert O. Wlecke, for example, understands Wordsworthian consciousness entirely in the dualistic terms of "intentionality" as defined by Franz Brentano: "This characteristic is, quite simply, the fact that consciousness in any of its acts always exhibits 'direction towards an object.' There is never merely consciousness but always consciousness *of*."[17] Wlecke locates consciousness in the percipient. Like Abrams's appeal to a vital reciprocity between mind and nature as the ground of Wordsworthian unity, Wlecke's understanding of consciousness as intentional and directional certainly conforms to the poet's efforts to exalt the generative powers of individual mentalities, but it does not escape the sense of the mind as one thing, the cosmos as something else. Readers influenced by the philosophical authority of such considerations must necessarily employ a dualistic terminology in their analyses of romantic creativity. Thus, Marilyn Gaull, in an overview of the entire romantic epoch, says with considerable confidence that the romantics' "interests were not in external nature itself but in how the mind relates to it" and that their poems "have a common concern: how the poet feels about the external world, how he relates to it, and what it means to him as an occasion, a metaphor, or a symbol."[18]

Much of Wordsworth's poetry, however, labors to hide or to obliterate the felt presence of a separate organizing or opposing self in favor of a prejudgmental, prereflective consciousness so deeply aligned with a perceived matrix of creative forces that it is impossible to say where the world's energies leave off and those of the poet begin. This deeper consciousness, coextensive with the world it illuminates, does not exist apart from, but is rather inclusive of, the mind presented in the Prospectus to *The Recluse*. I would like to explore this inclusive consciousness in the terms offered by Zen thought and art. Combining key elements of Mahāyāna Buddhism with Chinese Taoism, then carried later to Japan, where it was further refined, Zen is perhaps best understood as neither philosophy nor religion as such but as a spiritual practice that embraces both profound philosophical insight and deep religious experience. So far as we can think of it in philosophical terms at all, we are best served, perhaps, by Masao Abe's definition: "It is a philosophy based on a 'non-thinking' which is beyond both thinking and not thinking, grounded upon 'Self-Awakening', and arising from wisdom and compassion."[19] In like manner, Robert Linssen employs highly qualified terms in viewing Zen as a religion: "If religion means an organization of spiritual aspirations whose aim is to understand and pass beyond the tangible world by freeing ourselves from the impulses attaching us to it, then the various forms of Buddhism could be qualified as religious."[20] Neither a philosophy nor a religion in the conventional sense, Zen offers a perception of mind and world as a vital continuum, as a basic identity or unity beyond or prior to hermeneutic impulses to find meanings, to interpret the world in accordance with the projected needs and wishes of a discerning self and a specific cultural idiom. Tanzen, a nineteenth-century Japanese priest and philosopher who held the chair of Indian Philosophy at Tokyo University and who was later president of the Soto Sect College (now Komazawa University) in Tokyo, defines the Zen mind in terms remarkably similar in spirit to those expressed by Wordsworth in book 2 of *The Prelude*. Asserting that "In other religions and philosophies the so-called mind is looked upon as the governor of the body or the lord of things," a misconception "Which is the outcome of speculation, or stupid reason," Tanzen explains that

The law of the mind is above human understanding, for the mind is timeless and permeates all. Its function is not merely that of perception and cognition. It is limitless, containing all phenomena—mountains, rivers, the whole universe. A fan can soar skyward, a toad fly, yet never outside the mind.[21]

As in Wordsworth, for whom everything frequently appears like something in himself, an inward prospect, as it were, the mind for Tanzen is essentially subsumptive and combinatory, larger than its own processes and inclusive of the world.

What emerges in Wordsworth's poetry as an inclusive consciousness utterly continuous with the universe appears to Zennists as a state of "no-mind" or "one-mind," a perception that reflects the general Buddhist concept of '*śūnyatā*', or "the Void," as it is sometimes called. Buddhist thought is founded on the notion that because all things change, their reality, their suchness (Sanskrit, *tathatā*), is not their existential particularity, but a ubiquitous and eternally undivided ground variously called "the Void," "the Buddha-mind," "the Buddha-nature," "the Unborn," or, in Western terms, "the Absolute." The essential nature of this ground, so far as it can be said to have an essential nature, is its emptiness—a state beyond what might ordinarily be conceived as a spatiotemporal dimension. *The Heart of Perfect Wisdom*, a key text extracted from the *Prajñāpāramitā Sutra* and recited daily in Zen monasteries throughout the world, states the case succinctly: "form is emptiness and the very emptiness is form; emptiness does not differ from form, form does not differ from emptiness; whatever is form, that is emptiness, whatever is emptiness, that is form, the same is true of feelings, perceptions, impulses and consciousness."[22]

The Void or the Emptiness of Buddhist thought is not, however, a mere vacuity or a nihilistic vortex issuing from the perception of universal transience. It is predicated, rather, on the insight that the entire phenomenal world, all that exists, is tied together in a gigantic, interrelated, interanimative web of moving aggregates. Even individual human beings, as Thich Nhat Hanh explains in his commentary on the *Heart Sutra*, are a collection of five elements, called "*Skandhas*" in Sanskrit, which "flow like a river in every one of us." These forms, which are themselves currents of physical, mental, emotional, perceptual, and conscious being, cannot, according to Thich Nhat Hanh, exist individually: "Each can only inter-be with all the others."[23] In the Buddhist view, nothing possesses self-existence. Everything depends on everything else. Nothing remains unchanged. Yet each thing, so far as it comprises eternally moving aggregates, contains, indeed is an expression of, the Absolute. "Form is empty of a separate self," writes Thich Nhat Hanh, "but it is full of everything in the cosmos."[24]   Hua-yen Buddhism expresses this sense of interpenetrative fullness in what one philosopher, Steve Odin, calls "the summary formula: 'All is one and one is all.' " Predicated on an acute sense of the dialectical interpenetration of the one and the many, of subject and object, of unity and multiplicity, Hua-yen Buddhism sees the identity of form and emptiness as an eternally shifting spatiotemporal togetherness in which, Odin explains, "the large and small thus interpenetrate without the slightest obstruction" and "every event is virtually present or immanent in every other event."[25]

The oneness Zen thinkers proclaim, however, cannot be apprehended in the dualistic context of self and other, nor can it be ascribed to a separate creative force. Zen unity, according to Masao Abe, "is not a monistic or monotheistic oneness but rather a nondualistic oneness. . . . Monotheistic oneness does not include the element of self-negation and is substantial, whereas nondualistic oneness includes self-negation and is nonsubstantial."[26] There is nowhere to be found in the universe a separately existing logos, a creative center behind or above reality. "In the Buddhist perspective," writes Nolan Pliny Jacobson, "the source of everything is no determinate actuality but a creativity infinitely productive of actualities."[27]

The Zen Buddhist endeavors to experience this creative ground directly, not as a separate habitat, but as the lived and living essence of his own being. Zen master Sasaki Joshu writes: "Absolute being works as complete, perfect emptiness and embraces subject and object. If you want to see God or Buddha, you must manifest yourself as emptiness."[28] This condition of extreme egolessness reveals itself in the disposition to accept all things, to avoid discriminations based on a priori judgments, and to eliminate any thought of a distinction between one's own consciousness and the world one apprehends as seemingly other. Buddhists frequently see this state as a condition of harmony with the Tao or Way, "the origin of the universe and the source of life . . . the undifferentiated, complete reality that existed before Heaven and Earth . . . the life force of all things, animate and inanimate," as Sean Dennison defines the term.[29] Relating this concept of radical harmony to the notion of universal identity, Seng-t'san, in his famous treatise "On Believing in Mind," asserts that "In the Mind harmonious [with the Way] we have the principle of identity / In which we find all strivings quieted." This is a place where "All is void, lucid, and self-illuminating" and where "There is neither 'self' nor 'other.'"[30]   Eihei Dōgen, a thirteenth-century Japanese priest and philosopher generally credited with founding the Soto school of Zen, views the Buddhist understanding of universal identity as resulting from a process of self-forgetting and concurrently as a means by which the universe of myriad things realizes itself through the individual: "To study the buddha way is to study the self. To study the self is to forget the self. To forget the self is to be actualized by myriad things."[31]

For Zen Buddhists throughout the world, freedom from self is identity with all things, a means by which the perceived harmony of life is the actual lived and living center of one's being. "Zen is the essence of Buddhism, freedom is the essence of Zen," writes Thomas Cleary. In a later refinement of this definition, Cleary explains that "Liberation of the human mind from the inhibiting effects of mesmerism by its own creations is the essence of Zen."[32] The freedom that Cleary here remarks is not simply the freedom of the human individual to be and do as he pleases but the freedom of all things to emerge and to illuminate themselves in a field of consciousness at once individual and universal. What Wordsworth describes as seeing without "bodily eyes," to recall book 2 of *The Prelude*, the Zennist understands as a mode of self-illumination in which the seer's identity with that which he sees is also the means by which, for all practical purposes, things view themselves through the pulse of human perception cleansed of any conceptual frame. A philosophical-religious practice whose deepest insights and experiences issue from a condition of freedom from the very impulses that form the contents of human life, Zen is, then, a way of experiencing life in its deepest ranges without becoming attached to the cultural and psychological conditions that animate and define the moment. Reiho Masunaga, in a summary comment on the spiritual implications of the Buddhist process of self-emptying, remarks simply that "When the self dies, the universe flows in."[33]

Throughout his poetry, Wordsworth chronicles moments of self-forgetting extraordinarily similar in course and profile to the Zen experience of cosmic influx resulting from its formal procedures of self-emptying. As with Zennists, these occasions of self-forgetting form the spiritual basis of his art and the driving force behind his creativity.[34] Wordsworth's poetry issues from a radical spirituality inclusive of, yet beyond, all cultural systems and all modes of self-hood, a spiritual freedom that allows the poet to experience in a condition of profound detachment the very cultural and psychological phenomena that comprise his being at any point in time and space. "I was a Freeman," he tells us early in book 3 of *The Prelude*, "in the purest sense / Was free, and to majestic ends was strong" (89–90). Enlarging upon this condition of radical interior spaciousness, Wordsworth continues:

> I looked for universal things; perused
> The common countenance of earth and heaven;
> And turning the mind in upon itself
> Pored, watched, expected, listened, spread my thoughts
> And spread them with a wider creeping; felt
> Incumbences more awful, visitings
> Of the Upholder, of the tranquil soul,
> Which underneath all passion lives secure
> A steadfast life. (3.110–18)

As a vital, coherent, yet nonideological, body of thought and experience grounded in the perceived interactive oneness of all beings and things in the universe, Zen offers us an opportunity to understand the "tranquil soul" of Wordsworth's lines, what the poet later calls "the one Presence, and the Life / Of the great whole" (3.130–31), in nonmonotheistic, nonpantheistic terms. A comparison of selected poems in the Wordsworth canon with some of the leading documents in Zen literature and philosophy establishes a less self-conscious, less egotistical strain in Wordsworth's art, refines our understanding of the poet's engagement with the *unio mystica*, and creates for his work a less ideological, more universal context than what it has encountered among readers whose understanding of metaphysics is grounded in such traditional Western dualisms as self and other, subject and object, nature and spirit.

PART ONE

WORDSWORTHIAN CAPACIOUSNESS
AND
ZEN EMPTINESS

INTRODUCTION TO PART ONE

Book 8 of *The Prelude* is offered as a retrospective commentary on book 7. Both books deal with the period of Wordsworth's residency in London when he was about twenty-three years old. The theme of his commentary, Wordsworth tells us in the subtitle to book 8, is how love of nature led in his youth to love of humankind, enabling him to endure, indeed to conquer, the debilitating effects of what he later saw in London:

> With deep devotion, Nature, did I feel,
> In that great City, what I owed to thee,
> High thoughts of God and Man, and love of Man,
> Triumphant over all those loathsome sights
> Of wretchedness and vice. . . . (8.62–66)

The triumph recorded here finds its source and power in Wordsworth's efforts to reconcile his earlier conviction that humanity is "Subordinate" to nature, to "her awful forms / And viewless agencies" (8.485–86), with his growing awareness of humankind "As, of all visible natures, crown" and "As, more than anything we know, instinct / With godhead, and, by reason and by will, / Acknowledging dependency sublime" (8.634–40). Central to this reconciliation is the poet's early apprehension of an indwelling "Capaciousness and amplitude of mind" that reflects the capaciousness of "all objects" (8.757–59). The "godhead" Wordsworth acknowledges as instinctual to humans, therefore of the nature of life itself, and the "awful forms / And viewless agencies" of nature emerge in book 8 of *The Prelude* as a radical continuity whose leading attribute is a dynamic capaciousness empty of specific form. The path of love that leads from nature to humankind and that enables Wordsworth to triumph over the "loathsome sights" of London is not a linear movement from one point or perspective to another but an instantaneous opening to the essencelessness and emptiness, the inherent spaciousness, of all phenomena, including godhead. Zen thought helps us to understand this emptiness or spaciousness not as a form of nihilism but as the creative base of all reality and all human consciousness.

21

Books 7 and 8 of *The Prelude* reveal how Wordsworth's understanding of spiritual emptiness grew out of his developing sense of the innate immensity of all things both as a moving field of interactive forces and objects and as a mode of containment that has no structured center, no circumscribed nature, and no lasting identity in itself. Because it addresses an earlier period in his life, a time of rural experience that helped to form the consciousness he presents in book 7, we will examine book 8 first.

Chapter One

Capaciousness as Natural Process

Early in book 8, while describing shepherds at a fair beneath Helvellyn, Wordsworth depicts the attending figures first as moving about in an ambient magnitude, then as somehow larger than the very magnitudes that embrace them. "Immense," he says,

> Is the recess, the circumambient world
> Magnificent, by which they are embraced:
> They move about upon the soft green field:
> How little they, they and their doings, seem,
> Their herds and flocks about them, they themselves,
> And all which they can further or obstruct!
> Through utter weakness pitiably dear
> As tender infants are: and yet how great!
> For all things serve them: them the morning light
> Loves, as it glistens on the silent rocks;
> And them the silent rocks, which now from high
> Look down upon them; the reposing clouds,
> The lurking brooks from their invisible haunts;
> And old Helvellyn, conscious of the stir,
> And the blue sky that roofs their calm abode. (8.46–61)

The shift from a vision of human littleness in which the shepherds appear as "infants" to one of commanding human presence in which "all things serve them" destabilizes our sense of the boundaries

23

between human and nonhuman, small and great, even inner and outer. Recording far more than a mere projection of human qualities upon the external world, the passage hypostatizes love and consciousness as qualities of nature itself, revealing the shepherds as both figures in an immense environment and as giant recipients of the very processes they appear to serve. The result is a vision of human presence grounded not in a dramatic perspective that shapes the individual against a nonhuman backdrop, that is, against an otherness that allows the contours of the human form to emerge from the beholding eye's orchestration of determinant contrasts, but in a shifting perceptual field that displaces consciousness into all things in such a way that cognitive and emotional qualities ordinarily belonging to humankind are seen to participate in an amorphous and embracive environmental unity of seeing and feeling. Nature, we are told, serves the shepherds. The morning light loves them, as do the observing rocks, clouds, brooks, and sky; old Helvellyn itself is "conscious of the stir." One cannot locate the seeing eye, the feeling heart in a particular being or object. The perceiving I that first looked upon the fair beneath Helvellyn has disappeared into larger processes of seeing and feeling. Like the perforated water jars of the Danaides, consciousness appears as a moving web of perceptions continuous with nature itself. Immensity, the announced subject of the lines, is both embracive of and contained within the shepherds it alternately dwarfs and exalts, and is itself subject to perceptual motion, to the "stir" of it all.

Significantly, the source of this motion remains forever hidden or dispersed in what Wordsworth later calls simply a "quiet process." The term appears in a passage that records a moment when the poet, "while yet a very child" (8.82), comes upon a shepherd and his dog emerging from the valley mists:

> It was a day of exhalations, spread
> Upon the mountains, mists and steam-like fogs
> Redounding everywhere, not vehement,
> But calm and mild, gentle and beautiful,
> With gleams of sunshine on the eyelet spots
> And loop-holes of the hills, wherever seen,
> Hidden by quiet process, and as soon
> Unfolded, to be huddled up again:
> Along a narrow valley and profound

I journeyed, when, aloft above my head,
Emerging from the silvery vapours, lo!
A shepherd and his dog! in open day:
Girt round with mists they stood and looked about
From that enclosure small, inhabitants
Of an aerial island floating on,
As seemed, with that abode in which they were,
A little pendant area of grey rocks,
By the soft wind breathed forward. (8.84–101)

Once again we are presented with the seeming paradox of immensity confined, of motion motionless. Though bound by an apparent island, the shepherd is yet free of all constraints, journeying motionless in a floating, forward-moving world. The "quiet process" that makes all this possible, that both reveals and hides, is centerless, sourceless, mysterious, infinitely productive of manifest particularities and ceaseless, seamless unities in which humankind and nature appear perfectly continuous with and productive of each other: if nature evokes humanity in the form of the shepherd, humanity evokes nature as invisible process through the majestic poignancy of its rural inhabitants. We are left with the visual perception of humankind as the very mists out of which its occasional forms emerge in all their immensurable glory and into which they are forever disappearing.

It is the indeterminateness of the process, however, its mysteriousness, that forms the ground of Wordsworth's sense of human majesty, even when that majesty appears eclipsed, as in London, amid "all those loathsome sights / Of wretchedness and vice" (8.65–66). Recalling the shepherds of his youth, "stalking through the fog" (8.401), their giant forms "glorified / By the deep radiance of the setting sun" (8.404–5), the poet concludes:

Thus was man
Ennobled outwardly before mine eyes,
And thus my heart at first was introduced
To an unconscious love and reverence
Of human nature; hence the human form
To me was like an index of delight,
Of grace and honour, power and worthiness. (8.410–16)

Though Wordsworth traces his abiding sense of human greatness to nature—"With deep devotion, Nature, did I feel, / In that great City, what I owed to thee, / High thoughts of God and Man . . ." (8.62–64)— the nature he exalts and to which he later says he belongs is uniquely devoid of form and definitive presence. Thus, near the end of book 8, while describing the power he found in all things, he writes that

> nothing had a circumscribed
> And narrow influence; but all objects, being
> Themselves capacious, also found in me
> Capaciousness and amplitude of mind;
> Such is the strength and glory of our youth!
> The human nature unto which I felt
> That I belonged, and which I loved and reverenced,
> Was not a punctual presence, but a spirit
> Living in time and space and far diffused. (8.756–64)

The "quiet process" Wordsworth remarked earlier in book 8 as productive of all things and beings in the endless ebb and flow of departure and arrival, of disappearance and emergence, is itself displaced by spiritual power conceived not as an indwelling force of nature but as emptiness, capaciousness. Unlike the "presence," the "something far more deeply interfused," of "Tintern Abbey," the source of Wordsworth's natural reverence in book 8 of *The Prelude* entails a process of dispersal, of diffusion, that identifies the human, the spiritual, and the natural as a vital continuum of interactive forces without center and abiding form.

Even when the poet employs a dualistic terminology to describe his sensations, we do not gather the sense of a vital distinction between external and internal, natural and human. In the concluding lines to the above passage, Wordsworth writes:

> In this my joy, in this my dignity
> Consisted; the external universe,
> By striking upon what is found within,
> Had given me this conception, with the help
> Of books and what they picture and record. (8.765–69)

All sense of a separate creative presence in nature or in books, together with any sense of a separate coadunative, mediating self, of a mode of being removed in any way from the endlessly shifting motions of the universe, disappears into the ambient, sourceless perception of characterless immensity as a network of transient, eternally emergent identities. Wordsworth's vision of the relationship between humankind and nature, his sense of human nobility, his perception of the world itself as a "tract more exquisitely fair / Than is that paradise of ten thousand trees, / Or Gehol's famous gardens," as he writes elsewhere in book 8 (121–23), is based on the sheer immensity of the particular and on the corresponding absence of circumscription and abiding identity in himself.

Zen thought helps us to understand that the immensity Wordsworth here applauds is not vacuity. In terms remarkably close to those of Wordsworth, Herbert Guenther explains that the Buddhist concept of nothingness "names an openness that cannot be limited by an unvarying and exhaustively specifiable mode of being. It imparts to each and every complex individual an openness and profundity . . . misleadingly translated as emptiness or the Void. . . . "[1] Understood as a mode of dynamic openness, the Void, or the emptiness of things, according to Nolan Pliny Jacobson, "refers to the rich qualitative flow that is infinitely productive of all the forms of this world."[2]   The "qualitative flow" to which Jacobson refers is for Buddhists the creative aspect of change.   Reality, according to Jacobson, "is constituted by momentary *nows*, events interrelated and forever coming to be, none of which ever remains as it is." We cannot, therefore, think of nothingness as absence. "Nothingness is not nothing," Jacobson continues; "it is events in process." So far as we understand that the emptiness of things is the continually emergent creative process that forms the ground of all things, we can understand, to rely yet again on Jacobson, that "It is the emptiness-of-my-self-existence that the world is full of."[3] Masao Abe uses similar terms in describing the relationship between the individual's perception of natural process and his realization of his own emptiness. "Becoming, process, and flux are beginningless and endless in every possible sense, whether these notions are understood in terms of immanence or transcendence, substance or activity," writes Abe. "They are thoroughly realized existentially from within. They are grasped through the realization of Emptiness which opens up endlessly."[4]   Just as Wordsworth, in his highest and most creative moments of visionary insight, understands that there is a direct correlation between his sense of the capaciousness of all things and his own capaciousness, so the Buddhist understands emptiness as a mode of revelational conjunctivity in which, as Michael Adam says, "Emptiness does not create the many things, it reveals them by showing itself as them. It is not the sum of things, but is each thing wholly and only and always for the little while that each thing is— one russet leaf is autumn, a green leaf is spring. All things are One and that is No-thing."[5]

The openness and corresponding creativity Buddhists celebrate as the ground of all things, including the individual self, resonate closely with the capaciousness of Wordsworth's visionary reality. The absence of "punctual presence," as he calls it, results from the perceived diffusion of spirit among things that are themselves forever changing, forever emerging in the "quiet process" that constitutes the onward flow of the world. The things themselves, including the beings who view them, are vast emptinesses, dispositions of capaciousness, only in the sense that they are containments without boundaries, continuities without abiding form. The Zen master Dōgen explains this notion of continuity in metaphorical terms similar in effect to the shepherd images Wordsworth employs:

> When a fish swims in water, there is no end of the water no matter how far it swims. When a bird flies in the sky, fly though it may, there is no end to the sky. However, no fish or bird has ever left water or sky since the beginning. . . . But if a bird leaves the sky, it will immediately die, and if a fish leaves the water, it will immediately die. You must understand that the water is life and the air is life. The bird is life and the fish is life. Life is the fish and life is the bird.[6]

Dōgen's metaphors help us understand that the bird and the fish are absolute in themselves, life-forms perfectly continuous with the water and the air in which they live. Water cannot be viewed as something other than the fish. Air cannot be viewed as something other than the bird. Commenting on Dōgen's text, Francis H. Cook writes: "The metaphor of the fish in water and the bird in the air makes the point that every event, every condition, everything, is the absolute reality in which the individual, itself the same reality, is eternally emersed."[7]   Each of us, like the giant shepherds of Wordsworth's youth, is an emergent aspect of a continually moving absolute that comprises our being at all times. "We are never apart from this reality, just as the bird is never apart from the air," says Cook. "If it leaves the air, it dies, but in fact, it never does, nor are we ever, in life or death, apart from the ultimate reality."[8]

The effective displacement of separate presence as a quality of individual being or as a metaphysical principle thus reifies spirit not as in any way substantive, even in the Spinozistic sense of pantheistic force or argument, but as continuous with the very process by which all things are rendered dimensionless. Like Buddhist thought, Wordsworth's poetry in book 8 of *The Prelude* moves us away from the relational ethic in which things, beings, and ideas achieve identity through a system of signifying differences toward a realm of continually emergent, mutually productive unities in which all things, all forms, implode on each other or fold inward, as it were, in an eternally shifting matrix of creativity without source, center, and intention.

Given the shifting profile of this creative matrix, it is not surprising, then, that Wordsworth, in his concluding remarks on his continuing sense of the "unity of man," reveals, near the end of book 8, a note of diffidence regarding both the source and the countenance of his sensations as he looks back on them from the perspective of his residency in London. Recording how "every thing that was indeed divine / Retained its purity inviolate" despite the gloom of London, indeed "seemed brighter far / For this deep shade in counterview" (8.813–16), the poet writes:

> Add also, that among the multitudes
> Of that great city, oftentimes was seen
> Affectingly set forth, more than elsewhere
> Is possible, the unity of man,
> One spirit over ignorance and vice
> Predominant, in good and evil hearts
> One sense for moral judgements, as one eye
> For the sun's light. When strongly breathed upon
> By this sensation, whencesoe'er it comes,
> Of union or communion, doth the soul
> Rejoice as in her highest joy: for there,
> There chiefly, hath she feeling whence she is,
> And passing through all Nature rests with God.
>   (8.824–36)

The entire passage functions as a moving network of implosive synecdochic constructs that both illuminate and complicate the poet's sense of human unity. The bold simile, for example, that compares the "One spirit" of line 828 to the "one eye / For the sun's light" of lines 830-31 contrasts sharply with the cognitive uncertainty of lines 831–33, which record his submission to a mysterious "sensation . . . Of union or communion." Undoubtedly, Wordsworth experiences the sensation of human unity, a gracious moment of spiritual wholeness in which he encounters "One spirit over ignorance and vice," but he does not know whence the sensation comes or if its defining characteristic is one of union or communion. Union implies one whole or complete body; communion implies a shared bonding or relationship, a communing, of separate items. Even the syntax of Wordsworth's stated uncertainty is implosive and destabilizing, with the question of the sensation's source falling within the subsuming question of the sensation's profile as either union or communion. But if the uncertainty of the last six lines undercuts the confident drive toward the capping simile of the first eight in which the "One sense for moral judgements" is compared to the "one eye / For the sun's light" (830–31), it serves as well to amplify the passive construction of line 825, which, ironically perhaps, sets the passage in motion. The one spirit "was seen." But by whom?

The question, of course, is impertinent so far as it motivates a quest for generative locus and self. But it is immensely appropriate so far as its insolubility adumbrates a mode of spiritual unknowing that identifies the passive, implicate seer of line 825 with the moving soul of lines 833–36. Wordsworth's sense of the absence of boundary and specificity among things is caught up with, indeed is produced by, his very inability to locate the sensation of human unity in a particular source, including himself, and to describe its workings as an act either of union or of communion. But instead of causing a moment of frustration, the poet's confusion becomes an occasion of joy in the compensatory recognition of the ineffable unity of the soul with God or the absolute. Another instance of motion in motionlessness, the soul, remaining undefined, passes "through all Nature" to rest with God, the point from which, one gathers, she never departed. The soul is seen to "Rejoice as in her highest joy" at precisely the point where the individual human intellect she employs fails to determine her source, her features, and the boundaries of her unity with God. Wordsworth's vision of reality accrues through a dynamic progression of moral, psychological, and spiritual displacements that eliminate discrimination and preference in response to a perceived network of mutual identities. The "One spirit over ignorance and vice / Predominant" works, not in a hierarchical setting that distinguishes it from its contents, as if it were innately or inherently superior to ignorance and vice, but much in the manner of the sunlight to which it is compared, illuminating "in good and evil hearts / One sense for moral judgements."

In their appeal to a nondiscriminatory moral judgment that affects good and evil hearts alike, Wordsworth's lines bear a striking resemblance to the opening passages of the *Shinjin-Mei* (Chinese, *Hsin-hsin-ming*) of Seng-t'san, the Third Patriarch of Zen (Chinese, Chan). Composed sometime in the sixth century, and translated as "On Believing in Mind," the poem identifies the mind with the cosmic Tao or the Way of things:

> The Perfect Way knows no difficulties
> Except that it refuses to make preferences;
> Only when freed from hate and love,
> It reveals itself fully and without disguise;
> A tenth of an inch's difference,
> And heaven and earth are set apart. . . .

Explaining that "To set up what you like against what you dislike —/ This is the disease of the mind," Seng-t'san, in lines that compare remarkably with Wordsworth's earlier references to capaciousness of mind, asserts that

> [The Way is] perfect like unto vast space,
> With nothing wanting, nothing superfluous:
> It is indeed due to making choice
> That its suchness is lost sight of.[9]

Suchness (Sanskrit, *tathatā*) refers to the absolute, the true nature of all things. It is the condition of all things beyond all concepts and distinctions, beyond the realm of self-nature: "*Tathatā* as the thus-being of things and their nonduality is perceived through the realization of the identity of subject and object in the awakening . . . of supreme enlightenment."[10] Apprehension of the nonconditionality of all things can only occur in a state beyond discrimination and choice.

For the Buddhist, however, freedom from preference is not the absence of discretion; it is, rather, a condition of nonattachment to choice as it relates to the ego. Commenting on these lines from the *Hsin-hsin-ming*, Dennis Genpo Merzel writes: "Out of delusion and confusion arises self-clinging, our need to maintain the illusion of a separate self, or ego, which manifests in our forming preferences, in our picking and choosing."[11] The ability to have likes and dislikes and to experience emotions such as hate and love without clinging to them and to the preferences they effect is absolutely essential to the process of freeing oneself from the limitations of the ego in order to apprehend mind, which, as Merzel says later, "is vast and wide, boundless and limitless."[12] The Japanese Zen master Bunan relates this concept of mind to what he calls "essential human nature," whose emergence requires a detached response to matters of right and wrong:

> People think it is hard to perceive the essential human nature, but in reality it is neither difficult nor easy. Nothing at all can adhere to this essential nature. It is a matter of responding to right and wrong while remaining detached from right and wrong, living in the midst of passions yet being detached from passions, seeing without seeing, hearing without hearing, acting without acting, seeking without seeking.[13]

The mind that Bunan is here describing can be neither seen nor grasped because, as Merzel explains, it "does not have a shape, it does not have a form, it is not a thing, it is a no-thing."[14]

Wordsworth's appeal to a moral sense both inclusive of yet somehow beyond the good and evil of individuals relates closely to the dynamics of the Buddhist mind as a way or process both inclusive of yet beyond the very preferences it apprehends through individual consciousness. Recalling in moral terms the poet's earlier references to capaciousness, the "One spirit," like the sun, does not distinguish in a preferential dimension; it absorbs and illuminates while displacing the self from the center of perceptual engagements with reality.

A comparable pattern of displacement prevents our efforts to locate Wordsworth's use of such terms as nature, soul, God, and spirit in fixed meanings. The nature through which Wordsworth depicts the soul as passing, for example, is not other than the beings who inhabit it, as we saw in the shepherd passages. Similarly, nature cannot be viewed as substantively separate from the spirit Wordsworth earlier remarked as diffused through time and space. The soul's journey toward a state of rest in God must be viewed, then, not as a movement toward something conceived as an achieved or achievable end, but as an unveiling of what always was or as an awakening to a felt presence that, like the Buddhist mind Merzel describes, lacks characterization and definition but that is nevertheless always here. Distinctions arise and vanish in such a way that all is revealed as God, soul, nature, spirit. The terms are interchangeable.[15] Love of nature thus leads to love of humankind not through a narrative progression from one state of being to another but through a poetic process that entails the falling away of layers of distinction between one thing and another. In this mode of capaciousness, to employ Wordsworth's vocabulary, all is revealed as at once God, soul, nature, spirit, and individual human being: capaciousness answers to capaciousness through the tacit recognition of the emptiness of all things, an emptiness perceived as the absence of an abiding identity or selfhood in things.

Love of nature, then, leads to love of humankind through the individual's recognition that love of nature *is* love of humankind: the resulting perception of human unity, like the conscious love attributed early in book 8 to mountains, rocks, and morning light, is of the nature of reality. It is not the province of humanity alone. "A poetry that represents man in isolation from nature," says Aldous Huxley, "represents him inadequately. And analogously a spirituality which seeks to know God only within human souls, and not at the same time in the non-human universe with which in fact we are indissolubly related, is a spirituality which cannot know the fullness of divine being."[16] The spiritual fullness Huxley exalts as an analogue of poetic vision grounded in the perceived indissolubility of humankind and nature surfaces for Wordsworth in response to early childhood experiences of consciousness and love as aggregates of all things. If the self in such a visionary mode is displaced from the center as a perceiving agent

and is seen to disappear into larger cognitive and emotional processes, so also is the apparent selfness of all things seen to vanish into an
eternally immanent creativity beyond the ability of the intellect to
define it in relation to a particular cultural milieu. The moving soul
of lines 831–36, in her journey through nature, has no choice but to
rejoice in her unknowing. She has no place to go. All is present as
emergent possibility. The spirit diffused through time and space renders time and space mere designations of that which, though ineffable, characterless, and formless, is forever now and here. As Masao
Abe writes: "Thus, becoming is not simply becoming but Being in any
moment; process is not merely process but always the beginning and
the end at the same time; flux is not just flux but permanence [sic] at
any point."[17] Wordsworth's joyous sense of human unity arises similarly as a fold or layer in a larger, ever-shifting web of imploding identities. His poetry in book 8 of *The Prelude* explores and celebrates the
perceived integration of nature, soul, God, and humankind as a moving, capacious, seamless whole without center, source, and abiding
form.

CHAPTER TWO

CAPACIOUSNESS AS
RECEPTACLE

I f book 8 of *The Prelude* offers the theme of how love of nature
leads to love of humankind through the gracious experience of
capaciousness, book 7 reveals how the sense of universal emptiness enables the individual to escape the limits of conceptual thought
and to retain a vital sense of spiritual freedom in circumstances that
invite the opposite. For Wordsworth, the source of the problem is
London itself, a place both remote from the natural influences of the
beloved Lake District in which he was reared and threatening in the
density of its swarming masses and trivial pursuits to overwhelm the
calm majesty of the cosmic spirit he had encountered in his youth:

> Oh, blank confusion! and a type not false
> Of what the mighty City is itself
> To all except a straggler here and there,
> To the whole swarm of its inhabitants;
> An undistinguishable world to men,
> The slaves unrespited of low pursuits,
> Living amid the same perpetual flow
> Of trivial objects, melted and reduced
> To one identity, by differences
> That have no law, no meaning, and no end [.]
> (7.695–704)

Significantly, Wordsworth does not reject "the perpetual flow / Of trivial objects." He accepts the flow and so provides himself with an opportunity to affirm later, without condoning the slavishness of quotidian urban pursuits, an intellectual, moral, and spiritual independence that will enable him to convert London from an image of vacuous horror to one of refulgent capaciousness. Beneath the multitude of "self-destroying, transitory things" (7.739), the poet experiences an underlying unity, "among least things / An under-sense of greatest" (7.710–11).

Wordsworth's ability to perceive a deep and abiding unity beneath the surface chaos of London is owing, he tells us (7.721–27), to the continuing influence of natural forms. The "mountain's outline . . . By influence habitual to the mind," the "forms / Perennial of the ancient hills," through both their innate "virtue" and "The changeful language of their countenances," have shaped the poet's mentality to such a "pure grandeur" that he envisions London, confounded in the closing lines of book 7 with his own "perfect openness of mind," as a "vast receptacle" embracing all things:

> This, if still,
> As hitherto, with freedom I may speak,
> And the same perfect openness of mind,
> Not violating any just restraint,
> As I would hope, of real modesty,—
> This did I feel, in that vast receptacle.
> The Spirit of Nature was upon me here;
> The soul of Beauty and enduring Life
> Was present as a habit, and diffused,
> Through meagre lines and colours, and the press
> Of self-destroying, transitory things,
> Composure, and ennobling Harmony. (7.729–40)

The closely juxtaposed images of mind as a "perfect openness" and London as a "vast receptacle" are too compelling to ignore. More than a mere symbol, London emerges here as a kind of objective correlative of the poet's mind. Perceiving both his own mind and London as vital immensities, the one a perfect openness, the other a vast receptacle, Wordsworth does not succumb to discrimination and moral condescension, nor does he grasp at compensatory ethical, philosophical, or religious systems as buoys on a shifting tide, but he retains in the midst of destructive triviality and transience a powerful sense of "Composure, and ennobling Harmony" grounded entirely in cognitive freedom.

The "perfect openness of mind" Wordsworth here celebrates as a condition both adumbrated by and extended through the perceived image of London as a vast receptacle corresponds directly to the Buddhist concept of mind as refulgent void. Hui Neng (638–713), the most famous Dhyana master of the Tang dynasty, and the Sixth Patriarch of Chan Buddhism, describes the mind thus:

> We say that the Essence of Mind is great because it embraces all things, since all things are within our nature. When we see the goodness or the badness of other people we are not attracted by it, nor repelled by it, nor attached to it; so that our attitude of mind is as void as space.[1]

The ninth-century Zen master Huang Po focuses more specifically on the theme of unity or of oneness in his depiction of mind, asserting that "All the Buddhas and all sentient beings are nothing but the One Mind, beside which nothing exists. This Mind, which is without beginning, is unborn and indestructible." Yet for Huang Po, as well, the mind is primarily void because it does not, indeed cannot, exist independent of the world. "It is that which you see before you," Huang Po continues; "begin to reason about it and you at once fall into error. It is like the boundless void which cannot be fathomed or measured."[2] In a later sermon, Huang Po enlarges on the theme of the mind's fundamental inaccessibility to thought: "The Mind is no mind of conceptual thought and it is completely detached from form. . . . If you can only rid yourselves of conceptual thought, you will have accomplished everything."[3]

Ridding oneself of conceptual thought, however, is not for the Buddhist a nihilistic act by which the mind is simply made into a blank. "Learned Audience, when you hear me talk about the Void, do not at once fall into the idea of vacuity," warns Hui Neng, "because when a man sits quietly and keeps his mind blank he will abide in a state of 'Voidness of Indifference.'"[4] In his commentary on

Huang Po, John Blofeld explains: "If, conceiving of the phenomenal world as illusion, we try to shut it out, we make a false distinction between the 'real' and the 'unreal.'"[5] To understand, rather, that all distinctions are void, including the distinction between mind and other, is to realize, again in Blofeld's words, that "none of the attractive or unattractive attributes of things have [sic] any absolute existence."[6] This realization is for the Buddhist a state of absolute freedom in which one understands that knowledge of oneself is also knowledge of the nature of everything. The experience of a separate mind brooding upon reality simply disperses into what might best be termed a network of perceptions in which the boundaries between things, including those between perceiver and perceived, are seen never to have existed. "The single aim of the true Zen follower is so to train his mind that all thought-processes based on the dualism inseparable from 'ordinary' life are transcended, their place being taken by that Intuitive Knowledge which, for the first time, reveals to a man what he really is," writes Blofeld. "If All is One, then knowledge of a being's true self-nature—his original Self—is equally a knowledge of all-nature, the nature of everything in the universe."[7]

From the Zen perspective, Wordsworth could not have rejected as entirely unattractive what he saw in London, though he knew much of it to be invidious, because he understood intuitively, as we can tell from the early passages of book 7, the limits of conceptual thought, including the moral categories it prescribes, and the grounds of his own identity with all he perceived. Hence, his humble, almost self-effacing reference to "freedom" and to "perfect openness of mind" rather than—shall we say, perhaps in a more conventional Western vein—to an innate or indwelling human generosity of spirit or to a specific religious or cultural tradition as the source of "real modesty." From the beginning of book 7, Wordsworth was practicing what students of Zen would quickly identify as an ethics of freedom grounded in processes of self-emptying or self-displacement. Early in the narrative, for example, Wordsworth tells of how, awakened from a long and unproductive period by "A choir of redbreasts" (7.24), he experiences an unpremeditated "delight / At this unthought of greeting" (7.31–32). This delight carries him far into the deep, refulgent silences of a mind-state that will be nearly eclipsed, as he tells us later in book 7, by a litany of urban distractions:

> A delight,
> At this unthought of greeting, unawares
> Smote me, a sweetness of the coming time,
> And listening, I half whispered, "We will be
> Ye heartsome Choristers, ye and I will be
> Brethren, and in the hearing of bleak winds
> Will chant together." And, thereafter, walking
> By later twilight on the hills, I saw
> A glow-worm from beneath a dusky shade
> Or canopy of the yet unwithered fern,
> Clear-shining, like a hermit's taper seen
> Through a thick forest. Silence touched me here
> No less than sound had done before; the child
> Of Summer, lingering, shining by itself,
> The voiceless worm on the unfrequented hills,
> Seemed sent on the same errand with the choir
> Of Winter that had warbled at my door,
> And the whole year seemed tenderness and love. (31–48)

The syntax of these lines is worth dwelling on for a moment, because it points to the source of Wordsworth's intuitive powers and to his strength, his unique ability, to withstand the sensuous assaults of London distractions. "A delight," the poet says, "unawares / Smote me." Neither the delight nor the poet is situated; neither experiences self-existence, as it were. The verb "unawares / Smote me" can be read in two ways—as applying either to the delight itself or to Wordsworth. To be sure, the birds sing; the poet hears. But the delight is sourceless, located at once in the birds' singing and in the poet's receptivity. Wordsworth himself, however, remains mysteriously unaware of the experience as having direction, that is, as coming to him from the outside. The confusion is, I believe, deliberate, the result of a moment of self-displacement so powerful in its impact that the experience of delight must be viewed as disembodied, as well as unfocused, not only comprising the poet's entire being in the instant of hearing, but nullifying hermeneutic efforts to locate either the emotion itself or its aural impulse in a particular source, whether in the poet or in the birds.

To be smitten "unawares," however, to be confused about source, direction, and goal, is not to be displaced from the center of one's being or to be lost in a meaningless environment of chaotic impulses. It is rather to be so identified with the contents of perception as to have no clear consciousness of center as occupying a specific point in time and space. The syntactic profile of Wordsworth's recorded experience of delight recalls similar features of Japanese haiku, which, according to Robert Aitken, attempt to reveal at once "the empty infinity of the universe and of the self."[8] A uniquely appropriate example of the form is a work by the Zen poet Bashō (1644–94):

> In plum-flower scent
> Pop! the sun appears—
> The mountain path.[9]

On the surface, the poem appears to record simply a moment of startling receptivity: Bashō, wandering along a mountain path, sees the sun.   Upon closer examination, however, the poem emerges as a record of profound psychological and intellectual dislocation.   Like Wordsworth, lost momentarily in the creative vacancy of an unproductive period during his residence in London, Bashō, lost in the pervading scent of plum blossoms, is, for all practical purposes, without conscious center. When the sun appears suddenly to Bashō, it is, like the instant in which Wordsworth hears the choir of redbreasts, an action from both within and without.   Explaining the word *Pop* (Japanese, *notto*), Aitken writes: "*Notto* and 'pop' are the action itself—from the inside. Bashō's experience of nature was more than observation, more than commingling: the sun, as Bashō, went *notto*."[10]

For Wordsworth as well, all potential dualism between self and other, between singing birds and listening poet, between quality of being in the form of delight and recipient of being in the form of perceiving poet, that is, finally, between subject and object, implode in the instant of intuitive awakening to self-nature. The poet's subsequent address to the birds, informing them that he and they together will be "heartsome Choristers" and "Brethren" who "in the hearing of bleak winds / Will chant together," eliminates all thought of an essential distinction between individual and environment, human and nonhuman.   Like the birds, Wordsworth becomes the voice of summer, not simply a harbinger of something to come or a mediator between one thing and another. As Bashō emerges as another form of the sun itself, another means by which the sun sees itself, as it were, so Wordsworth is summer come forth in winter warblings. In this mood, he later sees a glowworm, experiences a silence that is virtually, like the earlier singing of the birds, the content of his being, and envisions the "whole year" as "tenderness and love." In this state of deep silence, even distinctions of time disappear: the year ceases to exist as an aspect or measure of time, as if time were mensurably different from reality, and becomes literally an emotional quality. Wordsworth seems to understand implicitly what the Buddhist acknowledges explicitly as the ontological ground of existence—that being and time are one and the same, not separable aspects of an eternally extant other called reality. So Dōgen writes, in the "Uji" fascicle of the *Shobogenzo*, that "time itself is being, and all being is time."[11] Time does not exist apart from the mutable phenomena of the world. "Time in itself is being," as another translation of Dōgen's statement reads; "all beings are time."[12]

In making these claims, however, I do not wish to obscure Wordsworth's problems with the theme of spiritual emptiness. There were times, certainly, when he had his doubts about the insubstantiality of being and when, as he reports in a Fenwick note to the Immortality Ode, he felt constrained to grasp at something, "at a wall or tree to recall" himself from what he calls an "abyss of idealism." Unable in such moments "to think of external things as having external existence," Wordsworth says: "I communed with all that I saw as something not apart from, but inherent in, my own immaterial nature" (*PW* 4:463n). Buddhist thought traces such grasping after a perceived substantiveness to an innate fear of the dharma—the cosmic law of emptiness or the "great norm," as it is sometimes called, of universal impermanence. "Men are afraid to forget their minds, fearing to fall through the Void with nothing to stay their fall," says Huang Po. "They do not know that the Void is not really void, but the realm of the real Dharma."[13] We sense something of this fear in Wordsworth's later revisions of *The Prelude*. The "heartsome Choristers" whom he hails as "Brethren" in 1805 and with whom he will chant "in the hearing of bleak winds" become, in the 1850 *Prelude*, "Associates" with whom he will sing "unscared by blustering winds" (7.30). Both versions of these lines convey an element of fear. But the 1805 *Prelude* presents the winds as part of the total psychic landscape of Wordsworth's experience. To sing "in the hearing of bleak winds" is to accept the very bleakness of life as a welcome part of its dynamics. It is to convert into music what cannot be discarded without discarding life itself. To sing "unscared by blustering winds," however, is to obtrude a stoic element that evokes the image of a resisting self, something that stands apart from the bleakness of the moment and opposes the forces of nature. The substitution of "Associates" for "Brethren" introduces a corporative tone that further undermines the original blending of human and nonhuman. What appears in 1805 as a shared enterprise, as a mutual singing in the hearing of bleak winds, becomes in 1850 an agreement or partnership designed to protect an endangered self.

Wordsworth's response to the perceived immateriality of life or to its fundamental continuity with his own being is further complicated by a deeply compelling realization of his vocation as a practicing poet, a realization that gave him specific identity in a changeful world but that also required a critical stance grounded in a necessary dualism. The original unity that Huang Po celebrates as a creative Void and that Wordsworth sees as an abyss of idealism frequently reveals itself in a blending or fusing of images that the poet, though perfectly happy to record as perhaps the most unique aspect of his experience, is sometimes unable or unwilling to accept when he assumes a critical stance toward the original holistic event. This critical stance is particularly visible in those moments when Wordsworth views the form of his efforts, the work itself, from the highly self-conscious, vocational perspective of a practicing poet. In book 4 of *The Prelude*, for example, Wordsworth, reviewing his efforts thus far, compares himself to "one who hangs down-bending from the side / Of a slow-moving boat" (247–48), and who

> Sees many beauteous sights—weeds, fishes, flowers,
> Grots, pebbles, roots of trees, and fancies more,
> Yet often is perplexed and cannot part
> The shadow from the substance, rocks and sky,
> Mountains and clouds, from that which is indeed
> The region, and the things which there abide
> In their true dwelling[.] (4.252–58)

Although he speaks of these blendings as "Impediments that make his task more sweet" (261), Wordsworth is nevertheless "perplexed" and feels the need to part shadow and substance, to divide that which is passing or which is reflected on the surface of the water "from that which is indeed / The region."

If Wordsworth in the confidence and abandon of youth felt the need to grasp at the distinctiveness of things to break the fall, as it were, into the depths of mind, how much more appealing would the sportive variety of life appear to the sensitive adult lost in the teeming masses of the London streets. In book 7, the motivation to give himself to the multiplicity and singularity of the passing show that London offers the eager spectator nearly obscures the deeper reaches of the mind:

> Through the night,
> Between the show, and many-headed mass
> Of the spectators, and each little nook
> That had its fray or brawl, how eagerly
> And with what flashes, as it were, the mind
> Turned this way—that way! sportive and alert
> And watchful, as a kitten when at play. . . .
> (7.465–71)

Amid the novelty and diversion of London, Wordsworth feels "the imaginative power / Languish" (7.498–99). Despite its appeal, however, Wordsworth does not yield entirely to the "sportive" mind. He sees it, rather, as a border region of consciousness, as a suburb that certainly has its appeal but that is nevertheless removed from the central vastness that forms its true dimensions:

> For though I was most passionately moved
> And yielded to the changes of the scene
> With most obsequious feeling, yet all this
> Passed not beyond the suburbs of the mind. (7.503–6)

Given the force of these passages, the reader is tempted to discern in Wordsworth's work two presences, two distinctly different, perhaps equally appealing, selves—the one given unashamedly to the mystic blendings accompanying a powerful spiritual life, the other rooted in the dynamic compulsions of a persistent ego with its demands for place and distinction. Yet even when a sense of his separateness from the course of events rises upon him in moments of fear for the self, Wordsworth is never far from a profound realization and appreciation of life's indwelling harmony and essential essence-lessness. Thus, in the 1850 *Prelude*, immediately following his reference to the choristers of line 29 as "Associates," he proclaims nevertheless that "the whole year breathed tenderness and love" (7.42). The figuration collapses the human and the nonhuman in a sourceless gentleness and compassion that renders nugatory the implicate fears of his earlier stoic posture.

In its appeal to and exploration of a mind-state beyond, yet inclusive of, the dualisms of self and other, Zen thought enables us to see Wordsworthian consciousness as primarily unitary, abiding in the subsumptive, the formless, and the unsituated—and so to avoid both the tensions and the contradictions inherent in readings that identify the spiritual as one thing, the critical or, as in book 7, the urban and the social as something else. Commenting on Zen consciousness in English literature, R. H. Blyth writes that "the mind has no locality in space, it is not inside the skull of a certain person."[14] We discern throughout Wordsworth's poetry this transpersonal, unsituated mind in his persistent refusal to identify human consciousness with specific intellectual or vocational goals or with any function ultimately beyond that of containment. "The mind of man is framed even like the breath / And harmony of music," he tells us early in *The Prelude*, and then proceeds in the same sentence with

> there is a dark
> Invisible workmanship that reconciles
> Discordant elements, and makes them move
> In one society. (1.351–55)

Like the music to which it is compared, the mind flows; it is in motion and cannot therefore be said to have stable form and center. So far as it can be identified at all, it is aligned or, as in Wordsworth's sentence, implicitly identified with a "dark workmanship" that produces association and cohesion. The workmanship is dark not only because it incorporates discordant elements but also because its features are neither fixed in a particular location, say human consciousness alone, nor conformable to a specific intellectual pattern or ideology.

The darkness and the corresponding invisibility Wordsworth assigns the reconciling powers of the mind comprise especially poignant indicators of how creative consciousness works through its essential alignment or identity with emptiness or the Void. And here again, Zen thought and art provide useful guideposts to our understanding. A particularly notable example of how darkness functions as a creative force occurs in yet another poem by Bashō—"The Goi":

> A flash of lightning;
> Through the darkness goes
> The scream of a night heron.[15]

Goi is both the ideograph for heron and the Japanese for Tung-shan's Five Degrees of Interfusion, sometimes called the Five Positions of Interfusion in order to avoid the connotation of progression from one state to another. These interfusing states are "particularity in universality," "universality in particularity," "enlightenment emerging from universality," "enlightenment arriving from particularity," and "enlightenment achieved between universality and particularity."[16] The darkness Bashō remarks is the undifferentiated wholeness of his own mind, which exists in both perfect continuity and perfect identity with nature. Like Wordsworth's "dark workmanship," it is not a separately existing energy so much as a positive force-field working not against light, as we might expect, but as a capacious enabling arena for all form and energy. In his commentary on Bashō's poem, Aitken explains that "for the poet and the student of religion in Asia, darkness is an organic metaphor of the undifferentiated absolute. . . . Absorbed in the darkness, Bashō is absorbed in the universe, timeless, without bounds." In this state of absorption, the particular and the universal fold on each other in much the same way that the flash of lightning and the heron's cry both adumbrate and emerge from the void they illuminate: "In these immediately consecutive experiences," writes Aitken, "the scream and the lightning are one with the darkness, and the sighs of the poet and reader alike."[17]

In giving himself to the dark, invisible workmanship of mind, Wordsworth, like Bashō, accepts the fundamental mystery of consciousness, together with its essential opaqueness to the light of discriminating intellect, and apprehends in himself a compensatory realm of mind beyond yet inclusive of the energies attaching to the pursuit of focused perspectives and the trauma that such quests necessarily involve:

> Ah me! that all
> The terrors, all the early miseries,
> Regrets, vexations, lassitudes, that all
> The thoughts and feelings which have been infused
> Into my mind, should ever have made up
> The calm existence that is mine when I
> Am worthy of myself! (1.355–61)

Wordsworth's very ability to make distinctions, to part shadow and substance, as well as to join with nature in a shared creativity beyond the quest for meaning, derives largely from his engagement with human consciousness as a moving process of realization that, in the words of two modern Zennists, "has no color, no form, no psychological movement, and no action of dualistic tendency."[18] Wordsworth's faith in the underpresence of a "calm existence" both inclusive of and beyond the compulsory vexations of thought and feeling enables him to live without attachment to the various mental states, to the endless flow of emotional and intellectual stimuli, forever bubbling up from within.

But to be nonattached is not to be aloof and unfeeling. It is, rather, to be so deeply in touch with one's thoughts and feelings, with the passing mood of the moment, as to allow them a vital life of their own apart from the critical self's need for first causes, for explanations of how experience fits the various intellectual or cultural schemas to which the individual mind is innately drawn. The "dark workmanship" Wordsworth exalts in the first book of *The Prelude* works in the seventh as a power that enables him to experience the "motley imagery" of London, "the quick dance / Of colours, lights, and forms; the Babel din; / The endless stream of men, and moving things" (7.150–58), with a depth of engagement and an intensity of response that would submerge less capacious minds bound by the cultural structures and the structure-making abilities of the human intellect. At one point, for example, the poet writes:

> How often, in the overflowing streets,
> Have I gone forwards with the crowd, and said
> Unto myself, "The face of every one
> That passes by me is a mystery!" (7.594–97)

At first, Wordsworth cannot accept the mystery. Asserting that in the midst of such flow he was often "oppressed / By thoughts of what and whither, when and how" (7.598–99), he complains that "all the ballast of familiar life . . . Went from me, neither knowing me, nor known" (7.603–6).

Yet, paradoxically, the very absence of ballast and, concomitantly, the presence or immanence of an uncentered field of knowing produce the moment of salvation from the condition of oppression generated by the critical mentality's quest for meanings, answers, goals—"the what and whither, when and how" of what he calls a "second-sight procession" (601). As in the opening to book 8 of *The Prelude*, the poet's recorded experience destabilizes conventional perceptions of human understanding. Wordsworth hypostatizes the act of knowing, asserting that the "ballast of life," that which creates balance, neither knew him nor was known by him. The tropic configuration of the lines ascribes knowing to the so-called ballast of life, as well as to the individual percipient, thereby obscuring, perhaps eliminating, the sense of boundary between the human and the nonhuman, between subject and object. Unable to satisfy the critical inclinations that drive his oppression, Wordsworth simply gives himself to the motion of it all or, as he says more explicitly, to being "lost / Amid the moving pageant" (7.608–9), and consents tacitly to a conscious state of unknowing beyond the "reach of common indications" (7.608).

In this state of unknowing, born along by the flood of images rather than by the quest for meanings, Wordsworth proclaims that

> 'twas my chance
> Abruptly to be smitten with the view
> Of a blind Beggar, who, with upright face,
> Stood, propped against a wall, upon his chest
> Wearing a written paper, to explain
> The story of the man, and who he was.
> My mind did at this spectacle turn round

> As with the might of waters, and it seemed
> To me that in this label was a type,
> Or emblem, of the utmost that we know,
> Both of ourselves and of the universe;
> And, on the shape of the unmoving man,
> His fixèd face and sightless eyes, I looked,
> As if admonished from another world.   (7.609–22)

The mind that turns round "As with the might of waters" is one that has been humbled, paradoxically, by the grandeur of its own dimensions in the moment of sensing the limits of the human intellect. That we cannot know the "what and whither, when and how" of the moving pageant is both subordinate and necessarily prerequisite to the more compelling experience of the fundamental dimensionlessness of human consciousness.

The pattern of Wordsworth's experience in these lines reveals a movement from intense doubt, together with an accompanying feeling of oppression brought on by the mind's quest for meanings, to a moment of release into a new sense of the majesty and mystery of individual life, even as it inheres in the humblest, seemingly most alienated of beings—in this instance, a blind beggar. The profile of Wordsworth's experience here corresponds remarkably with that of the Zen Buddhist's in his moments of greatest doubt just before the instant of illumination during which he drops through all sense of a separate self and its reliance on conceptual schemas into the creative void of cosmic being. Describing this period of radical skepticism, the Zen master Hakuin (1686–1769) writes: "Suddenly a great doubt manifested itself before me. It was as though I were frozen solid in the midst of an ice sheet extending tens of thousands of miles." Giving himself completely to this doubt, however, and without thought of or hope for conceptual relief, that is, for explanations and first causes, Hakuin, awakening suddenly to the wonder of eternal being as the ground of his own existence, proclaims loudly: "Wonderful, wonderful. There is no cycle of birth and death through which one must pass. There is no enlightenment one must seek."[19] Though Hakuin was to go on to deeper and more penetrating moments of spiritual illumination, he understood at this relatively early point in his life a central feature of the Zen breakthrough into enlightenment—that it is an end in itself, not a cause of or a starting point for further intellectual analysis. "All the emotions are exhausted, all the intellect has come to its extremity; there is not an inch for the discrimination to enter," writes Zenkei Shibayama of the moment of enlightenment. "You are thoroughly lucid and transparent like a crystal. Subject and object, in and out, being and nonbeing are just one, and this very one ceases to be one any longer."[20]

The sudden vision of the blind beggar, immobile, backed against the wall, produces in Wordsworth an end state similar to that which Shibayama describes. Recalling the dark but inclusive workmanship of book 1, the very blindness of the beggar, together with his emergence in Wordsworth's mind as a type or emblem of our condition of unknowing, displaces him from his position as an outsider, as alienated from the flow of the London streets, and repositions him on the cosmic ground of humankind's universal condition. From the Zen perspective, what the blind beggar sees is his self-nature. But it is a self-nature empty of specific form or identity. Hence, the seeing into one's self-nature is a process in which, as D. T. Suzuki writes, "all the logical and psychological pedestals which have been given to one are now swept from underneath one's feet and one has nowhere to stand."[21] To be fully awake, in the Zen sense, is to be utterly transparent, not something seeing something else, but the very act of seeing itself. The Zennist will frequently speak of such seeing in negative terms, as a kind of "no-seeing." As Suzuki explains:

So long as the seeing is something to see, it is not the real one; only when the seeing is no-seeing—that is, when the seeing is not a specific act of seeing into a definitely circumscribed state of consciousness—is it the "seeing into one's self-nature". Paradoxically stated, when seeing is no-seeing there is real seeing; when hearing is no-hearing there is real hearing.[22]

To see "into one's self-nature" is to understand that what one sees is what one is. As the modern Zen writer Wei Wu Wei puts it, "Whether someone sees waves or particles, cyclones or poached-eggs . . . all are objects and, whatever he thinks he is seeing—that is ultimately what is looking."[23] That which we see is the seeing of itself through us and, in a deeper sense, its coming into being through us, for we are what we see and our becoming is the world's becoming.

Viewed in this light, we can understand how the beggar's emergence as "a type / Or emblem, of the utmost that we know" produces in Wordsworth, not a moment of despair or a cause for further groping along a teleological ladder, but a new sense of center. The ballast that had been missing earlier is now present in "the might of waters," a simile that carries forward the implications of the mind's having both depth and motion, both oceanic and diluvial proportions. If it carries all before it in the onward sweep of its course, it also contains and preserves. Hence, a paradoxical imagery similar to that which Suzuki employs. Waters containing depths and currents that might ordinarily drown the individual become instead a form of ballast. With the might of waters comes a lightness of being that enables the poet to float upon the moving tide of his own mind's depth, freeing him from the oppression of the quest for meaning and place without denying him the necessity and the immediacy of that quest.[24]

The key to this freedom is Wordsworth's unique ability to displace the self from the center of his existence and, concurrently, to divert the self's need for meanings, for explanations and interpretations, into contexts beyond the directive energies of a critical intelligence. Released from the self as the center of the field of knowing, Wordsworth, like the blind beggar, comes to realize knowing as a state of clarity beyond, yet inclusive of, the perceptible boundaries of things, including the perceived boundaries of self and other. *The Song of Enlightenment*, composed by the Chan priest Yung Chia Hsuan Chueh (655–713) during the Tang dynasty (618–907), regards the field of perceptual clarity as a mirror state either lacking or simply beyond notions of inside and outside, of percipient and perceived:

> The mirror of mind reflects without interference;
> Its vastness and clarity radiate through countless worlds.
> Various phenomena all manifest themselves;
> To a perfectly illumined one there is neither inside nor
> outside.[25]

For the "illumined" Zennist, the act of knowing is not entirely a hermeneutic function, nor is it an effort to construe meanings in order to find a place for the self in the quotidian flow, but an act of being that is whole or complete in itself and that reflects the fundamental oneness of mind and world. As the modern Zen master Sheng-yen writes in his commentary on the *Song of Enlightenment*,

When the mind is truly clear, there is neither an inside nor an outside. . . . This mind of wisdom transcends space and time. It does not exist in a specific point in space; it exists in every location of space. It does not exist only in this moment in time; it exists through all of time. There are no limits or boundaries.[26]

The mind-state Sheng-yen describes as the essence of Buddhist thought and that Buddhists in turn consider the essence of spiritual experience in general is, I believe, the enabling power behind Wordsworth's poetry as well as the theme of books 7 and 8 of *The Prelude*. In book 7, London emerges as the objective correlative of the "openness of mind" Wordsworth celebrates as the source of his ability to understand and to appreciate quotidian life. But like his Buddhist counterparts, Wordsworth understands that vastness of mind, emptiness, could be reified as vacuity or as a conceptual phenomenon. As D. T. Suzuki, quoting Hui Neng, warns his readers not to conceive purity of mind as "a separate entity outside the 'one who sees,'"[27] so Wordsworth feels the need to elaborate upon the theme of openness he had introduced in book 7. Hence, the retrospective book 8 in which London as a metaphor of oceanic consciousness gives way to remembered images of swirling, interactive forces and objects in nature as the moving profile of capaciousness. The books complement each other. Perceiving life as a vast empty ground in which mind and world are identical to and continuous with each other, Wordsworth eludes a destructive and obsessive fascination with the quest for meanings in the recognition that the mind is larger than the contents of its own intellectual life.

Wordsworth seems to understand, as well, that this mind-state can be neither developed nor attained, that it is, in other words, a condition from which one can never really depart. From the unselfconsciousness of the opening passages of book 7 to the selfless receptivity of book 8, there is no linear psychic movement from one point to another. The cognitive action in both books is not progressive or directive so much as expansive and embracive. Wordsworth does not develop the empty ground of "Capaciousness and amplitude of mind," to recall the theme of book 8. He discovers it as the source or essence of his own being, as that which, in its continuity with nature, he is never without. Buddhists understand this empty ground as the Unborn. The *Udana Sutra* of the Pali canon describes it as follows:

> There is, O monks, a not born, a not come into existence, a not made, a thing not composite; because, if there were not something which is not born, has not come into existence, has not been made, and is not composite, there would not be any deliverance for that which is born, has come into existence, is made, and is composite.[28]

Selfless, formless, characterless, yet infinitely productive as well as constitutive of all forms, the empty mind-ground of Buddhist meditative experience and the swirling, inclusive capaciousness of Wordsworthian consciousness are deeply analogous. Its realization as the base of his being allows the poet depth and intensity of experience without the loss of center that characterizes mentalities focused in the ego. To understand this center, however, we must come to see the mind not as a thing in itself so much as a way or a process. Part 2 of this study will explore both the dimensions and the dynamics of this shifting, elusive, refulgent way-mind.

PART TWO

WORDSWORTH'S ENDLESS WAY
AND THE
TAO OF ZEN

INTRODUCTION TO PART TWO

From the foregoing discussion, we can see that the key to capacious mind in Wordsworth, as well as in Zen, is the individual's ability to give up not only the self but also the entire knowing mode as it relates to the self. For Buddhists, this yielding of the self in pursuit of a deeper knowledge or wisdom culminates in an intuitive grasp of what is generally called the "Tao" or "Way"—the primordial "source of the universe and the originator of all things," as Chang Chung-yuan puts it.[1] Normally, we think of a way or path in linear terms, that is, as a transit between two points or as a method or passage to a goal. The supreme way of Buddhism and Taoism, however, is neither a path or transit between two points nor a movement toward a perceived or expected goal. It is, rather, a path that is at once the goal itself, a method that is its own end. The *Tao Te Ching*, a sixth-century B.C. Taoist text that influenced the development of Buddhism in China and that continues to be read and studied as a primary document among Zennists, asserts that

> Something unformed and complete
> Before heaven and earth were born,
> Solitary and silent,
> Stands alone and unchanging,
> Pervading all things without limit.
> It is like the mother of all under heaven,
> But I don't know its name—
> > Better call it Tao.
> > Better call it great.[2]

For all its greatness, however, the Tao does not exist apart from what it creates. "Great means passing on. / Passing on means going far. / Going far means returning," says Lao Tzu, the putative author of the *Tao Te Ching*.[3] The return to which Lao Tzu refers implies a cyclic process that leads beyond the notion of origin as a prior state located in the past. Both transcendent and immanent, the "origin" of Taoist metaphysics is latent in its manifestations. Commenting, for example, on the Taoist relationship between cyclic return and human cognition, Henry Wei writes, "The mysterious cyclic movement from

55

essence to manifestations and from manifestations to essence is per-haps what makes some Taoists say that an enlightened person can see unity in multiplicity, quiescence in motion, and stability in change, and *vice versa*."[4]   The return is to that which is never absent. Paradoxically, the Tao, eternally present and unchanging, yet struc-tureless, centerless, and forever in motion, returns to itself. "It is at once the beginning of all things and the way in which all things pur-sue their course," says Wing-Tsit Chan. "When this Tao is possessed by individual things, it becomes its character or virtue (*te*)."[5] Yet its status as a creative priority in no way subverts the uniqueness and autonomy of the particular through which it manifests. Explaining, for example, that "*tao* in its broadest meaning is the 'spontaneous (*tzu-jan*),' or perhaps a better translation, 'self-evidencing,' process of all that is as it presences for a given particular," Roger T. Ames asserts that "In this paradigm, the particular achieves its own self-expression through patternings of deference: deferring to its environing condi-tions to establish an efficacious and fruitful integration while at the same time fully disclosing its own integrity as a particular."[6]

For Taoists and Buddhists, access to the Tao, the pattern of deferral Ames describes, accrues through a process of unknowing that steadily reduces all distinctions between the self as an acquir-ing agency and the world it apprehends as other. "Pursue knowledge, gain daily. / Pursue Tao, lose daily," explains Lao Tzu.[7] Knowledge is conceived here not as something to be acquired but as a practice of shedding that which stands between the individual and his own innermost nature, which is the nature of all things. "Lao Tzu does not really want people to be ignorant," says Chang Chung-yuan; "he merely wants them to follow the learning of unlearning."[8] Martin Heidegger, a Western philosopher deeply interested in Eastern thought, writes similarly: "Thirst for knowledge and greed for expla-nations never lead to a thinking inquiry. Curiosity is always the con-cealed arrogance of a self-consciousness that banks on a self-invent-ed *ratio* and its rationality."[9] Knowledge, then, or what we might bet-ter call "spirituality" or "wisdom," is not a body of fact and experience to be apprehended but a path in itself, a *praxis*, a process of unknow-ing that leads not to the acquisition of something new so much as to an awakening to the formless, eternally emergent and creative pre-sent, to what always was, is, and will be.

In Wordsworth, this process of awakening surfaces most visibly in poems that show the poet on a path or journey. A pervasive theme throughout romantic literature and philosophy, the journey motif in Wordsworth's poetry appears to most of his readers as a perilous quest in search of vocational independence and imaginative autonomy, as a secular variation of the Christian journey to spiritual renewal. M. H. Abrams, in a summary comment that underscores the romantic educational journey as a linear progress of the self from a fall into disunity to "a higher integration," argues that "the Romantic theme of the justification of evil and suffering" is "represented in the plot-form of a circuitous yet progressive self-education, self-discovery, and the discovery of vocation, in a life which terminates in this world." But the high terminus Abrams describes, though certainly a condition of integration with the world of everyday life, preserves nevertheless a dualism of self and other that qualifies spiritual unity as the achieved result of the focusing energies of a creative subject. Commenting, for example, on the spiritual journey in the last book of *The Prelude*, Abrams writes: "As in Hegel's *Phenomenology* the spirit, at the close of its educational journey, recognizes itself in its other, so Wordsworth's mind, confronting nature, discovers itself in its own perfected powers."[10]   However integrated with the surrounding world, the mind Abrams sees is one that confronts nature as other in its efforts to rediscover its own vital yet nevertheless separate powers. Like the dialectical progress to which Abrams alludes in his reference to Hegel's *Phenomenology of the Spirit*, a progress that leads from thesis, through antithesis, to a new synthesis, the process of integration requires that the individual mind shape the world around it, remake it, so to speak, in accordance with its need for place and order.   The implication behind such Hegelian readings of Wordsworth's spiritual journeys is that the mind acts upon the world so as to project upon the external the vital order of its own perfect powers. The loop reveals a fundamental subjectivism: the reference point for mind and world is the creative but nevertheless separate self, and the resulting unity occurs in the form of a relationship *between* rather than a continuity *with* that which the mind perceives initially as other.

Many of Wordsworth's poems, however, record not a progressive journey leading to a higher or more integrated relationship between the self as confronting mind and the world as requisite other but an aborted quest that breaks the linear pattern of motion toward a presumed end while dropping the sojourner through all notions of selfhood into an integration of identity rather than relationship. Such integration mirrors the state of enlightenment Buddhists and Taoists describe as the result of a process of shedding all that stands between themselves and the essential way of the world. Commenting on this act of shedding as a process of unknowing, Henry Wei writes that "when the knower and the known have become one, or when the illusory polarity between subject and object has disappeared, then there will emerge enlightenment or realization of Tao."[11] For Wordsworth, this condition of total integrative realization occurs most visibly in those moments when the self simply disappears into its own processes of seeing and hearing, that is, into the very patterns of apprehension that arrest its progress along a specified route and that help to form the poet's initial sense of his vocational identity.

CHAPTER THREE

"STEPPING WESTWARD"
AND
"THE SOLITARY REAPER"

Especially appropriate for our purposes is "Stepping Westward" (*PW* 3:76), a short but profoundly suggestive poem of twenty-six lines composed in 1805 and first published in 1807. Following a brief note explaining that he and his sister were traveling through a lonely region of Scotland near Loch Ketterine on their way to a hut where they had stayed previously, the poet records how an acute sense of an indwelling, benignant cosmic order rose upon him in response to a question put to him and his sister by two women whom they met in the solitudes: "What, you are stepping Westward?" For Wordsworth, what appears initially as a *"wildish* destiny" (2) through a region "dark and cold; / Behind, all gloomy to behold" (9–10) becomes a *"heavenly* destiny" (12) upon the occasion of the greeting:

> I liked the greeting; 'twas a sound
> Of something without place or bound;
> And seemed to give me spiritual right
> To travel through that region bright. (13–16)

Natural yet supernatural, familiar yet unfamiliar, the greeting evokes a sense of ambient humanity in which the finite and the infinite fold upon each other in a journey that now partakes of eternity itself:

The echo of the voice enwrought
A human sweetness with the thought
Of travelling through the world that lay
Before me in my endless way. (23–26)

Two aspects of the encounter recorded in this poem are uniquely similar to Zen experiences of the Void: Wordsworth's description
of the greeting as "a sound / Of something without place or bound"
and the quality of mind that enables him to appreciate the greeting
as giving him what he calls a "spiritual right" to journey through
what at first appeared to be a desolation. Having neither place nor
bound, the greeting is truly empty or, to put it another way, infinite
and eternal so far as it comes from nowhere and goes nowhere.
Although the address issues through specific individuals, its sound
is larger than they, conveying neither provenance nor end. Not the
greeting itself, but the echo of the greeting, attracts Wordsworth.
Coming, as it were, from nothing and everything, the greeting is both
hollow and full, both nonexistent and eternally existent, stimulating
in the poet the equally paradoxical sensation that he is journeying
at once toward an earthly location, the hut, and toward eternity as
embodied in the glowing western sky. Wordsworth's subsequent
apprehension of a "human sweetness" in the "endless way" of his
journey eliminates for him all meaningful distinctions between for-
eign poet and native interlocutor, between self and other, human and
nonhuman, and even between near and far, leaving him in the midst
of a refulgent cosmic togetherness, an ultimate community of form
and being, reflected in the contrasting destinations of distant western sky and imminent hut.

The seemingly paradoxical dimensions of this greeting, particularly its hollowness and its fullness, constitute a nearly perfect
metaphor of the Zen principle of the interdependence of being and
nonbeing. T. P. Kasulis explains this interdependence by invoking
what he calls "The Allegory of the Bell." Kasulis imagines a mountain traveler in Japan coming upon "a rudimentary hermitage with
a large temple bell suspended from a simple wooden pagoda." (The
Japanese bell has no clapper and is struck from the outside as if it
were a gong.) The traveler asks the temple priest about the age of
the casting and receives the following answer: "This is about five
hundred years old, but . . . the emptiness within—*that's* eternal."

The priest then asks the traveler: "Now please answer *my* question. Where did the sound come from—from the metal casting or from the emptiness inside?" For Kasulis, the emptiness within "truly *is* eternal. . . . The space within the bell's enclosure is in itself the same regardless of whether the bell encloses it or not, but for that period of time in which it is enclosed by the bell, its relatedness to the casting makes it *functional*."[1] Nonbeing relates to being in the same way that the emptiness within the bell relates to the bell's casting and corresponds to Lao Tzu's presentation of the Void in the *Tao Te Ching*:

> Thirty spokes join one hub.
> The wheel's use comes from emptiness.
> Clay is fired to make a pot.
> The pot's use comes from emptiness.
> Windows and doors are cut to make a room.
> The room's use comes from emptiness.[2]

Emptiness here is not vacuity or absence. It is the vital and refulgent center that moves and shapes all things and that holds them together but that is itself forever in motion, forever becoming. Commenting on emptiness as the universal creative out of which all things come, Michael Adam explains that "The world as we know it is a becoming, is ceaseless change. Change is the only unchanging fact. . . . The Tao cannot be told, but its way can be seen as creative, not chaotic. There is no Creator, there is *Creativity*."[3] Similarly, Walpola Sri Rahula, a Buddhist philosopher concerned with the way in which change and motion comprise both creativity and emptiness as the absence of abiding form and center, remarks that "There is no unmoving mover behind the movement. It is only movement. It is not correct to say that life is moving, but life is movement itself."[4] The priest's question in the example Kasulis employs, like the echoic greeting in "Stepping Westward," admits of no answer. As the sound of the bell emerges from both the casting and the emptiness within the casting, so the greeting Wordsworth encounters in the Scottish Highlands emerges from a multiplicity of things, from the entire surrounding landscape of hills and valleys as well as from the psychic landscape of surprise and appreciation. Both questions, that of the Japanese priest and that of the Highland women, call us back from the arena of specificity, that is, of particular identities, places, and expectations, to what Kasulis terms "the inner nondiscriminating, nonbifurcating core, the basis of all discrimination." Both Taoists and Buddhists try to return to this source. But while Taoists model their efforts after what they perceive as a metaphysical and cosmogonic principle, students of Zen, according to Kasulis, are interested "not in the source of the universe, but in the source of our experience of the universe."[5]

It is in this latter sense that Wordsworth's experience in the Scottish Highlands corresponds most directly to the Zen Buddhist's efforts to achieve enlightenment. Through meditation and self-discipline, the student of Zen learns to empty himself of attachment to conceptual thought, to eliminate all conscious discrimination in order to become one with the flow of events. Wordsworth achieves this state of consciousness by hiding or shedding all professional identity, anything that would set him apart as disposed to ordering the world around him in accordance with a preconceived set of vocational or social expectations. Hence the note at the head of the poem explaining that he and his sister were returning to a place where they had stayed before: the greeting addresses not a poet, a recognizably special person, but a pair of beings who, though apparently lost or isolated, participate in the same beneficent community of selfless concern that motivates their interlocutors to begin with. The hut, in its simple, impartial hospitality, is both an appropriate refuge for the travelers and a symbol of the universal, all-encompassing self that lies beneath its expression in individual egos much as the bell's emptiness lies both within and beyond the casting that gives it a voice. Wordsworth's appreciation of the inclusive depth and power of the greeting issues through his tacit realization of a formless, interior self that, paradoxically, is the ground upon which the unity of the cosmos is manifest.

Ruth Fuller Sasaki, an American-born Zennist, refers to this formless interior self as the "Great Self": "Though we have temporary individuality, that temporary limited individuality is not either a true self or our true self. Our true self is the Great Self; our true body is the Body of Reality."[6] In like manner, Shôei Andô asserts that the "essential self," as he chooses to call it, "is beyond good and evil, serene, peaceful, deathless, immortal, self-sufficing, and . . . is of the same nature and root as the universe itself."[7] Given the manner of the greeting itself and the way in which he received it, Wordsworth could not have experienced his journey as anything other than an "endless way," that is, as a nonlinear falling through the individual and vocational self into the eternity of a "heavenly destiny," the motionless motion of the nonself which forms the dimensionless source or ground of being at all times.

The displacement of the egotistical self into the larger mode of a self-illuminative cosmic consciousness is also visible in "The Solitary Reaper" (*PW* 3:77), a poem Wordsworth insisted on placing next to "Stepping Westward" in all the collective editions of his works and one that forms a nearly perfect complement to the previous piece. Here, as in "Stepping Westward," Wordsworth, depicting himself as journeying through a solitary region, is confronted once again with something boundless—a song that overflows the vale whence it issues to be carried, like the earlier greeting of the Highland women, into his heart, organizing his perceptions ("I saw . . . I listened") while conveying a sense of the harmony of the surrounding world. But the poet does not know the words of the song. Unable to understand the reaper's dialect, Wordsworth, in the two middle stanzas, comments about the universality of the music he hears, then speculates about the possible themes of her song. But finding no answer to his question, "Will no one tell me what she sings?" (17), he accepts the music and moves on:

> Whate'er the theme, the Maiden sang
> As if her song could have no ending;
> I saw her singing at her work,
> And o'er the sickle bending:—
> I listened, motionless and still;
> And, as I mounted up the hill,
> The music in my heart I bore,
> Long after it was heard no more. (25—32)

Most critics read the poem in dramatic terms: Wordsworth is the separate abstracting consciousness confronting a baffling and chaotic world. For Geoffrey Hartman, the drama centers around Wordsworth's struggle to control or to "veil" the apocalyptic tendencies of his imagination in order to effect a binding of the self with nature.[8] Jonathan Wordsworth argues that the poetic mind at the center of the poem employs the abstractive powers of the imagination to sing the world into existence, to take possession of the world by ordering its separate elements into acceptable fictions.[9] Both readings view the poet as actively engaging the world from a position of relative isolation.

The final lines of the poem, however, border on the tautological in their effort to evoke an abiding quietude and passivity in the image of the poet watching and listening "motionless and still." When he moves on, it is with the burden of a mystery taken inwardly without the active interpretations of a speculative consciousness. The suggestion throughout these lines is not that of a particular consciousness fronting an unknown world but an oceanic consciousness inclusive of the world. Unable to determine a specific source or theme for the reaper's music, yet perfectly capable of imagining a variety of themes for the song, Wordsworth simply abandons professional form-making, which includes the egotistical need to create specific fictions or abstractions for possessing the world, and instead unveils the fundamental continuity of world and consciousness by accepting the music in the interior stillness generated by the complete frustration of conceptual thought. Wordsworth does not solve the mystery of the song. He absorbs the song and so becomes the mystery itself. The result is a Zenlike emptiness or stillness reminiscent of the quiescence Lao Tzu exalts in the *Tao Te Ching* when he counsels his students to "Attain complete emptiness, / Hold fast to stillness." Claiming that by this means "Things grow and grow, / But each goes back to its root," Lao Tzu affirms that "Going back to the root is stillness."[10] What Lao Tzu calls the "root" is for Wordsworth, as well as for students of Zen, the formless but refulgent interior Void at once the provenance and end of all forms, all means of knowing.[11]

The way to this consciousness is not through conceptual thought, through the application of mind to world as if the two were separate. It is, rather, through the recognition that mind and cosmos are essentially one. "You cannot use Mind to seek Mind," says Huang Po in a passage that recalls Lao Tzu's advice to empty the mind of thought. "Let a tacit understanding be all! Any mental process must lead to error. There is just a transmission of Mind with Mind."[12] Mike K. Sayama, attempting to define this Zen concept of mind in terms of Jungian psychology, argues similarly: "The fundamental tenet of transpersonal psychology is that the universe is one mind evolving to see itself. . . . The task before us is no longer to differentiate from nature and develop the ego, but transcend the ego and realize the true Self that is one with the universe."[13]

For Wordsworth, as well as for students of Zen, the "transmission" Huang Po indicates and the transcendence Mike Sayama exalts follow a path that leads not upward, toward a commanding intellectual overview of the world, but downward, through the acquired detritus of conventional social expectations and conceptual thought, to the formless ground of intuitive acceptance and understanding. In "Stepping Westward," the journey through Scotland ceases, opening instead onto the cosmic unity of hut and universe, of human and nonhuman. There really is no place else for the poet to go. The greeting marks an end point. The cessation of linear movement results from the power of an aural and visual process in which the echoic sound of the human voice, cutting beneath the formal conventions of the very language the voice employs, reveals such an emptiness of specific form and being, such an absence of abiding identity, as to produce the sense of a united heaven and earth fully visible in the instant of present existence. Martin Heidegger refers to this process of opening as a regioning:

> Regioning is a gathering and re-sheltering for an expanded
> resting in an abiding. So the region itself is at once an
> expanse and an abiding. . . . Because that-which-regions
> regions all, gathering everything together and letting
> everything return to itself, to rest in its own identity. Then
> that-which-regions itself would be nearing and distancing. . . . a
> characterization which should not be thought of dialectically.[14]

Heidegger's suggestion that the open ground of cosmic vision is at once an expanse and an abiding corresponds to Wordsworth's depiction of the hut in "Stepping Westward" as both a resting place and an opening onto the universe. Each thing is a revealing of and a resting place for the infinite. Attainment of the Void by falling through the self, as Huang Po would have it, or by transcending the ego, as Mike Sayama would say, is nothing more nor less than a return to the open ground or to the suchness, as some call it, of one's essential nature, which is always and forever presencing in all things. As Masao Abe writes, "When you realize your own suchness, you realize the suchness of everything at once."[15]

In "The Solitary Reaper," the linear quest for perspective, for overview, together with the self's efforts at enhancement through vocational identity, ceases through the frustration of the very processes the mind employs as its means of understanding. Centering on a question that holds the poet in a state of unknowing, intellect displaces itself. Wordsworth hopes to engage the song, to understand it, by isolating its theme. But the analytic mind is denied access to the song. The poet's speculations about theme lead nowhere. Even if he were to learn the theme of the song, the knowledge would do him no good. It would not solve the mystery of the song's power, its ability to hold the observer in a condition of near stasis. Why, after all, one theme and not another? Knowledge of the song's theme would simply give the poet one more thing to think about, teasing him into an endless set of questions leading only to more questions that further the division between the self and the world it apprehends as seemingly other. "Our thinking process tends to dissect reality in order to better understand it," writes Chang Chung-yuan. "Even though these dissections be reassembled into a whole, they can never regain their original inner unity."[16] For Wordsworth, to think thus about reality, in this instance about the theme of the music that overwhelms him, is not to live it, to experience it. If he is to know the song in a manner equal to the song's power over him, his knowing must be a mode of apprehension beyond conceptual schemas, beyond the point where the self, through the intellect, can grasp what it apprehends through the senses. As in "Stepping Westward," where the poet had no choice but to stop and accept both the eternity of the present moment and the dimensionlessness of all things, so in "The Solitary Reaper" he must acknowledge, however tacitly, the understanding that all themes are possible and that the singer herself, like the vale from which the song issues, is of the world itself, carrying in its presencing through her the entire history of human and natural process. Hence, the dismissal of speculative thought: "Whate'er the theme, the Maiden sang / As if her song could have no ending." Of course the song could have no ending. It had no beginning and has no bounds. Entering the poet, who is now void not only of conceptual thought but even of the desire to apprehend the music through conceptual schemas, whether discerned or imagined, the music enters his heart, literally becomes one with him, is himself. He knows the song now, not as a separate construct accessible to the intellect, but as himself, as an extension of his own being.

Zen is particularly useful in helping us understand that what has happened here is not simply a form of solipsism or anti-intellectualism. It is, rather, a form of what might best be described as meditative knowledge. In terms of its effect on him, the poet's effort to answer the question, "Will no one tell me what she sings?" parallels the practicing Zennist's effort to eliminate all adherence to discriminatory thought and all distinction between himself and the world by focusing on what is called a "koan." The koan is a seemingly paradoxical question, problem, or anecdote that the Zen student, particularly in the so-called Rinzai tradition, is assigned to meditate. Typical koans may ask questions like "What is the sound of one hand clapping?" or "What was your original face before you were born?" Others may center on a brief story, as in Joshu's "Mu": "A monk once asked Master Joshu, 'Has a dog the Buddha Nature or not?' Joshu said, 'Mu'!"[17] Mu is a bewildering and nearly untranslatable word vaguely corresponding to "not" and evoking roughly the concept of nothingness. The student may contemplate such a koan for years, not with a view to achieving an intellectual understanding of Joshu's response so much as with the intention of attaining a spiritual breakthrough into an entirely different mode of perception. "Mumon exhorts the Zen student to work at mu," says Kasulis, "to become it, rather than to understand it."[18] The koan's purpose, so far as it can be said to have a purpose, is to tease the individual out of linear thinking by carrying her backward and downward through an endless set of possible answers until she realizes the utter futility of intellectual approaches to the deepest questions of being. To contemplate the features of one's face before one was born, for example, leads the practitioner to the eventual realization that each individual has no beginning and no end and that each thing is in some mysterious way the embodiment of all other things. "We cannot conceive the birth of anything," writes Thich Nhat Hanh. "There is only continuation." In a passage that recalls the echoic regioning or gathering of all things in Wordsworth's "Stepping Westward," Thich Nhat Hanh says that "I can see that in a former life I was a cloud . . . a river, and the air . . . a rock . . . the minerals in the water." Hanh argues, however, that "This is not a question of belief in reincarnation. . . . Everyone of us has been a cloud, a deer, a bird, a fish, and we continue to be these things, not just in former lives."[19]

To encounter such a condition of interbeing, however, one must get beyond mere contemplativeness. One must become the *koan*, as Kasulis says of *Mu* practice, in order to understand the dimensionlessness of one's own being as well as one's identity with all things. "The intensity of this inquiry is such that the mind is literally possessed by preoccupation with the koan," writes John Crook. "There is no room for anything else. In the course of the work all aspects of personal being are drawn into this central inferno of questioning. . . . When the mind is fully unified the whole person has gathered at one 'place.'"[20] The *koan*, then, like the reaper's song, ceases to exist as a mere problem to be solved and becomes instead a vehicle of recovery, a praxis leading the individual into the deepest reaches not simply of his own being but of all being or of that which, at the deepest levels of awareness, he shares with all being. In this way, the *koan* helps the practitioner annihilate all sense of separation between herself and her environment, her mental as well as her physical environment. The student awakens to discover paradoxically that there really was no barrier to begin with, that the original mind has always been with him. Explaining, for example, that "The title *Wumenguan* [*Mumonkan*, the collection containing the *koan* "*Mu*"] can also be read, 'The Barrier That Has No Door,' or 'The Bolt on a Nonexistent Door,'" Thomas Cleary says: "According to the central teaching of Buddhism, in reality nothing cloisters the mind but attachment to its own thoughts and projections. The meaning of Zen is to realize this fact in experience, in the experience of genuine freedom of mind."[21]

Like Joshu, whose response eludes the dualisms implicit in a simple yes or no, Wordsworth veers from the quest for an intellectual answer to his own question and, effectively, from the subjective security that such an answer may provide. In the absence of anything for the self to hang onto, any conceptual framework, whether perceived as a quality of the contemplated object or problem itself or as an ordering projection of the creative mind of the observer, Wordsworth, like the student of Zen in his moments of highest meditative absorption, experiences the reaper's song as himself, literally as part of his being. Zen views this experience of identity with the

object of consideration as *kensho*, the condition of profound awareness Huang Po refers to when he speaks of "a transmission of Mind
with Mind." The word "transmission" is, however, misleading. In
kensho, knowledge is not transferred from one mind to another or
even from one mode of consciousness to another. The process of
knowing, so far as we can speak of it as a process at all, entails a
steady, sometimes an abrupt, falling away of layers of distinction
between what is initially perceived as self and other or as subject and
object until there is no difference between perceived and perceiver.
Hence, Lao Tzu's description of the sage or the enlightened individual as someone for whom spiritual knowledge is not an object of
acquisition but a process of loss: "Pursue Tao, lose daily. / Lose and
again lose, / Arrive at non-doing."[22] Zen expresses this condition of
unknowing in a famous four-line maxim composed sometime in the
seventh century in China:

1. *Transmission outside scriptures*
2. *Not relying on letters*
3. *Pointing directly to one's Mind*
4. *Attainment of Buddhahood by seeing into one's Nature*[23]

Significantly, the maxim avoids any form of the verb to know. It
speaks, rather, of seeing into one's nature. As Wordsworth gives up
the effort to know the reaper's song through questions about its
theme, resorting instead to seeing, hearing, and finally to accepting
the music as an extension of his own being, so the student of Zen
looks beyond words as a medium of knowledge to the actual experience itself. Commenting on the line about direct pointing to the
Mind, Shibayama says, "Here Zen teaches that if we want to experience the Truth, the Reality itself, we must once and for all transcend
the blind alley of dualistic human intellect."[24]

By accepting the reaper's music in his "heart" without recourse
to thematic distinctions based on the perception of an identifiable
logos behind or above the experience of the moment, Wordsworth
accepts an entire cosmos of mutually creative forces virtually indistinguishable from the powers of his own prereflective consciousness.
He becomes, in effect, creativity itself or, to put it another way, a living web of perceptions through which the universal creativity of life
is seen to flow. As Kitarō Nishida says: "The merely conceptual is

not the real."[25] The world of actuality is rather the world of self-creation, a creative environment that goes on forming itself through the individual and is in turn formed by the individual. "We act as creative elements of the creative world, as the self-determinations of the absolute present," writes Nishida. "Our selves, existential monads of the world, mirror the world, and, at the same time, are the world's own creative expressions."[26] At the heart of Wordsworth's world, as of Nishida's, is not an ordering creator, whether singer or poet, but creativity itself issuing through an art form that appears eternal: the maid's song, which overflows the surrounding vale, can indeed have "no ending," for it comes, like the greeting in "Stepping Westward," from everything else, from an eternally creative void, and returns to the same source. The heart that receives the song bears the same relationship to universal creativity as the Japanese bell does to the emptiness within its casting.

Chapter Four

The
Alpine Crossing

The chief problem for Wordsworth's readers is the impenetrable autonomy of spiritual emptiness and its resistance to analysis from the dualistic perspective of subject and object. Despite the pattern of displacement in "Stepping Westward" and "The Solitary Reaper," as well as in other poems by Wordsworth, readers ascribe the poet's creativity and spirituality to a personal human source or power. "What is so precariously spiritual about Wordsworth," says Geoffrey Hartman, "and so difficult to separate from egotism, is the minute attention he gives to his own most casual responses, a finer attention than is given to the nature he responds to. He rarely counts the streaks of the tulip, but he constantly details the state of his mind."[1] Occasionally, however, the very mind to which the poet is so attentive retreats before the influence of what appears to be one of its own powers. If we view this displacement in the context of a presumed distinction between self and other, we are compelled to a dualistic perspective that regards Wordsworthian spirituality and its attendant productivity either as a failure of intellect requiring a subsequent binding of individual creative powers or as a condition of reciprocity grounded in the relational notion of mind and nature as deeply analogous but nevertheless separate entities. We see this dualism in critical discussions of the crucially important Alpine passage in book 6 of *The Prelude*.

The incident itself occurs in the summer of 1790. Following his third year at Cambridge, Wordsworth, together with his friend Robert Jones, undertakes a walking tour across France, through the

71

Alps, into Italy. The high point of the excursion is to be the Alpine crossing by way of the Simplon Pass. At some point, however, the two, separated from a group that is to be their guide, lose their way, journey on alone, and learn from a peasant that they have crossed the Alps without realizing it. Deeply disappointed in having missed the anticipated excitement of a view from the Simplon, Wordsworth and his friend continue along a downward course with "a dull and heavy slackening" (6.549) that culminates in a powerful vision of what the poet calls the "one mind" (6.568). Writing about the event fourteen years later, however, Wordsworth is uniquely joyous, for he discovers in the very act of writing both the reason for his disappointment and the high freedom of the dimensionless mind:

> Imagination! lifting up itself
> Before the eye and progress of my song
> Like an unfathered vapour—here that Power,
> In all the might of its endowments, came
> Athwart me; I was lost as in a cloud,
> Halted without a struggle to break through;
> And now recovering, to my soul I say—
> "I recognize thy glory": in such strength
> Of usurpation, in such visitings
> Of awful promise, when the light of sense
> Goes out in flashes that have shown to us
> The invisible world, doth greatness make abode,
> There harbours, whether we be young or old.
> Our destiny, our nature, and our home
> Is with infinitude, and only there;
> With hope it is, hope that can never die,
> Effort, and expectation, and desire,
> And something evermore about to be.
> The mind beneath such banners militant
> Thinks not of spoils or trophies, nor of aught
> That may attest its prowess, blest in thoughts
> That are their own perfection and reward,
> Strong in itself, and in the access of joy
> Which hides it like the overflowing Nile. (6.525–48)

Interpreting Wordsworth's spirituality as a "precarious" state intimately conjoined with the ego, Hartman argues forcibly and confidently that the poet records here "a failure of the mind vis-à-vis the external world" and reveals, as well, a struggle "to bend back the energy of his mind and of his poem to nature."[2] E. A. Horseman, on the other hand, claims that Wordsworth here is dramatizing the contrast between "the sterile activity of the mind haunted by itself and the creative activity of the mind in contact with the external world." For Horseman, the entire thrust of book 6 of *The Prelude* is to demonstrate "the extreme oddity of the relationship between the images in the mind and Nature's images outside it."[3] Both readings occupy the same proverbial coin. In the former, mind is subdued to nature. In the latter, nature emerges as the analogue of a mind whose projection upon that which appears external to itself is simply part of the scheme of things. Neither effort yields a sense of Wordsworthian creativity as inhering in a release of the poetic mind into a selfless and universally inclusive consciousness.

The central problem for readers is Wordsworth's reference to imagination as "an unfathered vapour" that intrudes upon the "progress" of his "song," leaving him stranded, uncertain, unable to break through the cloud of expectation he had formed at the beginning of his journey. His vision of imagination as an intrusive energy contrasts sharply with the more positive, certainly the more attractive, way in which the poet and his contemporaries describe the power in their critical writings. In his 1815 Preface to *Poems in Two Volumes*, for example, Wordsworth, quoting Charles Lamb, speaks of imagination as "that power which, in the language of one of my most esteemed Friends, 'draws all things to one, which makes things animate or inanimate, beings with their attributes, subjects with their accessaries, take one colour and serve to one effect.'"[4] Similarly, Wordsworth's friend and colleague, Samuel Taylor Coleridge, exalts imagination as a powerful coadunative energy focused in the individual mind. "The primary IMAGINATION I hold to be the living Power and prime Agent of all human Perception, and as a repetition in the finite mind of the eternal act of creation in the infinite I Am," says Coleridge early in his *Biographia Literaria*. Later in the same work, Coleridge asserts that imagination functions under the control of "will and understanding" and that it "reveals itself in the balance or reconciliation of opposite or discordant qualities."[5] Unlike the faculty described in such critical treatises, the power that rises upon Wordsworth in the Alps seems an alien energy that threatens to separate the poet from the very world he seeks so strenuously to engage. But when viewed against the possible self-loss attendant upon the individual's complete yielding to the world, to its features and its powers, the imagination, in its very ability to usurp its place as a coadunative faculty, emerges as "the poet's ultimate defense," to use Thomas Weiskel's vocabulary, "the final foundation of his individuality." For Weiskel, as for many Western readers, creativity is rooted in the dramatic and issues in defense of the self. Building on Bloom's *Anxiety of Influence*, Weiskel remarks: "In life, it is our defenses that enable us to exist and therefore to create. . . . The Imagination's usurpation issues for Wordsworth in triumphant self-recognition and self-vindication."[6] Imagination viewed in this light is the central theme of the Alpine passage and the hero of the moment because, no matter how threatening or usurpatory, it is rooted, to quote Weiskel once again, "in a domain properly human."[7]

The problem for the reader is made even more complex by the verbs the poet employs and the revisions he makes over the years. In the 1805 version of *The Prelude*, the "unfathered vapour" simply comes "Athwart" the poet in the "might of its endowments." In the 1850 version of the incident, however, imagination is an "awful Power" that rises "from the mind's abyss." Though he continues to regard it as "an unfathered vapour," it is now one "that enwraps, / At once, some lonely traveller" (6.594–96). The later version of the Alpine passage conveys a much more powerful sense of the imagination as an autonomous power with a life of its own, one that plays upon and extends the individual's distinction from the world through which he moves.

We must be careful, however, not to allow the critical, more analytic language of the later version of *The Prelude* to lead us into a dualistic reading of the original experience. From a spiritual perspective, the Alpine experience, conveyed more holistically, as it were, in the earlier than in the later version of the poem, occurred not in 1790 alone but over a fourteen-year period beginning in 1790 and extending through the writing of the text in 1804. The 1805 version of the passage, for example, deliberately confuses the distinction between the historical event and the writing of the poem. "Imagination! lifting up itself / Before the eye and progress of my song," we are told in lines 525–26, "came / Athwart me" (528–29). The syntax of Wordsworth's language here collapses distinctions between the present moment of composition, when imagination is seen "lifting" itself before the poet in the act of writing, and the past event in history, when it putatively "came / Athwart" him. One feels that the original experience and the act of writing about that experience are all one, that there is no distinction between present writing and past experience. The "song" has been going on, as it were, for fourteen years. And it is the song which seems important, not the singer. So far as we can speak of a singer, he is, like the eye to which he refers, in the song, of the song.

The 1850 version, on the other hand, distinguishes more clearly the present from the past by eliminating the participial "lifting up itself / Before the eye and progress of my song" and replacing it with the appositive "here the Power so called / Through sad incompetence of human speech" (6.592–93). The later version, which cuts directly to the past tense, reflects the intervening years between the strenuous efforts of the composing process in 1804, which seems to occur from within the event itself as in some way an ongoing phenomenon, and the later critical efforts that produced the "Essay Supplementary to the Preface," a work dominated by linguistic concerns. Reflecting, for example, a more analytic—one might say more scholarly—mind visibly separated from the material it observes, the "Essay" tells us that *imagination*, like *taste*, "is a word which has been forced to extend its services far beyond the point to which philosophy would have confined them." Earnest of the way in which "The word, imagination, has been overstrained" to serve "intellectual *acts* and *operations*," Wordsworth remarks that "Poverty of language is the primary cause of the use which we make of the word, imagination."[8] The appositive renaming of imagination in the 1850 version of *The Prelude* reflects the poet's distance from the actual dynamics of the event and his growing preoccupation with understanding imagination in the dualistic context of subject and object, a context that emphasizes definition and that views creative power as something to be grasped by the intellect and used, to give Weiskel his due, for the preservation of the self.

I do not wish to disparage Wordsworth's comments in the later
"Essay" or, for that matter, in the later *Prelude*. Both works convey
valuable insights into the limits of language and the need for greater
critical understanding of the terms we use to describe aesthetic experience. But there is a clear distinction between the earlier and the
later treatments of the Alpine incident, a distinction that we ignore
at great peril to our understanding of Wordsworth's spiritual genius.
The earlier text is clearly the more spiritually astute of the two and
reflects more accurately Wordsworth's intuitive grasp of the dynamics of infinitude as the ever-emergent and continually shifting
grounds of the true mind. Indeed, if we read the passage carefully,
we see that the Alpine event, extended across a fourteen-year period
from 1790 to the moment of composition in 1804, is not really about
imagination at all but about the mind and its ability to let go its need
for place, boundary, and distinction, that is, for identity itself. A Zen
reading of the Alpine passage enables us to see both the incident
itself and Wordsworth's later treatment of the event as the working
of a radical spiritual freedom at the base of life, a spirituality that
releases human mentality from egotism and dualism while concurrently arraying the self in the features of the world.

Following the coordinating conjunction *And* at the head of line
531 is Wordsworth's address, not to his imagination, but to his soul:
"to my soul I say— / 'I recognize thy glory'" (531–32). The theme of
usurpation applies both to the imagination as a usurping energy and
to the soul's ability to be usurped. Lines 532–37, with their reference
to "visitings" that illuminate the "light of sense," affirm the glory of
the "soul," not as an aspect or attribute of the soul's existence as a
separate entity, but as the mark of its self-dispersal. The soul ceases
to exist as a noun or as an object held together by a central core and
emerges as a verb, as activity best described, perhaps, as a shifting
constellation of forces. Greatness abides neither in what the soul
acquires as knowledge or experience nor in what defines its existence
as an actual entity but in what it loses, in its ability to be usurped:
"in such strength / Of usurpation . . . doth greatness make abode."
The agency of usurpation—in this instance the imagination—does
not stand in opposition to the soul or to nature, but services the soul's
ability to be usurped, to relinquish the need to hold together as a separate, abiding form, to hang on, as it were, to its own expectations as
the contents of its being. In other words, the soul's greatness abides

paradoxically in its ability to eliminate itself, to disappear, to exist in no place, in no time, and with no abiding content or faculty as the defining characteristic of its existence.

Viewed in this light, Wordsworth's reference to imagination as an "unfathered vapour" that halts the forward progress of his song, leaving him without direction, with no place to go and nothing to hang onto, conforms to the pattern of his spirituality as he has been experiencing it for some time. Like the echoic sound beneath the voice of the Highland women in "Stepping Westward" or the song of the Highland reaper, the imagination is sourceless. Hence the shift in lines 538–39 to the proclamation that "Our destiny, our nature, and our home / Is with infinitude, and only there." The most remarkable aspect of this infinitude is that it is not a static empty ground, a bottomless pit through which the spiritual sojourner falls, but a dynamic phenomenon of moving states, "hope that can never die, / Effort, and expectation, and desire, / And something evermore about to be" (540–42). The mind, "beneath such banners militant" (543), Wordsworth tells us, simply disappears, ceasing its efforts to call attention to itself as a separate phenomenon while giving itself instead to "thoughts / That are their own perfection and reward" (545–46)——thoughts which form a matrix of moving conditions that work ultimately without source or center to hide the very mind they compose. Imagination, then, is an alien energy only if viewed as a human power residing separately in a separate mind—the perspective we see displayed so convincingly in the later essays and one that conforms to the critical need to step back and analyze experience in the dualistic manner of the scholar-intellectual. So far as the Alpine imagination inhabits an eternally shifting matrix of sourceless forces, it is inaccessible to the critical mind, for this mind is hidden, having disappeared, "like the overflowing Nile," into its own workings. Of course Wordsworth is halted. As in "Stepping Westward," there is no place to go, for all places are absolute, are the end point of the journey. And, as implicit in "The Solitary Reaper," the going itself, if it does occur, must be inevitably, not toward a specific goal, but upward into the ever-emergent ambient wholeness of the eternally here and now. Wordsworth's use of the present participle *lifting* in the 1805 document, his perhaps instinctive confusion of the present moment of composition with the past incident in time and space, implies his intuitive understanding that in the selfless dimension of cosmic consciousness, particularly as Zennists understand the experience, there is no time, there is no place, that defines and confines us. "We never leave the Way for a moment," says Amakuki Sessan. "What we can leave is not the Way."[9] Ken Wilbur adumbrates the perspective at greater length:

> Now precisely because Mind is everywhere and everywhen, because it is always already the case, there is no possibility or even meaning in "trying to find It" or in "trying to reach It," for that would imply a movement from a place where Mind is absent to a place where it is present—but there is no place where it is absent. Mind, being everywhere present, abides in no particular place where we can finally grab it.[10]

But if the imagination and the shifting mind-ground to which it necessarily belongs is inaccessible to the critical, analytic intelligence, it is not beyond the range of spiritual consciousness. From the Zen perspective, Wordsworth's treatment of the Alpine incident marks a spiritual breakthrough, a moment of *satori*, as Zennists might call it, in which the individual falls through all notions of selfhood and its attendant confinements into the dimensionlessness or the "infinitude," to use Wordsworth's vocabulary, of cosmic being. The provocative impulse, the proverbial pebble, as it were, in the pool of consciousness, to appropriate an image Coleridge employs at the head of "Kubla Khan," is the imagination, which compares favorably, in this instance, with the Zen *koan*. As the imagination is sourceless and therefore beyond the critical ken of the self-bound analytic intelligence, so the *koan*, as we have already seen, is an insoluble case or problem the student of Zen is assigned to meditate, sometimes for years on end. Some of these *koans*, like the one that asks the practitioner to meditate the features of his face before his parents were born, impel the individual backwards and downwards through a regressive series of speculations that ends only with the student's breakthrough into a vital, nonintellectual experience of virtual identity with the universe and all things in it. This is what Kasulis means when he says that the student does not solve the *koan* in any intellectual sense. Rather, he becomes one with the *koan* and, so, one with the universe. "This very irrationality of *koan*, which refuses all the intellectual approaches . . . makes us realize the limitations of our discriminating intellect and finally drives us to despair of it," says Shibayama. In this despair, the student "comes to the extremity where no logic and no verbalisms are of any avail. His eyes are open, yet he is not conscious of seeing. He has ears, but is not conscious of hearing. He is actually in the state of no-mind, no-thought, where there is neither the self nor the world."[11] Like Wordsworth halted before the sourcelessness of his own imagination, the student comes to understand his mind in terms of what Masao Abe calls the "'Non-abiding Origin' through which all things are established."[12] The student has no choice but to surrender, not the intellect, but her compulsive need for intellectual answers, and to accept her essential oneness with the world around her in all its multiple features.

Among *koans* that exist in narrative form, one that strikes me as uniquely parallel to Wordsworth's Alpine experience is that of Tokusan, known in Chinese as "Te-shan Hsuan-chien" (ca. 781–867). One day Tokusan came to visit his master, Ryotan (Chinese, Lung-t'an Ch'ung-hsin). After spending the day with Ryotan, Tokusan got up to return home. As he was about to leave, he remarked that it was dark outside. The master lit a candle. But as Tokusan reached for it, Ryotan blew out the flame. At this instant, we are told, Tokusan "was awakened, and made a bow to the Master."[13] Like Wordsworth both in the Alps and in the act of writing his poem, Tokusan was halted with no place to go, compelled to accept the darkness in the understanding either that there is no specific home to go to or that all places and conditions are one's home. Commenting on Tokusan's dilemma, Shibayama remarks that "At the extremity of no mind, no self, where neither heaven nor earth exists, all of a sudden the moment of breaking through this no-mind was given. He was revived as the Great Self of no-self."[14]

For Wordsworth, the seal of this mind-state is the vision attendant upon the downward course of his journey through the Gondo Gorge subsequent to his meeting with the peasant. Bereft of expectation, stripped, as it were, of the egotistical need to discriminate one thing from another, one prospect from another, Wordsworth has a vision of reality as a boundless state of motion and interanimation in which all things—winds as well as waters—and all conditions—light as well as darkness, tumult as well as peace—play to, augment, and thwart each other in a gigantic moving web of perfect oneness:

> The immeasurable height
> Of woods decaying, never to be decayed,
> The stationary blasts of waterfalls,
> And everywhere along the hollow rent
> Winds thwarting winds, bewildered and forlorn,
> The torrents shooting from the clear blue sky,
> The rocks that muttered close upon our ears,
> Black drizzling crags that spake by the wayside
> As if a voice were in them, the sick sight
> And giddy prospect of the raving stream,
> The unfettered clouds and region of the Heavens,
> Tumult and peace, the darkness and the light—
> Were all like workings of one mind, the features
> Of the same face, blossoms upon one tree;
> Characters of the great Apocalypse,
> The types and symbols of Eternity,
> Of first, and last, and midst, and without end. (6.556–72)

One is constrained to yield all efforts to find a center and a source for this vision. There is no mind standing behind the events of this incident and making them happen. The "one mind" of this passage is the working of its own contents. The passage is all predicate. True, rocks "mutter," crags "speak." But to whom and for what purpose? As voice is neither centralized nor focused in a particular source, so tumult and peace, darkness and light are not separately existing phenomena, but necessary aspects of each other. Nothing is weighted or emphasized over anything else. All is an endless swirl of forces, objects, and events folding inward on each other to form the pulsatory eternity of the present moment, a totality that is always with us, that is for all practical purposes the coming forth of each thing in its own right. Surrendering the self that would make of reality a picture painted to the prescribed dimensions of an anticipatory individual mind, Wordsworth emerges as the vision itself—most assuredly the eye and progress of his own song. The entire frame of mind that would ask, What sees? What hears? has been displaced and is rendered, for all practical purposes, nonexistent. The vision simply occurs, erupts, as it were, from nowhere. Wordsworth, perfectly attuned, happily or not, to the fundamental dimensionlessness of his own being, his own mind, omits even to say, I saw; I heard. The entire vision occurs without a subject, conveyed, in simple obedience to the sourcelessness of its occurrence, in the form of an eternally evolving and revolving predicate. The vision is perfectly autonomous, beyond all notions of an observing subject and a separate creator.

If constrained to speak of the vision as having a center at all, we must employ a terminology grounded in an ontology of change and motion and focused in an aesthetic dimension both inclusive of and beyond the human. Nolan Pliny Jacobson provides a glimpse of what such an aesthetic may look like:

> Beyond the breakdown . . . of individuals and nations, beyond the frustration of human hopes, beyond the relentless sweep of time and destructiveness which ruin every other ground upon which one may take one's stand, there is the fullness of the aesthetic center of life, the flow of unstructured quality, unlimited in its intensification and stimulation of each moment in even the common and ordinary affairs of life, providing that one is able to penetrate the confinements of language and cultural pattern.[15]

In the absence of intention, in the frustration of anticipation, Wordsworth simply accepts the stream at hand and with it the ordinary flow of objects, events, and forces. In this moment of acceptance, all appears as indeed it really is—as extraordinary. We look in vain to ascribe the vision to a particular individual in a particular setting or even to a specific power of the mind.

The genius of Wordsworth's response to the imagination, then, is not in his restraining it and in his subsequent binding of himself to nature, as Hartman would have it, nor in his using it as a "screen . . . to block the emergence of the deeper, more terrifying and traumatic memory of Gondo Gorge,"[16] as Weiskel claims, but in his complete immersion in it, in his giving himself to the impulse in such a way as to allow it to pass through him so that the greater, more inclusive, nondiscriminating self emerges as the abyssal vision itself. In this state, no one thing or condition takes precedence over another. "Tumult and peace, the darkness and the light" are all the necessary workings of one mind. As Tokusan comes to understand that darkness is simply another aspect of the same moving, sourceless reality that produces light and that his going is simply another aspect of his eternal staying, so Wordsworth encounters motion as motionlessness in the "woods decaying never to be decayed" and in "The stationary blasts of waterfalls." Empty of preference, momentarily bereft of the need for specific pleasures, Wordsworth comes as close as any Western spiritualist to the condition of the Zennist in the moment he breaks the bonds of selfhood. Michael Adam describes this condition of mind as a state beyond seeking, beyond even the need for direction:

> The man of Zen, being "wholly empty, and nothing holy," lives without preference or judgment, as the sun itself in a world where all things may be seen to play their necessary parts. To find the world whole in this way is to have ceased seeking any one part of it. Without seeking, there is no seeker; with no one standing in the way, the light is freely allowed, all the ten thousand things are revealed.[17]

Significantly, Adam, like many Zen writers, resorts to the passive voice—"the ten thousand things are revealed"—in compliance with his understanding that what he is here describing is uncentered and sourceless. As there is no seeker and no seeking in this state, so there is no fixed perspective, no specific place from which the light emerges to illuminate each thing. Rather, the illuminative light is of the nature of the things themselves, an aspect of their eternal coming forth in the moment of vision subsequent to the lived experience of one's identity with all things. "Light is not a thing and so may not be sought," says Adam. "It is nothing and so may not be found anywhere but everywhere. To see anything wholly is to find the light that is on all things, is in them, *is* them."[18]

The light Adam here describes corresponds, I believe, to the way in which Wordsworth's imagination functions in the Gondo Gorge. So far as we can speak of the post-Simplon vision as the product of imagination, we are compelled to see this power not as a chastened energy disciplined to go forth from a self bound or committed to a world it perceives as other but as a power resident in all things as the shared ground of their existence. And here again, we have difficulty if we approach this field of vision from the critical perspective Wordsworth offers outside the intuitive range of his vision. In his "Preface to Poems" (1815), for example, Wordsworth argues that the

imagination "shapes and *creates*; and how? By innumerable processes; and in none does it more delight than in that of consolidating
numbers into unity, and dissolving and separating unity into number,—alternations proceeding from, and governed by, a sublime consciousness of the soul in her own mighty and almost divine powers."[19]
The Simplon passage in the 1805 version of *The Prelude*, however,
subverts the theme of the imagination as a separately existing coadunative power located in the individual mind. The structure of the
episode as recorded in the poem strips the imagination of any
ground, any perspective, outside the action of the events recorded.
Following upon the peasant's tidings, the two friends hurry downwards, entering "Into a narrow chasm" (553). The poet describes himself as totally immersed in his surroundings, dwarfed almost out of
existence, moving, if not reluctantly, then at least with no expectation
through a "gloomy pass" (554). There is no suggestion here of perspective, no stable height or eminence from which the poet, like the
wild-eyed prophet of John Martin's *The Bard*, commands the forces
and events of the abyss below. The poet, rather, is in the abyss,
indeed is of the nature of the abyss itself. The vision that comes upon
him comes, as well, out of him. So far as we might describe it as a
product of imagination, we are impelled toward the same movement
and condensation of prepositions Adam employs in his description of
the light of awakening—if imagination is a projection on, it is also in
and of the things it illuminates, *is* the things themselves.

From a Zen perspective, Wordsworth's experience in the Gondo
Gorge is pure in the truest sense, that is, devoid of egotistical intention and of any effort to cater to the needs of an expectant self. In the
absence of ego, subject and object, self and other, expectation and perspective are, according to Kitarō Nishida, "mutually submerged, and
the universe is the only reality." The submergence Nishida articu-
lates here cannot occur in the realm of speculative consciousness
viewed as servicing a separate self:

> To experience means to know events precisely as they are. It
> means to cast away completely one's own inner workings, and
> to know in accordance with the events. . . . When one experi-
> ences directly one's conscious state there is as yet neither sub-
> ject nor object, and knowledge and its object are completely
> united. This is the purest form of experience.[20]

The fourth-century B.C. Taoist philosopher Chuang Tzu adumbrates the problem the artist has in expressing this unity: "Heaven and earth were born at the same time I was, and the ten thousand things are one with me. . . . The one and what I said about it make two, and two and the original one make three. . . . Better not to move, but to let things be!"[21] Wordsworth's post-Simplon vision, sustained over a period of fourteen years, reflects his effort to express oneness from within the event of oneness, literally from within the gorge. The vision of one-mind results not from his own creative and projective efforts but from his letting things be, from his yielding all expectations of reality. To carve out a source for the vision is to project upon the moment of experience the egotistical need for a conceptual schema outside the vision itself and focused in the very realm of subject and object Wordsworth abandoned in the Gondo Gorge.

The entire Alpine episode, however, is made even more complex for us because Wordsworth himself had only the dimmest understanding of such experiences and resorted on many occasions to the very dualistic perspective his latter-day readers, burdened additionally with a post-Arnoldian tendency to critical rather than intuitive viewpoints, employ in their efforts to probe this exceedingly autonomous state. In book 2 of *The Prelude*, for example, shortly after remarking that there were times when he "forgot" that he had "bodily eyes" and that what he saw "Appeared like something in myself, a dream, / A prospect in my mind" (2.367–71), Wordsworth asserts that "A plastic power / Abode with me" (2.381–82) and that "An auxiliar light / Came from my mind, which on the setting sun / Bestowed new splendour" (2.387–89). Later in *The Prelude*, this "plastic power" or "auxiliar light" is identified as the human imagination, which expressly resembles the transforming power nature thrusts upon the world in "That domination which she oftentimes / Exerts upon the outward face of things" (13.77–78). Certain "higher minds," Wordsworth tells us near the end of *The Prelude*, carry this power with them and employ it in such a way that "They from their native selves can send abroad / Like transformation; for themselves create / A like existence" (13.93–95). Although we can see Wordsworth laboring to focus imagination in two places, in mind and nature, reflecting perhaps a persistent intuitive understanding that it crosses boundaries between self and other, the critical thrust of his poetry reveals the powers of mind as in some way a mimetic repetition of external forces rather than as an extension of those forces and hence identical with them.

To Zennists, such an understanding of the relationship between mind and world reflects a basic confusion about the nature and dimensions of human consciousness. The source of this confusion, according to R. H. Blyth, one of the first to discover elements of Zen in Wordsworth's art, is the poet's preoccupation with imagination as a transforming power rather than as an agency of disclosure. Blyth focuses on the Preface to *Lyrical Ballads*, especially on the passage in which Wordsworth says that his purpose in choosing "incidents and situations from common life" is "to throw over them a certain colouring of imagination" and "to make these incidents and situations interesting."[22] Arguing that the poet's theory of imagination "is not so much wrong as it [is] detestable," Blyth offers a definition of imagination that he believes is closer to the heart of Wordsworth's best poetic efforts: "*It is the power by which we become so united,—or better, by which we realise our original unity with persons, things, situations, so completely,—that we perceive them by simple self-consciousness.*"[23]

Imagination conceived as the power "*by which we realise our original unity with persons, things, situations*" exists, then, less as an attribute of the observing mind than as an indefinable creative ground or way through which all things emerge to voice their existence and their oneness with all other things. Wordsworth, in visions like that which occurred in the Gondo Gorge and in poems like "Stepping Westward" and "The Solitary Reaper," understands intuitively, in a context beyond the occasional critical perches of his poetry and prose, that we cannot trace creativity and spirituality to a particular source, that there is a realm of imagination deeper than the coadunative power the critical mind alternately applauds and fears. Like the sourceless light Adam exalts, a sort of ground-light, as it were, the Wordsworthian imagination, at its deepest levels, is a shifting constellation of forces so intimately conjoined as to be indistinguishable from each other and from the individual who appears to be observing the world from a position outside it. This imaginative ground does not take us to a perch outside or above the world we inhabit, nor does it take us to one that we reconstruct to meet the needs of a separate self; it enables us, rather, to fall through the self's need for perchings, returning us selfless, purged of egotism, to the world we have never really left.

CHAPTER FIVE

"THE BLIND
HIGHLAND BOY"

T he return to a deep and abiding creative ground upon which the imagination as a separate power dissipates is particularly visible in "The Blind Highland Boy" (*PW* 3:88–96), the work I would like to use to conclude this section. Composed in 1806, the poem was placed eventually at the end of *Memorials of a Tour in Scotland, 1803*, where it serves as a fitting conclusion to the spiritual pattern we see emerging in "Stepping Westward" and "The Solitary Reaper," its companion poems in the volume. The poem tells of how a blind boy, using an abandoned turtle shell as raft, sets off across his native lake in search of the high adventure and the distant lands described by the boisterous mariners he hears along the shore when the ships come in. But having journeyed only "The fourth part of a mile . . . ere he was seen / By any human eye" (158–60), the boy is rescued from the dangerous depths and returned to shore. Particularly significant is the absence of a prevailing mood of anguish in the boy's acceptance of the common life he was at first disposed to abandon in favor of an imaginative venture that moves him, as Wordsworth puts it, "in face of Heaven" (156). Though deeply disappointed in having been prevented from wrapping himself, as it were, in "that inward light / With which his soul had shone so bright" (211–12), the boy accepts the shore without struggle: "And, though his fancies had been wild, / Yet he was pleased and reconciled / To live in peace on shore" (243–45).

Reading this poem in the light of Hegelian thought, we might be inclined to view the boy's return as a new, achieved state of being,

87

as the result of a progress from a thesis rooted in fancy, through an antithesis comprising a denial of fancy, to a higher synthesis grounded in the notion of reconciliation. The boy accepts the joyous reality of his vision, as he had accepted the spiritual friendship of his God in the early stanzas of the poem: "For God took pity on the Boy, / And was his friend; and gave him joy / Of which we nothing know" (23–25). From the Hegelian perspective, the result is a new autonomy for the boy, one in which imagination is chastened and subdued, made to serve the boy's present needs rather than to drive him upon the depths of its own desires.[1] Such readings address the imagination as the central concern of the poem. Through denial of the apocalyptic imagination that leads him "in face of Heaven," the boy comes to a new and higher understanding of his own powers and preserves himself from psychic death or absorption in the object of imaginative desire. To see the imagination as the center of the poem is to see the poem's theme as one of self-preservation in the face of powerful, appealing, yet nevertheless dangerous, forces.

Reading "The Blind Highland Boy" in response to "Stepping Westward" and "The Solitary Reaper," however, and in light of the Zen doctrine of no-mind enables us to see that Wordsworth's concern here is not with self-preservation and autonomy of imagination so much as with consciousness and with the process of awakening to a deeper understanding of the grounds of consciousness. To see this, we must abandon the Hegelian notion of poetry as a progress toward an achieved synthesis and view the poem as a way or path that returns us to the infinitude of our own being. In "The Blind Highland Boy," this infinitude is conveyed through the image of the lake, the controlling metaphor of the poem. Described as "one of mighty size, and strange; / That, rough or smooth, is full of change, / And stirring in its bed" (53–55), the lake, like the infinitude Wordsworth depicts in book 6 of *The Prelude* as "Our destiny, our nature, and our home" (6.538), is a place of motion and complexity and is fundamentally inclusive:

> For to this lake, by night and day,
> The great Sea-water finds its way
> Through long, long windings of the hills,
> And drinks up all the pretty rills
> And rivers large and strong. (56–60)

The boy's journey across the lake in pursuit of dreams inspired by the mariners is a rejection of the very infinitude the lake represents. His rescue is important not because it preserves him from the watery abyss but because it enables him to awaken to a state beyond dreams: "So all his dreams—that inward light / With which his soul had shone so bright— / All vanished" (211–13). The action of the poem, dominated by the journey across the lake, corresponds remarkably to the spiritual action Wordsworth describes in his *Essay upon Epitaphs* as part of his discourse on the soul's progress toward its understanding of infinity:

> As, in sailing upon the orb of this Planet, a voyage, towards the regions where the sun sets, conducts gradually to the quarter where we have been accustomed to behold it come forth at its rising; and, in like manner, a voyage towards the east, the birth-place in our imagination of the morning, leads finally to the quarter where the Sun is last seen when he departs from our eyes; so, the contemplative soul, travelling in the direction of mortality, advances to the Country of everlasting Life; and, in like manner, may she continue to explore those chearful tracts, till she is brought back, for her advantage and benefit, to the land of transitory things—of sorrow and of tears.[2]

What the Highland boy awakens to is nothing less than the sheer dimensionlessness of the ordinary, to a recognition that the "Country of everlasting Life" and the realm of "transitory things—of sorrow and of tears" are one and the same. Evidence of this final recognition emerges in the poem's depiction of light and joy. Moving in quest of his dreams, the boy, we are told, is flushed with an "inward light" that dissipates upon his rescue. By the end of the poem, he is not ecstatic but "pleased and reconciled / To live in peace on shore" (244–45). From a Buddhist perspective, the boy's loss of ecstasy is not a falling off or evidence of a lesser spiritual existence. Rather, it marks a state of freedom from the pleasurable desires that drive the deluded individual on most occasions and that render him the pawn of phenomenal events. What the boy has lost is the self that would cling to such modes of ecstacy as that implied by the term "inward light." What he acquires, so far as we can speak of acquisition at all, is an expansive frame of mind that, like the lake above which he journeys, is both absorptive of and beyond, or independent of, the very contents that comprise its being at any point in time and space. The boy's final contentment is the sign of his understanding that ordinary and extraordinary experience are, if anything, interchangeable. For the Buddhist, the realm of true spirituality is not apart from the realm of everyday, ordinary existence. The message is particularly well conveyed in a brief Zen parable on the nature of spiritual light:

> A man of Zen was visited by a monk who said that he had come from the Monastery of Spiritual Light. "In the daytime, we have sunlight," said the man of Zen. "In the evening, we have lamplight. What is Spiritual Light?" The monk could not answer, so that the man of Zen spoke for him: "Sunlight, lamplight."[3]

The imagination that drove the blind Highland boy upon the dreamscape of its own making is, like the "Spiritual Light" of the Zen parable, partial and preferential and disappears in the very act of being pursued in the context of capaciousness. And here, as in the Alpine passage from *The Prelude*, the prevailing action is not one of acquisition but one of usurpation. Like Wordsworth in his effort to write from within the Alpine incident as an ongoing phenomenon, the blind boy, in giving up the self to the creative dynamic of the moment, arrives not at a new place, at a new state of being, but in what Buddhists argue has always been and always will be our true home—the mind. The Buddhist document *The Awakening of Faith* calls this home the "One Mind and Its Two Aspects": "The Mind in terms of the Absolute is the one World of Reality . . . and the essence of all phases of existence in their totality."[4] Commenting on the theme of totality in this passage, the Chinese patriarch Fa-tsang remarks that the absolute and the phenomenal "are not differentiated, but include each other. . . . The one World of Reality is nothing but the world of samsara. At the same time the world of samsara is nothing but the world of the Absolute."[5] Samsara, generally speaking, denotes the ordinary world of unenlightened reality. Here, Fa-tsang, like all Buddhist commentators in the Mahāyāna tradition, is asserting that the phenomenal world is essentially identical with nirvana, the goal of spiritual practice in Buddhism and the realm of freedom from the cycle of phenomenal effects. "The essential unity of samsara and nirvana is based on the view that everything is a mental representation," according to *The Shambhala Dictionary of Buddhism and Zen*, "and thus samsara and nirvana are nothing other than labels without real substance. . . . To the extent that one does not relate to the phenomenal aspect of the world but rather its true nature, samsara and nirvana are not different from one another."[6] In this view of reality, the absolute and the phenomenal interpenetrate each other, much as the mountain rills and the waters of the ocean mingle in the lake across which the Highland boy journeys. In his commentary on *The Awakening of Faith*, Yoshito S. Hakeda sees this intermingling of absolute and phenomenal in terms of mutual containment:

> The Mind necessarily contains within itself two orders or aspects—the transcendental and the phenomenal, the universal and the particular, the infinite and the finite, the static and the dynamic, the sacred and the profane, the Absolute and the relative. . . . The Absolute order, therefore, does not exist apart from the relative order; rather, they differ epistemologically but not ontologically. Man is presented as being located at the intersection of these opposing orders.[7]

So far as he accepts gracefully the loss of the inward light and is truly "well pleased," as the poem tells us, to live his life on shore, the Highland boy, like the Zen practitioner, has found the point of intersection between the absolute and the phenomenal and has discovered that ordinary reality is both extraordinary and nothing special. For the practicing Zennist, to abide in a special spiritual light apart from the mundane affairs of the world is to participate in the subtlest form of spiritual arrogance. The point is well made in story after story of Zen practitioners who, after making a significant breakthrough into a momentary experience of oneness, must be reminded of their considerable distance yet from true understanding. The Zen master Hakuin, for example, experienced a powerful moment of enlightenment in his twenty-fourth year, when, after a long period of intense meditation, he awoke to discover that "There is no cycle of birth and death through which one must pass. There is no enlightenment one must seek." Flushed with the joy of his discovery,

"Shouldering my glorious enlightenment," as he puts it, Hakuin goes to visit his master, Shoju, in the present-day Nagano Prefecture, to tell of his experience. But the master senses in his pupil's countenance an element of pride and a subtle attachment to the occasional ecstasy of high spirituality, what Hakuin himself would later identify in his poem "Zazen Wasan" (Song of Zazen) as a mode of discrimination, and denounces the monk as a "poor hole-dwelling devil." Several months later, still trying to understand the nature of his experience, Hakuin, while out begging one day for food, encounters a deranged person who beats him with a broom. Unexpectedly, Hakuin penetrates, in the instant of the beating, several *koans* he had been meditating and drops through all sense of a separate spiritual self and through all attachment to special states of mind. "After I returned to the temple I spoke of the understanding I had gained," he reports. "The Master neither approved nor denied what I said, but only laughed pleasantly. But from this time on he stopped calling me a 'poor hole-dwelling devil.'"[8]

In all these examples, those from the Wordsworth canon as well as those taken from Buddhist documents, the linear quest for perspective in the form of speculative understanding and for joy in the apprehension of high visionary experience ceases through the frustration of the very processes the mind employs as its means of engaging the world. The aborted quest erupts in the individual's breaking through the confined samsaric self to encounter a condition of pure freedom and acceptance one comes to understand as the basic ground of one's existence from the very beginning. There really was no place to go and nothing to seek. "In short," writes Urs App while comparing Eastern and Western "mystical" practices, "any striving towards a goal is seen as simply one more expression of the problem."[9] App, here, is relying on the well-known and seemingly paradoxical Zen notion that the way or path of true spirituality is the method of no method. Similarly, while responding to Huang Po's famous reprimand, "As long as you are concerned with 'by means of' you will always be depending on false media," the modern Zen teacher Richard De Martino says: "The basic method of Zen Buddhism tries to get the ego to realize that ultimately there can be no method for it to attain to its True-Self-Awakening apart from the awakening itself."[10] The Zen practitioner, like Wordsworth's Highland boy, comes to understand that one place is as good as another and that to interpose anything, be it intellect or imagination, between the self and its awakening to its true nature is to hamper severely the freedom available to all in the simple goalless acceptance of the moment. As Niu T'ou Fa Jung, a sixth-century disciple of the Fourth Patriarch, writes in his *Hsin Ming* (Song of Mind):

> Taking pleasure in Tao is calming,
> Wandering free and easy in reality.
> No action and nothing to attain,
> Relying on nothing, manifesting naturally.[11]

The breakthrough into such freedom conveys a sense of universal escape, but escape without place and direction. "At last I've broken Unmon's barrier!" declares the Zen master Daito (1282–1337) at a poignant moment of enlightenment. "There's exit everywhere—east, west; north, south. / In at morning, out at evening; neither host nor guest. / My every step stirs up a little breeze."[12]

The freedom and emptiness Zennists here describe correspond directly to what Wordsworth frequently encountered, especially on his tours. In a letter to Mrs. Thomas Clarkson, for example, Wordsworth's sister Dorothy explains how the conduct of the 1803 journey through Scotland eventuated in a high sense of freedom and joy only when she and her brother gave up all sense of moving toward an expected goal:

> we were very happy during our tour, particularly the last
> month, for at first we were but half weaned from home and
> had not learnt the way of enjoying ourselves—We seemed to
> consider the whole Tour as a business to be by us performed
> for some good end or other, but when we had fairly got forward
> the rambling disposition came upon us and we were sorry to
> turn back again.[13]

Not until they had relinquished the self's need for goals and expectations and had given themselves completely to the dynamics of the journey at precisely the point in time and space at which it was unfolding before them were Dorothy and William able to accept fully the world through which they moved. They had discovered what Wordsworth frequently described in his poetry—that the method of the journey is its own end, that the Way or the Tao of the spiritual quest leads not to a specific end but only back to the method itself, to the processes of a mind emptied of self and its need for special states.

The following chapters will explore various aspects of this mindscape as the dynamic spiritual ground constitutive of poems that touch on such important themes as solitude, poverty, suffering, mutability, spiritual depth, and beauty.

PART THREE

ZEN MOODS
AND THE
POETRY OF EMPTINESS

Introduction to Part Three

The mind emptied of self and of the self's need for abiding perspective and for special states of feeling and spirituality is strongly resistant to intellectual analysis. A path or way that is its own end, the mind of emptiness, though eternally present, creative, and emergent in and as all things, is unsituated, formless, and essentially indefinable. It is not, however, inaccessible. Though it eludes the best efforts of thought and language to confine it within a specific system of philosophical principles and linguistic signifiers, it can be apprehended through a range of emotion known as the four dominant moods of Zen art: *sabi* (isolation), *wabi* (poverty), *aware* (impermanence), and *yugen* (mystery). Unlike feelings expressed purposely in art designed to produce specific effects, "These moods are not consciously created," writes Lucien Stryk; "they are experienced as we experience the light of the sky, hardly aware of the delicacy of its gradations."[1] As expressed in Zen poetry, these moods differ from ordinary passions in that they occur primarily in states of high meditation accompanying experiences of self-displacement aligned with the breakthrough to spiritual enlightenment. "Poems of satori [enlightenment] and death are poetic expressions of the Formless Self at the most significant moments of life, of satori and death respectively," says the modern Zen master Taigan Takayama. "Poems on general subjects are likewise versifications in various situations of that void Self."[2] What Taigan Takayama calls "versifications . . . of that void Self" Shin'ichi Hisamatsu describes as "the self-expression of the Formless Self."[3] For the Zennist, spirituality precedes aesthetics. Zen literature is an expression of the spiritual. Or, as Takashi Ikemoto writes, "Zen literature is an expression of the Inexpressible, and Zen poetry is a typical example."[4]

Similarly, William Wordsworth, explaining how emotion informs his poetry, claims, in his Preface to *Lyrical Ballads* (1802), that his art results not from "a distinct purpose formally conceived" but from "habits of meditation" that form feelings that "carry along with them a *purpose*."[5] Wordsworth's reference to "habits of meditation" suggests a level of creative spirituality beneath the expression of emotion for its own sake and beyond the self-conscious pursuit of vocational intentions. Viewed in relation to the four dominant moods

97

of Zen art, Wordsworth's poetry, like the art of Zen, emerges as an expression of the Formless Self that lies beneath all creativity.

In part 3, I would like to examine this creative spirituality through an intertextual perspective that inverts the dialogic procedures of earlier chapters. Whereas I have tried previously to bring Zen to Wordsworth in order to demonstrate the English poet's accessibility to Buddhist culture, I would like now to explore the depth and range of his universality by applying his poetry to the Zen context. "In spite of difference of soil and climate, of language and manners, of laws and customs, in spite of things silently gone out of mind and things violently destroyed," says Wordsworth elsewhere in his Preface to *Lyrical Ballads*, "the Poet binds together by passion and knowledge the vast empire of human society, as it is spread over the whole earth, and over all time."[6] As Zen moods are not exclusively the province of Eastern spiritual and aesthetic communities, so the "passion and knowledge" Wordsworth exalts as synoptic forces in human society need not be viewed as functioning only in the sphere of Western cultural traditions. Focusing on the dominant moods of Zen art as a basis for comparison enables us to employ the work of a major Western writer to elucidate an important aspect of Zen aesthetics, thereby enriching both sides of the East-West dialogue while contributing a sense of Wordsworth's innate vitality and internationality.[7]

CHAPTER SIX

SABI: THE SPIRIT OF
SOLITUDE AND FREEDOM

C hief among the moods of Zen—and the one that, for all practical purposes, forms the bedrock of Zen enlightenment—is *sabi*, the spirit of nonattachment or freedom. Associated with the period of early monastic training, "*Sabi* may be defined as the feeling of isolation," writes Lucien Stryk, "or rather at a midpoint of the emotion when it is both welcome and unwelcome, source of both ease and unease."[1] The feeling of isolation results from the strong sense of the emptiness of all things and surfaces most poignantly in those moments of spiritual breakthrough accompanying deep meditation, especially during concentration on a *koan* or public case. After long meditation on Joshu's *Mu* or Nothingness, for example, the fifteenth-century Japanese master Saisho wrote:

> Earth, mountains, rivers—hidden in this nothingness.
> In this nothingness—earth, mountains, rivers revealed.
> Spring flowers, winter snows:
> There's no being nor non-being, nor denial itself.[2]

For the Zennist, the experience of nothingness, the sense that there is no abiding nature within things and no separately existing force or power beyond things, does not produce feelings of despair. Rather, she experiences a radical freedom at the heart of all things, including her own existence, and comes to understand that the terms *being* and *nonbeing* are alike inadequate to express the depth of one's own nature. The meditator realizes that no conceptual schema and no system of emotional preferences command his allegiance. "There is never any expectation in Buddhism of acquiring a conceptual system in which the deepest secrets of life are explained," writes Nolan Pliny Jacobson. "No Buddhist has ever provided a manual for living which describes and explains the entirety of nature as though from a lofty transcendental position."[3] To be free of conceptual schemas is, in a sense, to be isolated. Such freedom leaves the individual without the security of an abstract code on which to rely in all circumstances. But it does not, by the same token, abandon the individual to a mere web of relativity nor does it cast her upon a frozen tundra, as it were, of arbitrary choices. Rather, by freeing the individual from all conceptual schemas and the emotional responses they necessarily produce, Zen identifies the person with the situation, allowing the existential unity of the moment, the common ground of event and respondent, to determine the content of action. T. P. Kasulis, commenting on what he calls "the context of *mu*," asserts that "To be freely responsive, to act as the situation demands, one must have no vested interest in a conceptual scheme. Having one's meaning as a person tied to no context, one can express each situation or occasion (*jisetsu*) as it is."[4] We can see why, in the context of *Mu*, Saisho would depict nothingness as both hiding and revealing. Nothingness itself is beyond conceptual logic, eluding all efforts of definition, presencing only in and through each thing and each individual's experience. Hence, Kasulis's reference to the person not as responding to but as expressing each situation.

Central to the notion that the individual is both a participant in and an expression of each situation is the understanding that one has no self. "In the final analysis, the Zen person has no *intrinsic* meaning," writes Kasulis; "there is no person at all."[5] What Kasulis means is that there is no ego-entity, no separately existing self to respond to situations conceived as other than the composite dynamics of one's living in the present moment. "Grounded in the prereflective base of experience, the Zen Buddhist changes his or her meaning as the contexts change," says Kasulis.[6] To engage the prereflective base Kasulis describes is to encounter radical freedom not as a context in which one does as one pleases but as the very ground of one's own being. One is not free to do. One is freedom itself. It is this freedom that Zen as a philosophic and aesthetic discipline attempts to give its practitioners by encouraging them to yield all notions of selfhood, to break through all reliance on the self and on those systems of thought and feeling that fuel the ego process. *Sabi*, or freedom in the sense of nonattachment to the self and to the concept of 'selfhood', is a primary concern of Zennists because it is perhaps the most difficult of all the Buddhist principles to realize as the actual living base of one's own existence. "Men cling hardest of all to the illusion that at the core of their being there is an indestructible, unitary, coherent Soul," writes Jacobson. "Men fabricate this supposititious Self and use it disastrously as the living centre of their behaviour."[7] But once the breakthrough is made, once the individual comes to understand the self as an illusory entity standing between the composite elements of his being and the limitless depths of his existence as a cosmic manifestation, he is free to enter upon the river of being as that which is continuous with his own nature. "All minds have, in fact, the great 'Stream of Being' as their indispensable condition," says Jacobson; "it is this life-continuum, and not a unitary soul or self, which sustains each individual in his struggle."[8] The "life-continuum" Jacobson here exalts in place of self as the vital center of existence emerges, then, not as a form of anarchy or nihilism but as a condition of universal interdependence in which one is all and all is one.

In Zen Buddhism, the document that perhaps best describes this process of self-loss in relation to the practitioner's growing understanding of emptiness as the ground of existence and of nonattachment as the means to that ground is Ching-yuan's famous sermon on mountains and waters:

> Thirty years ago, before I began the study of Zen, I said, "Mountains are mountains, waters are waters."
>
> After I got an insight into the truth of Zen through the instruction of a good master, I said, "Mountains are not mountains, waters are not waters."
>
> But now, having attained the abode of final rest [that is, Awakening], I say, "Mountains are really mountains, waters are really waters."[9]

Ching-yuan understands that to be truly free, one must be free even of the idea of emptiness. Commenting on the third stage of awakening, what Ching-yuan calls "the abode of final rest," Masao Abe remarks that "Emptiness empties itself, becoming non-emptiness, that is, true Fullness. Herein, all forms of anxiety and all forms of attachment, open and hidden, explicit and implicit, are completely overcome."[10]

Among Wordsworth's poems, a work that comes noticeably close in theme and structure to reflecting the Zen experience of *sabi* and the attendant process of self-displacement is "Resolution and Independence" (*PW* 2:235–40). The poem records an incident in which a traveler comes upon a leech-gatherer, "The oldest man he seemed that ever wore grey hairs" (56). The old man's words and manner alter the narrator's perception of himself and his world, leaving him in a state of rest and independence remarkably comparable to that which Ching-yuan records as the third stage of awakening.

The poem opens with an image of the narrator wandering unselfconsciously in a world of delighted eye and ear: "I saw the hare . . . I heard the woods and distant waters roar; / Or heard them not, as happy as a boy" (16–18). Like Ching-yuan in the first stage of his life, the world for Wordsworth's narrator is that of ordinary dualistic vision. Though certainly pleasant, it is not the realm of high spiritual restfulness Ching-yuan describes as the final stage of insight. Evidence of the narrator's dualistic relation with his surroundings emerges most poignantly in stanza five, when the traveler withdraws from the simple act of seeing and hearing to reflect upon his life from the perspective of one outside the events of his own responses: "Even as these blissful creatures do I fare; / Far from the world I walk, and from all care" (32–33). The narrator's judgment of his state as a blissful condition distinctly different from the ordinary world of care reveals his distance from the very objects of eye and ear that so charm him. The early seeing and hearing are valuable to him only so far as they provide him with escape from the frenetic pace of ordinary vocational life. They do not help him when vocational doubts surface to cloud the moment with fears of death and failure:

> I thought of Chatterton, the marvellous Boy,
> The sleepless Soul that perished in his pride;
> Of Him who walked in glory and in joy
> Following his plough, along the mountain-side:
> By our own spirits are we deified:

We Poets in our youth begin in gladness;
But thereof come in the end despondency and madness.
    (43–49)

So far as he sees the realm of care as distinctly different from the
happiness and freedom he experiences in his present idyllic surroundings, he inhabits what Abe, writing of Ching-yuan's first stage,
calls a world "grasped from the outside, not from within."[11] In this
dualistic context, thought comes to the narrator not in support of his
blissful kinship with the world he sees and hears but as an intruder
that both services and frets an ego concerned primarily with fame
and security.

Nearly overwhelmed by the "fears and fancies" (27) that come
to him, the narrator, "by peculiar grace" (50), as he calls it, encounters an old man sitting "Beside a pool bare to the eye of heaven" (54).
Compared first to a "huge stone . . . Couched on the bald top of an
eminence" and later to a "sea-beast crawled forth, that on a shelf /
Of rock or sand reposeth, there to sun itself" (57–63), the old man seems
"not all alive nor dead, / Nor all asleep" (64–65). In contrast to the
traveler's frenetic pacing between delight and dejection—"As high as
we have mounted in delight / In our dejection do we sink as low"
(24–25)—the old man's stability forms a perfect image of the motionless motion of nature itself: "Motionless as a cloud the old Man
stood, / That heareth not the loud winds when they call; / And moveth
all together, if it move at all" (75–77). Like the pool beside which he
is sitting and the cloud that reflects his motion, the old man embodies the cosmic emptiness of Zen consciousness, an emptiness of selfhood that, to recall Dōgen's description of Zen, reflects the world
itself: "To forget the self is to be actualized by myriad things."[12]

In his stillness and equanimity, and in his apparent oneness
with the world around him, the old man appears as the very embodiment of what Zennists call "zazen," loosely translated as "sitting
meditation":

In its purest form *zazen* is dwelling in a state of thought-free,
alertly wakeful attention, which, however, is not directed
toward any object and clings to no content. . . . If practiced
over a long period of time with persistence and devotion, *zazen*
brings the mind of the sitter to a state of totally contentless

wakefulness, from which, in a sudden breakthrough of enlightenment, he can realize his own true nature or buddha-nature . . .
which is identical with the nature of the entire universe.[13]

Zazen, as we can see from this definition, is not simply the act of
sitting cross-legged, nor is it a condition of thoughtlessness. It is for
the Zennist a state of being that one carries with him throughout his
enlightened life and that defines his manner on all occasions. "In the
midst of all good-and-evil," says Hui Neng, the Sixth Patriarch of
Chan (Zen), "not a thought is aroused in the mind—this is called za.
Seeing into one's Self-nature, not being moved at all—this is called
zen."[14] Explaining that zazen means "not to give rise to discriminating consciousness," Shibayama, in his commentary on Hui Neng's definition, writes: "In other words, zen is to awaken to our fundamental
Self-nature, and not to be disturbed by the superficial waverings of
our minds."[15]

The old leech-gatherer's posture and manner—his stillness in
motion, his motion in stillness, as conveyed through the cloud simile—constitute the posture of zazen itself. Indeed, the cloud image is
so powerful among Buddhists that the Chinese patriarch Xu Yun
(1840–1959) adopted the term Empty Cloud as his name. "Like all
the great Masters of Chan before him," writes Upasaka Wen-Shu of
Xu Yun, "he laid stress on the non-abiding mind which is beyond
reach of all conditioned relativities, even as they arise within it, a
paradox that only the enlightened truly understand." Commenting
on Xu Yun's name, which conveys the very essence of sabi or nonattachment to the conditions of one's mind, Wen-Shu continues: "He
symbolises the 'great man' hidden in ourselves and his name 'Empty
Cloud' reminds us of that greater, 'undiscovered Self' that we are all
fated to explore."[16] Evidence of the leech-gatherer's freedom, of his
distance from or nonattachment to the "conditioned relativities" of
his own mind, surfaces in his response to the narrator's question,
"What occupation do you there pursue?" (88). In a matter-of-fact
tone, and with perfect equanimity, in words "above the reach / Of
ordinary men" (95–96) and with voice "like a stream / Scarce heard"
(107–8), the old man explains that "gathering leeches, far and wide /
He travelled; stirring thus about his feet / The waters of the pools
where they abide" (121–23). The picture of the old man partially submerged in the various ponds he visits, sharing his blood with the

lowliest of creatures, is an image of oneness too powerful to ignore. It is precisely what Dōgen means when he speaks of self-forgetting as the process by which we are "actualized by myriad things." In the "Uji" fascicle of the *Shobogenzo*, Dōgen elaborates on this notion of self-realization by explaining that "The way the self arrays itself is the form of the entire world."[17] Commenting on this line from Dōgen, Joan Stambaugh remarks that "The self set out in array . . . is, so to speak, a meeting-place or confluence for the presencing of all things in a total situation."[18] Though he is worried about a dwindling number of leeches, the old man does not allow his worries to intrude upon the powerful equanimity of his manner. And he never reveals any concern about the lowliness of his profession. In tacit realization of the larger field of identity he shares with all things, the old leech-gatherer's worries simply emerge and disappear in the motion of the moment. There is no place for these worries to abide, nothing to which they can attach themselves, for the ego-self in which they would dwell is simply nonexistent.

Given the magnitude of the old man's spirituality, it is not surprising that the narrator describes him in religious terms, seeing in him a kind of teacher whose very being, like that of the Zen master, conveys the lessons he has to offer. Comparing the old man's speech to that of "Religious men, who give to God and man their dues" (98), the narrator finds it easier to think of the leech-gatherer in terms of his nonexistence, his emptiness:

> And the whole body of the Man did seem
> Like one whom I had met with in a dream;
> Or like a man from some far region sent,
> To give me human strength, by apt admonishment.
>   (109–12)

Like the very world in which he is arrayed, the leech-gatherer both is and is not there. To seek for any principle of vocation that might ground his identity in a specific function is as futile as the quest for a final cause to justify the existence of the cosmos. The old man, in the absence of ego, simply *is*, and he is all things.

Small wonder, then, that Wordsworth ceased calling the poem "The Leech Gatherer" and gave it the title "Resolution and Independence."[19] By the end of the work, the narrator, ashamed of his earlier concerns for the self, declares:

> I could have laughed myself to scorn to find
> In that decrepit Man so firm a mind.
> "God," said I, "be my help and stay secure;
> I'll think of the Leech-gatherer on the lonely moor!"
>   (137–40)

The old man inhabits the "abode of final rest," to use Ching-yuan's vocabulary, the condition Abe exalts in claiming that in the final stage of awareness, "Emptiness empties itself . . . becoming true fullness" and the condition the narrator approaches in aligning security in godhead with thoughts of the leech-gatherer. The narrator's resolve—to "think of the Leech-gatherer on the lonely moor"—is grounded in the notion that freedom is not a context that serves the development of the individual self but the fundamental nature of all reality. The ultimate freedom is the understanding that all modes of selfhood, all forms of allegiance to particular conditions and identities, are illusory. The resolution accompanying such a sense of freedom works not to solve problems or to establish only pleasant states of being but to accept all conditions as the passing contents of mind. "Pleasures and pains, joys and sorrows are merely accidents of life," writes Soyen Shaku. "They do not enter into its essential fabric."[20] The "essential fabric" of life, so far as we can speak of life's having any fabric at all, is its freedom from all form in the very midst of passing form as the necessary mode of its expression. The individual's resolve, then, is not to remove himself from life or protect himself in a shell of autonomy or of conventional ideology but, like the leech-gatherer, so to identify with the nonabiding nature of life as to be the ground of its contents at all times.

Bunan, a Japanese Zen poet of the seventeenth century, views this condition of identity as a shared thingness:

> The moon's the same old moon,
> The flowers exactly as they were,
> Yet I've become the thingness
> Of all the things I see![21]

Freedom defined as nonattachment to the conditions of being does not imply the absence of condition. It is, rather, the true fullness that comes with the self-forgetting Dōgen remarks as the object of Zen study. It is, for the practicing Zennist, a state of purity that by its very nature admonishes those yet aligned with the ego. "When we are able to live a life of non-attachment—like the water flowing in the river—there will be no stagnation and no stale conditions," says Gyomay M. Kubose. "Life will be always fresh and clean."[22] How could the narrator of "Resolution and Independence," with his narrow self-concern and his vocational fears, confronted with the perfect "thingness" of the partially submerged leech-gatherer at the envisioned point of his union, of his virtual identity, with sky-reflecting lake and blooded leeches, be anything but admonished? Like Bunan, the old man, in his freedom from both the worries and the joys that partially form his being, is the transpiring image of life itself in all its refulgent purity.

Indeed, throughout the Wordsworth canon, one senses that the many references to freedom and solitude, whether direct or implicit, celebrate not a resistance to the conditions of experience nor a transcendence to a higher state beyond the vicissitudes of life but an abiding acceptance so complete in itself that all moods, all states of being, are in some way positive and contributive. "Expostulation and Reply" (*PW* 4:56), for example, a short poem composed and published in 1798, implies a happy freedom from all experience as the requisite ground of wisdom beneath the visitations of human will:

> The eye—it cannot choose but see;
> We cannot bid the ear be still;
> Our bodies feel, where'er they be,
> Against or with our will. (17–20)

Wordsworth's response to this condition of choiceless seeing, hearing, and feeling is a "wise passiveness" (24) that eschews seeking beyond what is in essence always here:

> Think you, 'mid all this mighty sum
> Of things for ever speaking,
> That nothing of itself will come,
> But we must still be seeking? (25–28)

In "The Tables Turned" (*PW* 4:57), a companion poem subtitled "An Evening Scene on the Same Subject," relinquishment of the seeking mind erupts in "Spontaneous wisdom" and truth aligned respectively with health and cheerfulness. Counseling his interlocutor to "Come forth into the light of things" (15), the speaker says of nature:

> She has a world of ready wealth,
> Our minds and hearts to bless—
> Spontaneous wisdom breathed by health,
> Truth breathed by cheerfulness. (17–20)

Significantly, the "Spontaneous wisdom" of the third line and the cheerful truth of the fourth are unsituated. They exist as aspects of a total situation, not as products of individual effort. Wisdom that is literally breathed by health and truth that is breathed by cheerfulness emerge from the very ground of being itself. As we cannot determine where breath begins and ends, so we cannot establish a source for such wisdom and truth, for there is no recorded boundary between the individual as putative respondent and the world he sees and hears presumably as other.

Similarly, the sense of wisdom and truth is not presented here as the result of a corporative effort culminating in what we might think of as a Hegelian movement from thesis, through antithesis, to a synthesis in the form of a marital bonding or uniting of the individual with nature. Like the "mighty sum" of the previous poem, the totality productive of spontaneous wisdom and cheerful truth exists as a unity prior to the division of self and other. In this prior unity, we see and hear from the perspective of a deeper, unsituated self identical to what the modern Zen philosopher Keiji Nishitani determines to be the midst of things themselves. "Precisely because we face things on a field separated from things, and to the extent that we do so, we are forever separated from ourselves," says Nishitani. "Or, to put it in positive terms, we can get in touch with ourselves only through a mode of being that puts us in touch with things from the very midst of those things themselves."[23] To see and hear from the midst of things themselves is to be in touch with, indeed is to be the very breathing forth of, the deepest reaches of our own being and so to arrive at an end point where further seeking is futile.

We should understand, however, that such an end point does not displace thought, emotion, and desire. Rather, it enables one to encounter one's experience, whether sad or happy, whether invited or not, free of attachment to the condition, free of the need either to retain it as a profile of the self or to use it to extrapolate philosophical principles and theories. Commenting, for example, on the high joy accompanying *satori*, the Zen term for the experience of awakening, the modern Zen priest Takayama says, in words similar in spirit to Wordsworth's insistence on a wise passiveness as the appropriate response to the realization that "Our bodies feel, wher'er they be, / Against or with our will": "Satori will make it possible for you to live constantly in a state of joy. But remember that one needs further discipline to rid oneself of this joy, for there must not be even the shadow of attachment, any kind of attachment, in Zen."[24] Similarly, writing on the place of will and desire as they relate to feeling, Katsuki Sekida says of Zen nonattachment: "It is not that you are without desires, but that while desiring and adhering to things you are at the same time unattached to them."[25] Like the *satori* of Zen, the "wise passiveness" of Wordsworth's poems is a condition of freedom, not submission.

So far as we can speak of the individual, then, as doing anything, that is, as being active in any significant way or as performing anything that could be construed as culminatory, we must think in terms of renunciation or withdrawal, though these terms, too, are inadequate to the extent that they imply something to renounce. Wordsworth seems to understand the problem because his speaker in "The Tables Turned" counsels his listener to "Come forth into the light of things" rather than necessarily to shed light on things as if what one sees is the projective result of individual effort. To encounter the "light of things" themselves, one must relinquish the notion of light as emerging from a separate source. Indeed, one must relinquish the notion of separateness itself. To come into the light of things, one must become the things themselves, must see through things as things. Nishitani calls this mode of seeing the "self-realization of reality." Appropriating the English word *realize*, with its twofold meaning of "actualize" and "understand," Nishitani remarks that in the state of unity prior to the division of self and other, "our ability to perceive reality means that reality realizes (actualizes) itself in us; that this in turn is the only way that we can realize (appropriate through understanding) the fact that reality is so realizing itself in us; and that in so doing the self-realization of reality itself takes place."[26] Wordsworth understands tacitly and implicitly that such realization requires a yielding of or a distancing from the analytic intellect, what near the end of "The Tables Turned" he calls "Our meddling intellect" which "Mis-shapes the beauteous forms of things" so that "We murder to dissect" (26–28). The "meddling intellect" does not seek only to know. It obtrudes itself upon the conditions of experience in such a way as to impose concerns of the illusory separate self and its attendant will upon processes of consciousness that cut to the sources of life itself, to the seeing and hearing that lie beneath and beyond the very self they appropriate in the total, interanimative process of mutual realization.

To awaken to the light of ordinary things, then, is to be free of the intellect that, in its quest for the principles behind things, tends to value that which appears to eye and ear only so far as it services the self's need for theoretical answers and explanations. The modern Zen author Michael Adam compares this quest for answers to the way in which conventional religions and philosophies "seek meaning in things, so to find 'tongues in trees, books in running brooks, sermons in stones and good in everything.'" Warning, however, that one may find what one seeks, Adam continues: "One finds tongues, books, sermons, and good, but the trees, the brooks, the stones are missed, the bad is overlooked, the ten thousand things are lost."[27] In a manner that recalls the question put forth in "Expostulation and Reply" regarding the quest for meaning "'mid all this mighty sum / Of things for ever speaking," Hui Neng, the Sixth Patriarch of Chan, asks: "Why should we formulate any system of Law when our goal can be reached no matter whether we turn to the right or to the left?"[28] Like the Zennist and like the speaker of "Expostulation and Reply," the meditative persona of "The Tables Turned" counsels the seeker to give up the "dull and endless strife" of books, to listen instead to "the woodland linnet," for "There's more of wisdom in it" (9–12), and to look beneath the discriminatory, analytic mentality to the realm of consciousness aligned with the very pulse of being itself: "Come forth, and bring with you a heart / That watches and receives" (31–32).

Zen helps us to understand that the watchful heart, the wise passiveness, of these poems, like the deep tranquillity of the leech-gatherer, is neither a form of submission to mere instinctual awareness nor a state of being that simply opposes intellect with an alternative mode of consciousness. It is, rather, a condition of freedom in which the mind is allowed to expand to dimensions subsumptive of intellect. It does not displace intellect so much as offer a ground of freedom beyond the relationship of mind and nature as necessary contraries. Like Wordsworth, for example, the Zennist is intrigued with seeing and hearing as transintellectual and transvolitional conditions. A famous Zen poem remarkably similar in spirit and tone to the direct simplicity of the lines on seeing and hearing in "Expostulation and Reply" turns on what we might call a dangling modifier that deliberately conjoins subject and object in seer and seen: "Nightingale's song / this morning, / soaked with rain."[29] All is soaked with rain, with song. The nightingale and the perceived listener are one and the same, intersoaked, as it were, with sound and rain. The soaking is all. There is no I, no separate singer, no separate listener. Like the "Spontaneous wisdom" and the happy "Truth" of "The Tables Turned," the activities of this poem are grammatically undistributed, unsituated, focused neither in a perceived watcher nor in a nature separate from a watcher but in both at the same time. The poem thus builds on what Hisamatsu views as the identity of form and content as reflecting the union of the subject and the subject's expression in Zen literature: "What is of greatest significance in this literature . . . is not so much that it gives objective expression to Zen, as that Zen is present as a self-expressive, creative subject. In other words, that which is expressing itself and that which is expressed are identical."[30] What Hisamatsu sees as the "self-expressive, creative subject" Thomas Merton, writing on Zen insight, views as the means by which being sees itself through the individual: "Zen insight is not *our* awareness, but Being's awareness of itself in us."[31]

To encounter this awareness, one must relinquish all thoughts of a self-nature distinct from the world, together with all thoughts of any separately existing essence or indwelling spiritual substance to which one relates. "This is not a pantheistic submersion or a loss of self in 'nature' or 'the One.' It is not a withdrawal into one's spiritual essence and a denial of matter and of the world," says Merton. It is, rather, a mode of self-realization grounded in the absolute identity of individual and cosmos. In words that parallel Nishitani's concept of Zen experience as the "self-realization of reality," Merton continues:

On the contrary, it is a recognition that the whole world is aware of itself in me, and that "I" am no longer my individual and limited self, still less a disembodied soul, but that my "identity" is to be sought not in that *separation* from all that is, but in oneness (indeed, "convergence"?) with all that is. This identity is not the denial of my own personal reality but its highest affirmation.[32]

The stillness of the leech-gatherer, the "wise passiveness" of "Expostulation and Reply," the awakening to "the light of things" through the watching and receiving described in "The Tables Turned" result not from a relational process culminating in the joining of self and other but from a transintellectual, transvolitional recognition of the essential identity of humankind and nature in the absence of ego.[33]

CHAPTER SEVEN

WABI:
THE SPIRIT OF POVERTY

I f *sabi*, the spirit of nonattachment and freedom, is the necessary
precondition of Zen awakening, *wabi* or the spirit of humility and
poverty is, perhaps, the chief ideal of the sect and in many ways
its most visibly charming feature. But *wabi* conveys a sense of poverty grounded not in the idea of privation or denial so much as in what
Stryk calls an "antirelativism," a refusal, so to speak, to participate
in questions like "what's good? what's bad? what's valuable? value-
less?"[1] The mood is particularly visible in the Zen tendency to celebrate the common, simple things of life in as unobtrusive a manner
as possible. A classic example is Bashō's famous haiku on the
Nazuna: "When I look carefully— / *Nazuna* is blooming / Beneath
the hedge."[2] Bashō's poem is not simply a sentimental gesture
toward the commonplace *nazuna*, normally regarded as a weed. It
reflects, rather, an effort to elude relativistic standards in general.
Commenting on Bashō's poem, D. T. Suzuki writes, "Once off human
standards which are valid only on the plane of relativity, the *nazuna*
weeds match well with the peonies and roses, the dahlias and
chrysanthemums."[3] The mood is most poignantly evoked in response
to objects hitherto ignored emerging suddenly as exceedingly precious and significant.

A particularly good example of *wabi* among Wordsworth's
poems is the series devoted to the daisy. In "To the Daisy" (*PW*
2:135–38), composed in 1802 and published in 1807, the flower's
humility is a function of its poverty, of its nonattachment to its own

113

responses, rather than of any self-conscious or willed devotion to a principle of modesty:

> In shoals and bands, a morrice train,
> Thou greet'st the traveller in the lane;
> Pleased at his greeting thee again;
>   Yet nothing daunted,
> Nor grieved if thou be set at nought. (17–21)

The daisy's humility is rooted in a profound autonomy predicated on the implicit understanding that we are all, perhaps, alone and that the response of the world is certainly less important than the gesture to the world, the offer of greeting freely given without expectation of return. The condition is notably set forth in a famous "Fisherman" poem by the eleventh-century Japanese priest Honei:

> On wide waters, alone, my boat
> Follows the current, deep/shallow, high/low.
> Moved, I raise my flute to the moon,
> Piercing the autumn sky.[4]

Stryk explains that among Chinese Buddhists, "a simple woodcutter (or fisherman), who necessarily discovered the Truth for himself, was to be preferred to the scholar of the Scriptures."[5]

Wordsworth honors the daisy in much the same way. Affirming that the daisy "liv'st with less ambitious aim" (29) than "violets in their secret mews" (25) and the proud rose "with rains and dews / Her head impearling" (27–28), the poet declares:

> If stately passions in me burn,
> And one chance look to Thee should turn,
> I drink out of an humbler urn
>   A lowlier pleasure;
> The homely sympathy that heeds
> The common life our nature breeds;
> A wisdom fitted to the needs
>   Of hearts at leisure. (49–56)

If acceptance of common life is the key to the daisy's wisdom, as acceptance of the current informs the Chinese fisherman's wisdom, the emotional content of all life forms and, putatively, of those who respond to them is peacefulness. Thus, Wordsworth concludes another poem entitled "To the Daisy" (*PW* 4:67-68) with lines in which the daisy's humble wandering compares favorably with the wandering acceptance of all conditions attaching to the fisherman's life:

> Thou wander'st the wide world about,
> Uncheck'd by pride or scrupulous doubt,
> With friends to greet thee, or without,
>   Yet pleased and willing;
> Meek, yielding to the occasion's call,
> And all things suffering from all,
> Thy function apostolical
>   In peace fulfilling. (17–24)

The daisy's ministry, in line with the flower's deep humility, is offered, like the apostolicism of the practicing Zennist, in the complete absence of any self-conscious devotion to a prescribed piety. The modern Japanese poet Miyazawa Kenji views such ministry in terms of an ideal to which he aspires as a private individual. Hoping for "a stout body," as he calls it, that yields neither to rain nor to wind, neither to snow nor to summer heat, "without greed / never getting angry / always smiling quiet / ly" and "in everything / not taking oneself / into account," whether abiding "in the shadow of pine trees in a field" or "in a small / hut thatched with miscanthus," Miyazawa asks nothing for himself, looks for strength to nothing beyond himself and his present conditions, and wants only to nurse the sick, to tend the old and destitute, to make peace where there is strife. Accepting the condition of being "lost / called / a good-for-nothing / by everyone," he concludes with

> neither praised,
> nor thought a pain
>   someone
>   like that
> is what I want
>   to be.[6]

Visibly missing from this poem is a sense of moral intention grounded in a specific theological or ideological imperative. Like

Wordsworth's daisy, which "wander'st the wide world about," Miyazawa presents himself as homeless, unchurched, so to speak, his humility and his goodness evolving from the nature of things themselves, that is, from the conditions of his own existence, and present in the shade of pine trees in a field or residing beneath a thatched roof. There is no Kantian-like appeal to a categorical initiative working in some morally separate context beyond the simple coming forth of the ordinary events of life. Reminiscent of the image of the Zen fisherman's giving himself to the current at hand, the life Miyazawa celebrates in the poem follows the mystical current of ordinary quotidian existence. "This is a very mystical life," says the modern Zen priest Dainin Katagiri in his commentary on Miyazawa's poem, "just like a stream of water."[7]

What is so appealing about Miyazawa's poverty of selfhood and the humility of Wordsworth's daisy is their ordinariness. Zen refers to this nonideological ordinariness and the accompanying piety it supports as "wu-shih" (Chinese) or "buji" (Japanese), roughly translated as "nothing special." It carries with it the sense of being perfectly natural and unaffected, of embodying a simplicity that, according to Hisamatsu, "means being sparse, not being cluttered" and of having "something in common with naiveté and abandon." Such simplicity, Hisamatsu continues, is closely aligned with freedom from all forms of holiness: "If, as the negation of holiness results [in] the freedom of non-holiness, then simplicity as the negation of clutter may be spoken of as being 'boundless'—there is nothing limiting, as in a cloudless sky."[8] Emerging from the state of what the Japanese call "mushin," the condition of "complete naturalness and freedom from dualistic thinking and feeling,"[9] the humility of Wordsworth's daisy and Miyazawa's persona is the perfect reflection of unselfconscious emptiness at the heart of one's being, what Zennists understand as emptiness emptied of itself. As Masao Abe says, while explaining the Indian philosopher Nāgārjuna's association of emptiness with "wondrous being," "Precisely because it is Emptiness which 'empties' even emptiness, true Emptiness (absolute Nothingness) is absolute Reality which makes all phenomena, all existents, truly be."[10] The Zennist is aware that emptiness can be reified as a kind of content and so seduce the individual into a condition of spiritual pride based in the conviction that one has attained to something rather than having returned to a prior state of being. Wordsworth's daisy, Bashō's nazuna, Miyazawa's persona exhibit no sense of spiritual distinction:

their ministry is perfectly natural—not grounded, that is, in the human or the social. Hence, Katagiri's comparison of Miyazawa's mystical life to a stream. For Zennists, as for Taoists, flowing water is the natural symbol of beneficent humility. "Best to be like water, / Which benefits the ten thousand things / And does not contend," says Lao Tzu in the *Tao Te Ching.* "It pools where humans disdain to dwell, / Close to the Tao."[11] As the Tao or Way of things is frequently compared to water—

> Great Tao overflows
> To the left   To the right.
> All beings owe their life to it
> And do not depart from it.
> It acts without a name.
> It clothes and nourishes all beings
> But does not become their master[12] —

so the daisy's ministry flows, as it were, from the very processes of nature itself and not from any false or artificial sense of its own emptiness. In its perfect suchness, it thus reflects the purity of "Emptiness which 'empties' even emptiness," to recall Abe, and so also the freedom from selfhood that Zennists see as the leading quality of all genuine spirituality. As Kitarō Nishida remarks, "if we assume that reality is spirit and that our spirit is simply a small part of it, then there is no reason to feel wonder at breaking beyond one's own small consciousness and realizing one great spirit."[13]

A major indication of the breakthrough Nishida mentions is the ability to step back from things, to let things speak or be as if from the depths of one's own nature. A famous example of such noninterference occurs during a sermon by the Chinese master Dabei. One day, during *zazen* (formal sitting meditation), Dabei, trying to convey to his disciples the proper attitude toward the waves of thought and feeling that come and go during meditation, said, "No suppressing arrival, no following departure." His purpose, of course, was to help his students practice *sabi*, nonattachment to the conditions of one's own mind. At that very instant, a weasel shrieked, breaking the silence of the meditation hall. Dabei responded with the following poem:

> I'm at one with this, *this* only.
> You, my disciples,

Uphold it firmly—
Now I can breathe my last.[14]

"This" refers to both the weasel's cry and the pure suchness of the situation. To avoid any effort to obtrude the self between the events of nature and the experiencing of those events is to encounter pure experience, in this instance, pure hearing, and so to be that which one hears. The effort to sermonize upon the event or to extrapolate meaning from it falls short of the immensity of the event itself. "How much more real," says Stryk, commenting upon the sermon, "how much more relevant to the spiritual quest than even the wisest words is Nature's least manifestation, when accepted for the profound thing it is."[15] In the poverty of selfhood that accompanies recognition of the "one great spirit" Nishida mentions as the result of breaking beyond one's own small consciousness, Dabei's simple imperative to his students—"Uphold it firmly"—can be seen to come from the weasel itself.

Zen literature abounds with such moments of noninterference. A notable example is a famous haiku entitled "The Morning Glory," by the Japanese poet Chiyo-ni: "The well bucket / Taken by the morning glory; / I beg for water."[16] Like Bashō's piece on the *nazuna* and Wordsworth's poems on the daisy, Chiyo-ni's haiku turns on the feeling of surprise, of mild shock accompanying our perception of the consummate absoluteness—the perfect rightness, beauty, and preciousness—of something hitherto ignored. The humility Chiyo-ni expresses by going off to beg for water rather than disturbing the morning glory emerges from a deep and abiding sense of her own identity with the vine and of the naturally perceived inappropriateness of her visiting upon this other aspect of herself the momentary needs of her body. "Her mind was filled with the flower," writes D. T. Suzuki, "the whole world turned into the flower, she was the flower itself."[17]

A similar unwillingness to interfere in the processes of nature informs much of Wordsworth's poetry and, as in the work of many Zennists, derives from a vital modesty, a deep poverty of selfhood, that expresses an innate wisdom beneath conventional ways of knowing. A case in point is an early poem, "Anecdote for Fathers" (*PW* 1:241–43), composed in 1798. The poem turns on a conversation in which a doting father, remembering earlier pleasures at "Kilve's delightful shore" (10), where

> The green earth echoed to the feet
> Of lambs that bounded through the glade,
> From shade to sunshine, and as fleet
> From sunshine back to shade (17–20),

asks his son whether he had "rather be . . . On Kilve's smooth shore, by the green sea, / Or here at Liswyn farm" (29–32). The boy chooses Kilve. The father, obviously disconcerted by the answer, indicates that at Liswyn there "are woods, hills smooth and warm" (41) and presses the child to give a reason for his choice: "There surely must some reason be / Why you would change sweet Liswyn farm / For Kilve by the green sea" (42–44). Unwilling to respond either because, as he says, "I do not know" (39), or possibly in fear of disappointing his father, but succumbing finally to repeated questioning, the boy spies "Upon the house-top, glittering bright, / A broad and gilded vane" (51–52) and remarks simply, "At Kilve there was no weathercock; / And that's the reason why" (55–56).

Viewed in response to the poem's subtitle—a line from Eusebius that translates as "Restrain that vehemence of yours, for if you force me I shall tell you lies"—or in response to Mary Hutchinson's note, which offers in explication a passage from Porphyry containing "the Delphian oracle's rebuke to those who tried to extort an answer by force" (*PW* 1:363), the boy's answer is a lie, and the poem's chief purpose is to counsel parents against forcing responses from their children. Comparing "Anecdote for Fathers" to other works in *Lyrical Ballads*, for example, F. B. Pinion writes that the poem "shows the meddling intellect of the adult at work; here, in its zeal to promote adult reasoning in the child, it provokes spurious answers."[18]

On a more spiritual level, however, the child's pointing to the weather vane as the reason for his disappointment with Liswyn farm is the honest, perfectly appropriate, spontaneous reaction of a wisdom that cuts beneath all social concerns to an intuitive awareness of the individual's inherent alignment with forces beyond all measure. The gilded weather vane, like Liswyn itself, reflects an intrusion upon the naturally continuous ebb and flow of interactive forces beyond human efforts to predict and control. These forces appear in the poem through the father's aural memory of the earth's echoing of the lamb's feet and through his visual memory of the alternations of shade and sunshine at Kilve. Taoists and Buddhists might identify

such interactive forces as aspects of yin and yang, the two basic cosmic principles that form the *T'ai Chi* (Supreme Ultimate) or the
Eternal Tao, as it is sometimes called, or the Unnameable. "Yin,
being the passive principle, corresponds to Earth or Matter, Yang,
being the active principle, corresponds to Heaven or Spirit," writes
Henry Wei. "It is the interplay of the two cosmic principles that produces the ten thousand things."[19] Identified frequently as shade and
sunlight respectively, yin and yang compose the moving unity of the
cosmos. "The ten thousand things carry shade / And embrace sunlight," says Lao Tzu; "Shade and sunlight, yin and yang, / Breath
blending into harmony."[20] Access to this harmony, according to Lao
Tzu, occurs only in response to a radical humility that eschews all
vanities and contention. Indicating, for example, that Great Sages,
as he calls them, "Do not display themselves / And therefore shine"
and "Do not assert themselves / And therefore stand out," Lao Tzu
affirms that "The Sage's Tao / Acts and does not contend."[21]

In Wordsworth's poem, it is the father's memory of Kilve that
suggests these forces at work in the universe, but it is the boy who,
ironically, grasps these principles intuitively as the function of his
own being and who expresses them through his own humility. The
boy may not be able to articulate the pleasures of Kilve, but in pointing to the weathercock, he indicates what Kilve is not and demonstrates the need to step back and allow the processes of life their own
vital play. Like the Japanese poet Chiyo-ni, he demonstrates a tacit
contentment with simple being and an unwillingness to exploit
nature to serve boyhood pleasures. Indifferent to the conventional
amusements adult society foists upon its young, the boy exhibits a
form of realization beyond ordinary knowledge, a kind of unknowing,
as it were, that is both more visible and more accessible at places like
Kilve in the absence of such vain contrivances of measurement as
those represented by the weather cock. Like the Taoist sage who, in
his modesty, is "Cautious, / Like crossing a winter stream" and
"Hesitant, / Like respecting one's neighbors," as well as "Polite, / Like
a guest" and "Yielding, / Like ice about to melt," or like the Zennist
who is counseled to regard herself "as a fan in winter, the universe as
a straw dog,"[22] the boy sets aside all self-concern, defers to the father,
and reveals an intuitive consciousness that the purer world of Kilve
has deeper, though less intelligible, pleasures to offer than the more
commonly apprehensible but necessarily "gilded" amusements of

Liswyn. Little wonder, then, that the father, humbled before the
genius of his son's deeper realization, concludes with

> O dearest, dearest boy! my heart
> For better lore would seldom yearn,
> Could I but teach the hundredth part
> Of what from thee I learn. (57–60)

Elsewhere in Wordsworth's poetry, humility conceived as poverty of selfhood emerges as a source of strength and joy. In "The Oak
and the Broom" (*PW* 2:130–34), a little-known pastoral composed and
published in 1800, Wordsworth resorts again to a dialogue in which
the lesser or humbler voice expresses the deeper understanding of
self-forgetfulness. The oak, crowning "a lofty stone / As ever tempest
beat" (11–12), and presented as "a giant and a sage" (19), regales a
broom nestled at the feet of the crag with warnings of imminent
destruction by landslide: "Look up! and think, above your head /
What trouble, surely, will be bred; / . . . For such a Thing as you"
(25–30). The oak asserts, somewhat jealously, that the birds attending the broom and the shepherd boy who sleeps occasionally in her
bower will perish because of their association with her. Responding,
however, that "Frail is the bond by which we hold / Our being,
whether young or old, / Wise, foolish, weak, or strong," the broom
counsels the wisdom of acceptance and unlearning:

> Disasters, do the best we can,
> Will reach both great and small;
> And he is oft the wisest man,
> Who is not wise at all. (58–64)

Taoists understand the broom's wisdom as a form of mastery
predicated on noninterference. "Take the entire world as nothing,"
writes Lao Tzu; "Make the least effort, / And the world escapes you."[23]
As opposed to the oak, whose learning is preoccupied with self-
preservation and with enduring the forces of nature—"Eight weary
weeks, through rock and clay," he says, "Along this mountain's edge, /
The Frost hath wrought both night and day, / Wedge driving after
wedge" (21–24)—the broom speaks from a wisdom that uses knowledge of herself and her surroundings to forward and enhance her

delight in her own existence as it serves the needs of others. "What cause have I to haunt / My heart with terrors?" she asks; "Am I not / In truth a favoured plant!" (72–74). The broom celebrates her "branches . . . so fresh and gay" (78) with flowers that invite the butterfly—which "To me hath often flown, / Here in my blossoms to behold / Wings lovely as his own" (82–84)—and with shade that invites the mother ewe and her infant lamb: "And the sweet joy which they partake, / It is a joy to me" (89–90). For the broom, mortality is not an occasion of despair but an opportunity to rejoice in the miracle of interbeing, in the sense that her own existence is so closely bound up with that of other beings as to form a composite unit of shared beauty and joy.

The contrast between the oak's weariness as it stands against the forces of nature and the broom's lambent happiness as it delights in its humble adjustment to those forces marks, in Zen terms, the difference between secular and religious knowledge. Explaining, for example, that "In the forward progress of everyday life, the ground beneath our feet always falls behind as we move steadily ahead" and that as we take "a step back to shed light on what is underfoot of the self" we come to a "horizon of nihility at the ground of life," Nishitani asserts that the religious apprehend "a conversion from the self-centered (or man-centered) mode of being, which always asks what *use* things have for us (or for man), to an attitude that asks for what *purpose* we ourselves (or man) exist."[24] Wordsworth's broom appears either to have undergone this conversion or to have been born with an attitude of service to others, for she is completely without concern for the self yet perfectly aware of the nihility at the ground of existence.

The distinction here between secular and religious attitudes also marks the border region between pleasure experienced as an acquirement or aspect of the self and pleasure understood as an entitlement of nature and emergent in moments of self-displacement. The broom's blithe spirit, in its reverent service to the butterfly and to the ewe and her lamb, cuts far beneath a mere *carpe diem* effort to resist the destructive forces of life by grasping at fleeting pleasures. In the poverty of self that characterizes an innate humility at the root of her being, the broom's pleasure in her own serviceable existence is the pleasure of existence itself come forth in the form of broom. That the "careless Broom," as she is called in the last stanza, survives the storm which carries off the oak, but survives only "To live for many a day" (110) rather than happily ever after, indicates that the deepest pleasures are those aligned, after all, with the entire moving spectacle of life rather than with the phenomenon of the self as a separate being on a field of nihility.

The distinction between a mode of pleasure based on an attitude of soaring resistance to or transcendence of life and one grounded in a humble effort to hide the self amidst the moving forces of nature appears even more poignantly in an untitled poem in which Wordsworth contrasts a nightingale and a stock-dove (*PW* 2:214). The song of the nightingale, who is presented as having a "fiery heart" (2), comes forth as a "Tumultuous harmony and fierce" (4). Like the oak of the previous poem, though without the oak's seriousness, the nightingale opposes nature, singing "in mockery and despite / Of shades, and dews, and silent night; / And steady bliss" (7–9). Her notes "pierce and pierce" (3) the night. The tautology emphasizes her distinction from the world around her. The stock-dove's "homely tale" (12), however, emerges from a deeper, undisturbed nature, from a voice "buried among trees, / Yet to be come-at by the breeze" (13–14). Like the broom, she sings "of love, with quiet blending . . . Of serious faith, and inward glee" (17–19), which, says the poet in a tautology that offsets the earlier self-insistent piercings of the nightingale, "was the song—the song for me" (20).

The sepulchral image of a voice "buried" in nature signals an earlier death of the separate self. The resultant sound produces what Zennists regard as the "spirit" of *zenki*—"the sense of a spontaneous activity outside the established forms, as if flowing from the formless self."[25] The Japanese Zen master Bunan, writing in the seventeenth century, describes the pleasure of such moments as a function of the death of the self:

> When you're both alive and dead,
> Thoroughly dead to yourself,
> How superb
> The smallest pleasure![26]

The pleasure of such experiences carries one well beyond a mere sense of appreciation for the beauty of common things previously neglected. It displaces the self, opening the individual in perfect humbleness of response to the deepest reaches of her spiritual and moral nature, and constitutes what Wordsworth in his Preface to *Lyrical Ballads* calls "the grand elementary principle" by which humankind "knows, and feels, and lives, and moves."[27] According to Robert Aitken, such pleasure forms the basis of human morality. Explaining, for example, that the pleasure Chiyo-ni took in her perception of the morning glory precedes and makes possible compassion and charity, Aitken writes: "Emerging from this enjoyment is the great compassionate heart, to beg for water rather than to disturb the vine. Emerging from this enjoyment we greet one another; we take care of each other's children; we resist inhumanity and injustice."[28] Chiyo-ni's begging for water would be understood in the East as a perfectly honorable response to the situation. Indeed, begging for food, as far as Buddhists are concerned, is an honorable and necessary discipline for chastening the heart and reducing the ego of both the receiver and the giver. "In the East," Christmas Humphreys explains, "the Buddhist Bhikkhu [one who begs for food] does not thank the donor for his bowl of food, but regards the giver as fortunate that he will acquire such merit for his generosity."[29]

The merit Humphreys remarks, however, does not apply to the self understood in terms of ego, but to the attainment of nonself as the experienced reward of the moment beyond which there can be no other rewards. Thus, Humphreys writes:

> Experience shows that when the motive is right the law of the vacuum obtains. "Give, and it shall be given unto you"; when the self is emptied Tao flows in, and bread cast upon the waters returns in strange and devious ways. For the root of it all is in the heart's sure knowledge of its own eternal unity. The man that loves his fellow men is above all argument. He knows that the Buddha-Christ is shrined in Everyman, that all that stands between the Light and the heart's enlightenment is man-erected, and though the Way be long, it bears its own infallible reward.[30]

Achieving this condition of extreme poverty of self is certainly more difficult from the side of the *Bhikkhu* than from that of the giver. "Anyone can give, and most would if the gift were small enough," says a *roshi* (Zen master) from the Meiji era to his disciples. "But receiving something, particularly something small, is very difficult."[31] In the sense offered here, the receiver is also a giver. And the pleasure obtained is that of self so emptied as to be the place of the eternal Tao.

The connection between the pleasure Aitken identifies as the enjoyment we take in the existential fact of life, in the very emergent being of things themselves, and the compassion Humphreys views as the source of a transpersonal charity that merges donor and receiver appears with remarkable vigor in Wordsworth's "The Old Cumberland Beggar" (*PW* 4:234-40). Composed in 1797 and published in *Lyrical Ballads* (1800), the poem describes an old solitary

> So helpless in appearance, that for him
> The sauntering Horseman throws not with a slack
> And careless hand his alms upon the ground,
> But stops,—that he may safely lodge the coin
> Within the old Man's hat. . . . (25–29)

The poem is remarkable for what it does not convey. There is no sense of condescension among those who give alms to the beggar, and there is, in turn, no sense of fawning gratitude from the old man. The act of giving and receiving is simple, direct, as spontaneous or unpremeditated as any act of charity can appear. People tend the beggar as they would a flower—for its own sake. He elicits from those around him a natural rather than a social response or one grounded in the perceived workings of a separate will to generosity or in obedience to some vaguely realized categorical imperative. Nothing, no doting parent, no finger-wagging school marm stands behind the cycling post-boy who, coming upon the old man from behind, "Turns with less noisy wheels to the roadside, / And passes gently by, without a curse / Upon his lips or anger at his heart" (41–43).

The old man, for his part, is the very image of poverty. Yet it is a poverty aligned with neither abject privation nor soaring obedience to some high religious principle of sacrifice. With "eyes for ever on the ground" (52), he embodies the eternal commonplace beneath all selfhood and reflects that which is forever present in the motionlessness of endless motion that characterizes the moving nature of reality itself:

His staff trails with him; scarcely do his feet
Disturb the summer dust; he is so still
In look and motion, that the cottage curs,
Ere he has passed the door, will turn away,
Weary of barking at him. (59–63)

The old man's solitude and humility remind one of Bashō's haiku, "This Road": "This road! / With no one going— / Autumn evening."[32] Bashō's aloneness is not an expression of self-pity. It is, rather, the Buddhistic solitude of the essential self, which is no-self. Each individual is nothing more than an empty way or road along which numerous thoughts, feelings, reactions are forever appearing and disappearing. "It is this very road itself, with no people going along it," says Robert Aitken in explication of the poem.[33] In Wordsworth's poem, even the dogs cease barking at the old man, certainly in weariness of the beggar's pace, but also, perhaps, in instinctual awareness that there really is no self there to apprehend. His actions reflect no ego. What he receives, for example, he appears to receive in absolute purity of heart, in the complete absence of self-conscious concern, and so reflects the condition of charity as a pure act of life itself. Zen understands such action as itself the content of the form: it is not a being who acts but action itself that emerges through and forms the being much as a river or a stream forms its own banks or bed as it flows. Quoting Yamada Koun Roshi's famous injunction " 'When you stand up, there is only that standing up, with nothing sticking to it,' " Aitken remarks that "Whatever the experience, if it is pure, there is nothing else in the whole universe."[34]

To experience charity as a pure act, whether in giving or receiving, is to approach an understanding of what Buddhists seek to apprehend as the gateless gate of the great way of spiritual enlightenment. The concept of the gateless barrier derives from a famous poem, "The Gateless Barrier of Zen," by the Chinese Chan master Wu-men Hui-K'ai (Japanese, Mumon Ekai):

Gateless is the Great Tao,
There are thousands of ways to it.
If you pass through this barrier,
You may walk freely in the universe.[35]

Viewed in the light of Zen thought and experience, the old beggar's radical humility, the freedom from selfhood at the heart of his
every move, works not as a drag on the community but, like the daisy's
smiling countenance and the stock-dove's homely song, as an unselfconscious ministry that inspires mutual compassion while rendering
nugatory commonplace social considerations based in utilitarian value
systems. "But deem not this Man useless" (67), says Wordsworth
shortly before chastising those who would rid the world of such figures
by condemning them to a "House, misnamed of Industry" (179). To do
so would be to separate donors and receivers from the realm of active
good that forms the basis of natural morality:

> 'Tis Nature's law
> That none, the meanest of created things,
> Of forms created the most vile and brute,
> The dullest or most noxious, should exist
> Divorced from good—a spirit and pulse of good,
> A life and soul, to every mode of being
> Inseparably linked. (73–79)

Buddhism similarly eschews institutional responses to the problems
of poverty, preferring programs "based on the fluidity of events," as
Cleary writes: "Zen Buddhism is particularly strident in its warnings against trying to institutionalize the 'good' or the 'holy' because
of the sentimental attachments built up around these ideas, and the
hypocrisy that feeds on these attachments."[36] For Buddhists, sentimental attachments augment the ego-self, hindering access to the
deeper reaches of pure experience so necessary to the development of
the true Self.

In Zen terms, the goodness Wordsworth proclaims for all things
is the self-realization of the universal reality that constitutes the
ground of individual existence. "The good, conceived of as the development and completion of the self, amounts to our obeying the laws
of the reality called the self," writes Nishida. Asserting that "to unite
with the true reality of the self is the highest good," Nishida explains
that "The laws of morality thus come to be included in the laws of
reality, and we are able to explain the good in terms of the true
nature of the reality called the self."[37] So far as Wordsworth's old

Cumberland beggar has in the sheer purity of his humility cut beneath all forms of limited selfhood identified with any one aspect of human culture, say a church or an economic institution, he emerges as the focus of goodness located not in a separate or transcendent humanism but in the nature of things themselves. He ceases to exist, then, as an object of charity and becomes instead the center of an ambient field or matrix of charity productive of unity:

> While from door to door,
> This old Man creeps, the villagers in him
> Behold a record which together binds
> Past deeds and offices of charity,
> Else unremembered, and so keeps alive
> The kindly mood in hearts which lapse of years,
> And that half-wisdom half-experience gives,
> Make slow to feel, and by sure steps resign
> To selfishness and cold oblivious cares. (87–95)

The ambient selflessness evoked by such deeds of charity is both a product and a reflection of an abiding unity at the heart of all things: "We reach the quintessence of good conduct only when subject and object merge, self and things forget each other, and all that exists is the activity of the sole reality of the universe," writes Nishida.[38] Simply put, the old Cumberland beggar enables the villagers to forget the self and partake of a deeper goodness than mere utilitarian and religious institutional strategies can reach.

This deeper charity makes possible for Wordsworth's villagers a condition of pleasure comparable to the level of enjoyment Aitken sees at the base of Chiyo-ni's response to the morning glory:

> The mild necessity of use compels
> To acts of love; and habit does the work
> Of reason; yet prepares that after-joy
> Which reason cherishes. And thus the soul,
> By that sweet taste of pleasure unpursued,
> Doth find herself insensibly disposed
> To virtue and true goodness. (99–105)

The habit of love inspired by the old man's rounds, together with the unintentional pleasure evolving from a sense of virtue and goodness

aligned later with what Wordsworth offers as the understanding
"That we have all of us one human heart" (153), enables the villagers
to encounter through the beggar the vast solitude of existence not as
an empty desert of impaired or partial relationships based in social
place or function but as the sublime nihility that comprises each
being's home ground:

> And while in that vast solitude to which
> The tide of things has borne him, he appears
> To breathe and live but for himself alone,
> Unblamed, uninjured, let him bear about
> The good which the benignant law of Heaven
> Has hung around him: and, while life is his,
> Still let him prompt the unlettered villagers
> To tender offices and pensive thoughts. (163–70)

In Buddhist terms, the "vast solitude" in which the old man
appears to live "but for himself alone" corresponds to the vital
nihilum at the ground of all existence and the attendant ineffability
of all things. "Seen essentially . . . as existing in nihility and as manifest in nihility," says Keiji Nishitani, "everything and everyone is
nameless, unnameable, and unknowable."[39] In Wordsworth's poem
the catalyst of both unknowability and unnameability is the pleasure
the villagers encounter in a process of giving that obliterates ordinary distinctions between donor and receiver. As each serves the
other, who then is the beggar, who the donor? The process of the
poem renders the terms meaningless. The villagers and the beggar
meet on an empty ground where each party supports the other in
ways that move beyond conventional identities. Explaining that "In
short, it is only on a field where the being of all things is a being at
one with emptiness that it is possible for all things to gather into one,
even while each retains its reality as an absolutely unique being,"
Nishitani affirms the high presence of a "home-ground" in which
things both are and are not themselves:

> To say *that a thing is not itself* means that, while continuing
> to be itself, it is in the home-ground of everything else.
> Figuratively speaking, its roots reach across into the ground of
> all other things and helps [sic] to hold them up and keep them
> standing. It serves as a constitutive element of their being so

that they can be what they are, and thus provides an ingredient of their being. *That a thing is itself* means that all other things, while continuing to be themselves, are in the home-ground of that thing; that precisely when a thing is on its own home-ground, everything else is there too; that the roots of every other thing spread across into its home-ground.[40]

For Nishitani, this "circuminsessional system," as he calls the home-ground elsewhere in his study, "is only possible on the field of emptiness" and is the place "where religion emerges from man himself, as a *subject*, as a self living in the present."[41] Wordsworth implies the same when he suggests that "The good which the benignant law of Heaven / Has hung around" the old beggar functions as an ambient field in which individuals both are and are not themselves in the composite condition of the "one human heart" inspired by the beggar's rounds.

In his poverty of selfhood and in his freedom from conventional functional identities, Wordsworth's old Cumberland beggar, omitting, like the Buddhist *Bhikku*, to thank his donors and appearing to live for himself alone, comes as close as any Western literary figure to what Zen Master Hakuin calls "the True Man without Rank," a figure whose identity, aligned with the essential Buddha-nature of all things, cuts beneath all forms of fame and profit, all social conditions, and all modes of emotional and intellectual explication.[42] Wordsworth leaves him wandering among the hills and valleys of his native region, one with nature, "free of mountain solitudes" (183) and bearing with "him, whether heard or not, / The pleasant melody of woodland birds" (184–85). The old man stands alone, as we all do at the deepest levels of being, ultimately unknowable by conventional means, his humility and poverty (*wabi*) coming in aid of his freedom and nonattachment (*sabi*), and reminds us of the absolute, ineffable nature from which we emerge, into which we go, and of which we are at all times. "As in the eye of Nature he has lived, / So in the eye of Nature let him die!" (196–97), says Wordsworth at the end of his poem, reminding us finally that true poverty of self is indistinguishable from the lived and living process of nature.

CHAPTER EIGHT

AWARE: THE SPIRIT OF IMPERMANENCE

I n some ways the most powerful of all the Zen moods, *aware* is also exceedingly difficult to define. Lucien Stryk, for example, asserts that "*Aware* is the sadness that comes with the sense of the impermanence of things, the realization that they are lost to us even as they are found."[1] In illustration of the emotion and of the way in which Zen writers engage it, however, Stryk cites a fourteenth-century poem in which the sadness accompanying the realization of impermanence hardly surfaces at all:

> Refreshing, the wind against the waterfall
> As the moon hangs, a lantern, on the peak
> And the bamboo window glows. In old age mountains
> Are more beautiful than ever. My resolve:
> That these bones be purified by rocks.[2]

Whatever sadness the Zen master Jakushitsu may have felt when he composed this poem is either subsumed or displaced by the accompanying feeling of unity with all things. The poet's recognition that "In old age mountains / Are more beautiful than ever" illustrates a centrally important theme expressed by yet another fourteenth-century Zen writer, Kenko Yoshida: "The beauty of life is in its impermanence."[3] For Stryk, who cites Yoshida as well, the beauty of things perceived through *aware* is not an escape from or a transcendence of sadness but an indication of the "spirit of acceptance, of oneness with what *is*, whatever it happens to be."[4]

Other readers, however, deemphasize the sense of beauty associated with *aware*, preferring instead to see the mood as indicative of
a state of trauma. Explaining that it "is not quite grief, and not quite
nostalgia," Alan Watts, for example, says that "*Aware* is the moment
of crisis between seeing the transience of the world with sorrow and
regret, and seeing it as the very form of the Great Void."[5] In illustration of his definition, Watts presents two haiku. One turns on the
image of a stream disappearing amidst autumnal grasses: "The
stream hides itself / In the grasses / Of departing autumn." The other
compares the image of autumn leaves falling atop one another with
the dark image of rain beating on rain: "Leaves falling, / Lie on one
another; / The rain beats on the rain."[6] Unlike Jakushitsu, whose
recognition of impermanence culminates in a joyous sense of the
beauty of all things, the authors of these haiku exhibit no stated
relief from the pressures of transience. The beauty of the disappearing stream and of the departing autumn in the first poem, of the
falling leaves and the beating rain in the second can certainly be
inferred. But, owing possibly to the brevity of the haiku form, the
condition is not specified. The poems are content with suggesting the
trauma of the human perception of transience as an emotional end in
itself, a state no less compelling, perhaps, to the individual's experience of the Void than is the condition of sadness to one's ability to
perceive the beauty of life.

Comparing the two commentaries on *aware*, then, we can see
that one is clearly interested in the aesthetic dimensions of the term,
the other in its metaphysical applications, that is, in what it enables
us to see as reality. But if both analyses offer important insights into
aware, their differences indicate the need for a broader and more
inclusive definition of the term. It is with this need in mind that I
define *aware* as the spirit of impermanence and put forward in illustration of the mood several poems by Wordsworth. Whether viewed
as a form of sadness necessary to our vision of the beauty of things
or as a state of crisis equally necessary to our understanding of the
Void, *aware* is clearly associated with the undeniable fact of change
and with the equally undeniable fact that we cannot deal effectively
with mutability outside the arena of human emotion.

To appreciate the centrality of *aware* to the Zen experience of
emptiness, we must understand the Buddhist concept of imperma-

nence. "Everything moves, is transformed, both materially and psychologically," says Robert Linssen. Explaining that this notion of movement as transformation is "the fundamental declaration of Buddhism," Linssen goes on to assert that "There is not really any continuous entity always identical with itself but a perpetually changing succession of 'cause and effect'. There is no static 'I-process', but a continuously moving and fluid succession of moments of consciousness stripped of all permanent individuality."[7] The claim that "Everything moves, is transformed" is for Buddhists an absolute. Everything here does indeed mean everything. There can be no thing or essence, whether conceived as material or spiritual, undergoing the process of change. Buddhism contends that change itself is absolute, that change is of the nature of things themselves, that change changes.

We get a glimpse of the difficulty the Western mind encounters with the Buddhist concept of impermanence by contrasting Linssen's rejection of a "static I-process" with Friedrich Schiller's thoughts on change, particularly as they apply to the ego. A centrally important contributor to the European romantic movement that shaped the philosophic background of Wordsworth's thought, Schiller writes:

> The person that is revealed in the eternally persisting ego, and only there, cannot become, cannot have a beginning in time; the reverse is rather the case—time must begin in it, because something constant must form the basis of change. There must be something that alters, if alteration is to occur; this something cannot therefore itself be alteration. In saying that the flower blooms and fades, we make the flower the thing that persists through the transformation and lend it, so to say, a personality in which both those conditions are manifested.[8]

Schiller's insistence that "something constant must form the basis of change" recalls Aristotle's pursuit of a *hypokeimenon*, an unchanging and fixed substance or substratum against which change is measured. A Buddhist reading of Schiller's thoughts on change would argue confidently that the philosopher is caught in a web of dualism that can be traced all the way back to the grounds of Western thought in Greek philosophy. Nishida, for example, asserts that "Greek philosophy considered that which transcends time, the eternal, to be true reality, and, on the contrary, that which moves in time to be imperfect."[9] For Nishida, as for all Zen thinkers, there can be no unchanging individual substances. He does not deny the existence of individual entities, nor would he deny what Schiller calls the "personality" of the flower. But such things, he would insist, cannot be fixed and unmoving, because the individual personality is intimately conjoined with, indeed is the expression of, the universal, which is forever in motion, forever emerging through the individual. Explaining that "apart from the individual there is no universal," Nishida claims: "That which is truly universal is the concealed power behind the actualization of the individual; the universal is located within the individual as the power that causes the individual to develop." This development is what Nishida calls "personality." "The demands of the personality are the unifying power of consciousness and, at the same time, an expression of the infinite unifying power at the base of reality; and so to actualize and fulfill our personality means to become one with this underlying power."[10] To actualize and fulfill our personality is to become one with the infinite unifying power at the base of reality. That power, like the reality whose base it helps to form, is forever changing, forever in motion.

Summarizing Nishida's thoughts on change as they relate to the Buddhist concept of personhood and individuality, as well as to the Greek philosophy of permanence, Robert E. Carter writes: "Everything is change, or impermanence . . . and yet it is precisely as change that persons and things are what they are. As with Aristotle's *hypokeimenon*, there is that which endures change, but it is not as unchanging."[11] In Buddhist terms, the individual cannot exist as an entity undergoing growth and change. The individual is not a product of the universe. The individual is, rather, the activity of the universe. As such, the individual is activity itself. To be one with "the power that causes the individual to develop" is to be that power, to be activity, to be change itself.

By denying the concept of an 'I-process,' then, Linssen, as a Buddhist thinker, implies his understanding that change cannot be grasped from the outside, cannot, in other words, be objectified as something different from that which changes. If change is to be understood as the dynamic absolute of the universe itself, it must, to revisit Masao Abe, be "thoroughly realized existentially from within."[12] Just as emptiness, according to Abe, must be understood to empty itself if it is to be accurately "realized," literally made real through the individual, so flux, as Abe remarks elsewhere, "is not just flux but permanance [sic] at any point."[13] Abe here is underscoring Dōgen's claim that impermanence is the Buddha-nature and, like Nishida, affirming that the concept of subjectivity, whether conceived as personhood, individuality, or thingness, is activity: "For Dōgen, impermanence itself is preaching impermanence, practising impermanence, and realizing impermanence, and this, as it is, is preaching, practising, and realizing the Buddha-nature."[14]

Among Western poets, Wordsworth is, I believe, unique in his highly Buddhistic grasp of impermanence as the moving, interactive base of reality and consciousness so conjoined as to be mutual affirmations of each other. One of his later poems, "In a Carriage, upon the Banks of the Rhine" (*PW* 3:169), compares remarkably well, particularly in its autumnal mood, with Jakushitsu's vision of mountains in his old age. Composed in 1820, when Wordsworth was fifty years old, "In a Carriage, upon the Banks of the Rhine" reveals how acceptance of change from the perspective of motion itself works to incorporate sadness into the moving landscape of reality, thereby freeing the individual from the very emotions that render the moment precious beyond all measure:

> Amid this dance of objects sadness steals
> O'er the defrauded heart—while sweeping by,
> As in a fit of Thespian jollity,
> Beneath her vine-leaf crown the green Earth reels:
> Backward, in rapid evanescence, wheels
> The venerable pageantry of Time,
> Each beetling rampart, and each tower sublime,
> And what the Dell unwillingly reveals
> Of lurking cloistral arch, through trees espied
> Near the bright River's edge. Yet why repine?
> To muse, to creep, to halt at will, to gaze—
> Such sweet way-faring—of life's spring the pride,
> Her summer's faithful joy—*that* still is mine,
> And in fit measure cheers autumnal days. (1–14)

Unlike Jakushitsu, who only implies sadness at the base of his experience, Wordsworth records the emotion, offering in his discursiveness a more trenchant revelation, perhaps, of the depth and complexity of the processes of *aware* as they unfold in the moment.[15]

Much of the uniqueness of Wordsworth's exposition of impermanence in this poem hinges on the way in which he avoids a direct
confrontation, as it were, with the sadness occasioned by change and
allows motion in general so to inform consciousness as to displace the
trauma of a separate self's realization of mutability. In the first ten
lines of the poem, between the opening sense of a heart deprived of
its illusions of happiness and the question that invites his subsequent resolve to accept the "way-faring" nature of life, Wordsworth
depicts himself in a moving carriage on the river's banks, his forward
motion, perhaps a kind of yang force, contributing to the backward
flow, the yin, of images that dominate his consciousness. The picture
is not that of an individual confronting and enduring, however nobly,
forces over which he has no control but that of an active observer
who, in motion with the river, with the Tao, so to speak, or the Way of
the moment, becomes a moving web of consciousness through which
the forces and images of life are forever streaming. He is, in a sense,
the very motion he perceives as seemingly other. If in the Buddhist
mind-set impermanence, as Abe says, preaches impermanence,
motion in Wordsworth both creates and adumbrates motion, becoming, in the end, the content of consciousness and the Tao-like way
that is both the source and end of our efforts: the musing, the creep-
ing, the halting at will, the gazing, all comprise a sweet "way-faring"
that *is* the individual, "is mine," says the poet, and that cheers "in fit
measure." We cannot in such moments think of the individual as in
time or in change, as if time and change were ambient contexts.
Rather, we must regard the individual as time, as change itself.

In keeping with the forward motion of the carriage and the
backward flow of images, the "fit measure" that controls the mood of
the moment remains, like the perceiving eye of the traveler, unsituated, moving with the movement of the world. The poem suggests
measure but skillfully eludes reference to a specific set of principles,
that is, to a philosophical system or belief structure to which the
mood of the observer can be fitted, and to an aesthetic form that
might define or restrict thought and feeling. Indeed, much of the

genius of this poem, as of other sonnets in the Wordsworth canon, inheres in the poet's ability to burst the confines of the very form he uses. Here, the series of nominatives that adumbrate "the venerable pageantry of Time" with glimpses of things seen in motion forms a moving syntactical bridge between octave and sestet, enabling the mind to flow *koan*-like back and forth between problem and conclusion with no clear sense of division or distinction between the two. By the time the reader arrives at the question "Yet why repine?"— planted already two lines into the sestet—he has been involved in the very freedom of motion the concluding lines assert. The problem conventionally set forth in the octave and concluded in the sestet is not resolved so much as displaced or subsumed by the forward motion of the observer and the backward sweep of images. Thought and feeling have no place to rest, no conclusion to seek, no ultimate form in which to occur. The poem thus displaces the sequential dynamic of linear thought processes, presenting instead an ambient field of consciousness in which all is motion and nothing has abiding identity.[16]

This field of consciousness bears a striking resemblance to the "mind" presented in the twenty-ninth case of the *Mumonkan*. Entitled "Neither the Wind nor the Flag," the *koan* tells of two monks arguing about a flag flapping in the wind: "One said the flag was moving; the other said the wind was moving." Hui Neng, the Sixth Patriarch, intruding upon the argument, asserts that "It is neither the wind nor the flag that is moving. It is your mind that is moving."[17] Though Hui Neng's reference to mind appears to have settled the issue, later commentators find his response inappropriate, even a little embarrassing, for it tends to present mind, even when understood as the shared consciousness of monks and cosmos, as located in time and space and accessible to the specificities of language. Thus, Mumon, commenting on the event five centuries later, asserts flatly that "It is neither the wind nor the flag nor the mind that is moving," and he offers the following critique of both Hui Neng and the monks:

> The wind moves, the flag moves, the mind moves:
> All of them missed it.
> Though he knows how to open his mouth,
> He does not see he was caught by words.[18]

Like Wordsworth, who recognizes the existence of measure but who avoids locating the phenomenon in a fixed principle or form, Mumon understands that mind is motion grounded in the principle of freedom from conceptual restrictions. "It is moving, yet there is no movement. It is standing still, yet there is no standstill," writes the modern Zen master Shibayama in his analysis of the *koan*. "This is the freedom of Zen, which transcends subject and object, movement and nonmovement, and real peace is enjoyed only when one lives with this freedom."[19]

In Wordsworth's poem, the "real peace" of the moment surfaces in the cheerfulness that comes with the traveler's acceptance of mortality as liberative and purifying, of the moving nature of life itself. Though his work does not provide us with anything quite so stark as the bleached bones of Jakushitsu's poem, Wordsworth, like the Japanese author, avoids any effort to escape into a more artful world or into one that might in any way delude him into thinking that he is not of this earth and subject to its processes. He labors instead to fit his mood to the evolving forms and powers of the present, careful not to discriminate proudly among the various objects and scenes offered him. The "Thespian jollity" of the poem's imagery is an index of acceptance rather than an avenue of resistance to or stoical endurance of the endless destructiveness of mortality. Grounded in a mood that integrates the sadness of time's passing with the joy of appreciative vision, Wordsworth experiences from the perspective of change itself a condition similar to what Buddhists call "the form of the formless."[20] The experience is associated with enlightenment and is encountered as an absolute or seamless openness to reality conceived as perfectly set forth in and as the individual yet also completely beyond conventional methods of understanding and analysis. Explaining, for example, that "Enlightenment cannot be bodily grasped (*attained, perceived, etc.*), for the body is formless; nor mentally grasped (*etc.*), for the mind is formless; nor grasped (*etc.*), through its essential nature, since that nature is the Original Source of all things," Huang Po asserts that "In reality, there is nothing to be grasped (*perceived, attained, conceived, etc.*)—even not-grasping cannot be grasped."[21] Wordsworth's poem, like the experience of enlightenment, leaves us in motion, as motion. To be so, and to accept being so, is to be free of the need to grasp, free, as well, of the need for foundation and stability conceived as unmoving absolutes.

Such freedom, however, is neither anarchic nor chaotic. Despite its elusiveness, the formless Void has voice and image such that we acquire, in moments of selfless vision, a sense of unity as a moving web of continually imploding relationships. In "Composed in Roslin Chapel, during a Storm" (*PW* 3:266-67), a late poem that grew out of Wordsworth's visit to Walter Scott in 1831, these relationships come to light through a dynamic set of aural and visual images that fold inward on each other in such a way as to form a kind of three-dimensional or holographic reflection of the Void as mind in motion:

> The wind is now thy organist;—a clank
> (We know not whence) ministers for a bell
> To mark some change of service. As the swell
> Of music reached its height, and even when sank
> The notes, in prelude, ROSLIN! to a blank
> Of silence, how it thrilled thy sumptuous roof,
> Pillars, and arches,—not in vain time-proof,
> Though Christian rites be wanting! From what bank
> Came those live herbs? by what hand were they sown
> Where dew falls not, where rain-drops seem unknown?
> Yet in the Temple they a friendly niche
> Share with their sculptured fellows, that, green-grown,
> Copy their beauty more and more, and preach,
> Though mute, of all things blending into one. (1–14)

As in the haiku cited earlier, where the river is forever hiding itself among the grasses, the leaves and rain eternally falling, as if each were a different form of the other, the images of "Roslin Chapel" disappear into each other, suggesting a process of mutual displacement and preservation. The new "organist," in the formless form of wind, punctuates the chapel's present emptiness while evoking simultaneously the imagined music of past services, thereby conflating emptiness and fullness. The mysterious "clank" of the first line, an image of flat vacuity that plays dynamically to the "blank / Of silence" put forth in lines 5–6, cannot be separated from the deep quietude following the sumptuous harmonies of ancient masses. Nothing is terminal. Aural images of present emptiness evoke a sense of past fullness; notions of past fullness collapse in turn into present emptiness. Present and past do not simply concur, as if the two dimensions were separately existing phenomena negotiated into a relationship mediated by a third force or party. Rather, like emptiness and fullness, they contain each other, require each other, so to speak, in order to exist at all. The motion from present to past, from past to present, is not linear or directional, nor is it simply fluctuant; it is involutional, allowing past and present the opportunity to embrace each other, to form each other, in the dynamic immediacy of present vision.

A similar process of involutionary motion governs the poem's visual imagery. The sculptured leaves on the walls of the chapel, "green-grown" over the years, have become nearly indistinguishable from the leaves of the live herbs. As Dorothy wrote, when she and her brother first saw the chapel in 1803, "the natural product and the artificial were so intermingled that at first it was not easy to distinguish the living plant from the other, they being of an equally determined green, though the fern was of a deeper shade."[22] William's poem, composed many years later, when he felt himself momentarily a "prisoner" of the chapel during a storm, as he tells us in a Fenwick note to the text, eschews even the desire to distinguish between the living and the artificial, preferring instead to dwell in what he calls "the movements of the mind." Contrasting himself with the painter in a similar situation, Wordsworth writes:

> Here this Sonnet was composed, and if it has at all done justice to the feeling which the place and the storm raging without inspired, I was as a prisoner. A Painter delineating the interior of the chapel and its minute features under such circumstances would have, no doubt, found his time agreeably shortened. But the movements of the mind must be more free while dealing with words than with lines and colours; such at least was then and has been on many other occasions my belief, and, as it is allotted to few to follow both arts with success, I am grateful to my own calling for this and a thousand other recommendations which are denied to that of the Painter.[23]

The accuracy of Wordsworth's perception of the limitations of painting is for our purposes subordinate to his understanding that freedom constitutes the base of what he calls the "movements of the mind." These movements are shrouded in mystery and seemingly content with mystery. In the poem itself, the early statement that "We know not whence" comes the "clank" of line 1 and the later questions "From what bank / Came those live herbs? by what hand were they sown / Where dew falls not, where rain-drops seem unknown?" combine to evoke a sense of mind as intellect while skillfully denying that very intellect access to specific answers. As the artificial flows into the natural, the natural—through the phenomenalistic blurring of consciousness—into the artificial, the mind, teased not so much out of thought as out of position construed as a separate perspective, yields the need for explanation, for claims to solution and determination, and gives itself instead to motion, to the dynamic process of change unfolding in and as the present moment. Unlike the painter who, as Wordsworth's note implies rightly or wrongly, is limited perhaps to a specific perspective, certainly to line and color, the poet is free to be motion itself, to encounter motion as motion. It is from within the process of change, indeed as the very process of change or impermanence, that Wordsworth envisions unity not as a static oneness but as an eternal "blending into one," as an eternally moving, eternally forming, interanimative conjoining.

Hua-yen Buddhism, particularly helpful here, views this perception of eternal blending as "thought-instants" dynamically expressive of and constituted by the process of the mutual interpenetration of the past and the future in the ever creative and emergent present. Entire eons "Are identical to a single thought-instant," writes Uisang in his "Ocean Seal."[24] Normally, we think of time as linear and of causation as flowing from the past to the present. The Hua-yen conceptual system, however, views causal influence as resulting from the mutual blending of past, future, and present. According to Steve Odin, time, for the Buddhist, is constructed "so that all events—past, present and future alike—interpenetrate harmoniously together into a single thought-instant without any obstruction or hindrance whatsoever."[25] As the flat "clank" that accentuates the present emptiness of the ruin in Wordsworth's poem is contained within the refulgent silence concluding past services in Roslin Chapel, thereby collapsing future and past into the amorphous sphere of present interactive aural dimensions, so, for the Buddhist, time is a matter of symmetrical causal relations in which, as Odin puts it, "efficient causation flows from past, present and future directions with equivalent force, thus establishing simultaneous interpenetrative harmonization and unhindered mutual containment between all events in the three periods of time."[26]

So far as we engage these emergent unities as "thought-instants," we encounter the Buddha-mind that evokes intellect only to set it aside, as it were, in a process of cognitive dispersal that eventuates in the percipient's identity with that which is seen and heard. "Roslin Chapel" reveals this process of cognitive dispersal by structuring itself around the displacement of the knowing mind, which abides conventionally in a stable perspective outside the events it perceives, and its replacement by what Wordsworth, in his note, refers to as "the movements of the mind." After remarking, for example, that we do not "know" the source of the "clank" that "ministers for a bell / To mark some change of service," Wordsworth asks about the source of the "live herbs" and the hand that sowed them, but leaves his questions unanswered. As in "The Solitary Reaper," the answers potentially available to the observing persona could in no way account for the effect of the present conditions, which suggest an infinite set of speculative permutations. What conceivable difference would it make, for example, to know the source of the "clank" that serves as the chapel's present bell? An answer, were it forthcoming, and were we truly committed to the linear process of source seeking, would only beg the further question of what lay beneath the source of that source. Similarly, how could we benefit from knowing the source of the live herbs and the identity of those who placed them "Where dew falls not, where rain-drops seem unknown"? Such answers could not possibly articulate the transtemporal and transspatial effect of the images haunting Wordsworth's mind. By evoking aural and visual conditions that both mimic and contain their artifactitious counterparts in the form of the signal bell of earlier masses and the sculptured leaves of the original chapel, the poem displaces or undermines the human intellect's ability to apprehend events in a rational context predicated on the existence of a stable perspective beyond the fluid occurrences themselves. The result is a kind of profound discomfort, a condition of lostness that could, if engaged outside the dimensions of egoless spirituality, regard the "blank / Of silence" as a state of cosmic oblivion rather than one of religious fulfillment.

For the selfless spiritualist, however, particularly in the Buddhist mind-state, the discomfort of not knowing is the prerequi-

site to attaining the unattainable. "The intellect is to be left aside for
a while," writes D. T. Suzuki, "in spite of a certain sense of intellectual discomfort, so that we may plunge into that nothingness beyond
the intellect, as if into a threatening abyss opening up at our feet."[27]
But this abyss, as Wordsworth shows us in his reference to "a blank /
Of silence" that literally thrills what the poet imagines to have been
the "sumptuous roof" of the ancient chapel, is nothing more than that
which lies directly before us in its perfect "just-so-ness," to employ
Suzuki's terminology again. "The Unattainable is attained as such
in its just-so-ness," writes Suzuki, "and the strange thing is that
when this takes place the intellectual doubts that made us so uncomfortable are dissolved."[28] Wordsworth's hearing of the "clank" that
marks the emptiness of the church while underscoring the unity of
self and world dissolves all intellectual doubts. What Wordsworth
hears as that which simply exists in its marvelous flatness appears
to Suzuki as that which is "right here before us in full revelation":

> The great earth with its mountains and rivers, plants and ani-
> mals, rains and winds—are they not all revealing themselves
> in front of us, for us to see, and to hear, what they are? They
> are just waiting to make us become conscious of "the sense of
> nondiscrimination" (*avikalpa-jñāna*) that is dormant within us
> this very moment. This *jñāna* (cognition) is to be distin-
> guished from intellection: intellection helps us discriminate,
> dichotomize, dissect, and finally kill the objects it attempts to
> understand. The *jñāna* is inborn, indefinable, unattainable,
> but ultimately leads us to the self in its just-so-ness.[29]

Suzuki's effort to distinguish between cognition and intellection
recalls Wordsworth's earlier attempt to adumbrate the boundaries of
intellect in "The Tables Turned" (1798): "Our meddling intellect /
Mis-shapes the beauteous forms of things: / We murder to dissect."
    To displace the intellect so as to see that which is forever reveal-
ing itself right before us, however, is not to reject intellect. Nor is it
a form of anti-intellectualism. It is to understand, rather, that the
mind's true dimensions are not limited to the phenomenological and
hermeneutical quest for meanings. For Wordsworth, to see the
chapel from within the chapel is to see change from within the
dynamics of change and so to see "the movements of the mind," to

recall his note to the poem, from within the mind itself. His own mind and the mind whose movements he perceives as apparently other are one and the same, cognitive enfoldments whose mental activity, like the mutual enfoldment of natural and artificial ferns in an infinitely emerging oneness, comprises both the objective and the subjective grounds of the world. To see change from within this mind-state is to be the very dimensions of change one perceives and so to be the greater self, the cosmic mind or Buddha-self that is always here, forever constitutive of our nature, but available to consciousness only in those moments of active intellectual displacement which render nugatory all efforts of the ego to find comfort in answers to the why and wherefore of it all, that is, in perspectives outside the dynamic events of the eye's seeing and the ear's hearing.

Given the force of these considerations, of the sense of unity as the lived and living dynamic of one's own being in a process of eternal change, it is little wonder that Wordsworth in "The Trosachs" (*PW* 3:267), the next poem in the *Yarrow* sequence and the perfect companion to "Roslin Chapel," returns to the theme of *aware*, of the sadness accompanying change, but with a renewed sense of the pensive vitality of the emotion:

> There's not a nook within this solemn Pass
> But were an apt confessional for One
> Taught by his summer spent, his autumn gone,
> That Life is but a tale of morning grass
> Withered at eve. From scenes of art which chase
> That thought away, turn, and with watchful eyes
> Feed it 'mid Nature's old felicities,
> Rocks, rivers, and smooth lakes more clear than glass
> Untouched, unbreathed upon. Thrice happy quest,
> If from a golden perch of aspen spray
> (October's workmanship to rival May)
> The pensive warbler of the ruddy breast
> That moral sweeten by a heaven-taught lay,
> Lulling the year, with all its cares, to rest! (1–14)

Here, as in the Rhine sonnet from the 1820 *Memorials*, the sadness of the moment is neither displaced nor transcended but allowed to fuel the basic understanding that change is the requisite dynamic of life—

a condition not to be eluded by aesthetic efforts to arrest the flow from morning's growth to evening's withering by fixing the mind on forms and structures that promise permanence and stability. As sadness is not incorporated into a compensatory understanding that softens the confrontation with mutability, so art must not underwrite elegiac impulses to preserve the self with appeals to future safety in a static haven beyond change. Rather, the emotion of the moment and the aesthetic frame it evokes embody change, celebrate it, express it not only as a "heaven-taught lay" but as the only sure refuge for the human consciousness. The reference to the nooks within the Trosachs as various confessionals evokes the implicate religiousity of the previous poem and identifies as innately spiritual the impulse to move beyond all forms of selfhood by unburdening the self of its cares, its fears for itself. The result is a kind of "Thrice" happiness or higher joy grounded in the freedom to accept sadness as the attendant emotion of a necessary mutability rather than in the compulsion to elude change and melancholy. The "pensive warbler" of line 10—an image, perhaps, of the poet himself in his later years—does not lift us as on angels' wings toward a higher resort dissociated from change but carries us downward through the changing forms of nature— "Rocks, rivers and smooth lakes"—to a place of deep repose.

In Zen terms, Wordsworth has gazed upon the face of nothingness from the viewpoint of change and has discovered a restfulness that is yet dynamic and productive. What is lulled to rest is not life itself, but the "year," a designation of time, with the cares and concerns for selfhood which a time-bound mentality brings to the experience of change. What remains is a new sense of life as both permanent and impermanent, what Robert E. Carter, commenting on the Zen perception of the relationship between nothingness and change, calls a "seamless web of existence" prior to all notions of individuation and distinction:

> All things are "lined" with nothingness. Things are not only changing. Both the individuation and the change are distinctions within a seamless web of existence. Prior to rational-linguistic selection, prior to the distinction between a particular and whatever else it is contrasted with, prior to the taken for granted distinction between subject and object, self and other, there is the universe as unselected, undifferentiated.[30]

Carter's reference to nothingness as a kind of lining that underlies mutability and makes possible our perception of individuation and change as moving aspects of a "seamless web of existence" conforms to the Buddhist notion that emptiness cannot be reified as a substantive other that stands over and against things. Appropriating the Sanskrit term śūnyatā for emptiness, Keiji Nishitani explains that nothingness is a self-emptying phenomenon both productive of and identical with the things it underwrites:

> Emptiness in the sense of śūnyatā is emptiness only when it empties itself even of the standpoint that represents it as some "thing" that is emptiness. It is, in its original Form, self-emptying. In this meaning, true emptiness is not to be posited as something outside of and other than "being." Rather, it is to be realized as something united to and self-identical with being.[31]

Like Wordsworth, who understands intuitively that access to the movements of the mind occurs in a context beyond the dimensions of a specific perspective, so Carter and Nishitani understand that the apprehension of nothingness as that which is identical to the very things it creates or makes possible as features of its own face requires the surrender of all reliance upon viewpoints outside change, outside the moving nature of things and the seamless web of being they are forever forming. If nothingness is the lining of all things, change is the lining of nothingness.

Viewed in this light, the priority Carter affirms for nothingness is not a condition of time, an anteriority, as it were, that precedes the present and helps to produce it in linear fashion, nor is it a purely psychological state that forms the present sense of unity as an emergent state of being resulting from human efforts to establish a new way of seeing. It exists, rather, as an eternally present, though seldom glimpsed, basis of cognition grounded in the perception, however momentary, of the contradictory identity of all things. This way of seeing includes a logic of paradox in which, as Carter remarks, "A is A; A is not-A, therefore A is A. I see the mountains. I see that there are no mountains. Therefore, I see the mountains again, but as transformed. And the transformation is that the mountains both are and are not mountains."[32]

Carter argues that this logic of paradox, the ability to see that things both are and are not, evolves out of a perceived unity that "is not the unity of oneness, as the mystic would likely express it, but the unity of self-contradiction. It is *both* one and many; changing *and* unchanging; past and future in the present."[33] Kitarō Nishida, defining the relation between the unity of consciousness that lies at the base of such thinking and the process of change that forms the ground of all reality, employs similarly paradoxical terms that resonate well with Wordsworth's earlier experience of Roslin chapel as the movement of the mind: "All unity of consciousness transcends change and must be clearly unchanging; and change comes to arise from this, i.e., it is that which moves and does not move."[34] To see the world from the viewpoint of change is to understand, as well, that consciousness is larger than change, that change itself evolves from within consciousness, that, to employ Wordsworth's terms, the movement one sees is none other than the movement of the mind in a state of absolute restfulness. Mind is utterly continuous with or identical to what we normally call "reality." So far as we can speak of this condition of understanding as a state of consciousness, it is, according to Suzuki, a state free of intellection, the place where the individual comes face-to-face with God or the Absolute as the felt center of one's own being: "One feels free, independent, one's own master. Experiences at the level of intellection are restrictive and conditioning, but the 'inner' self feels the way God felt when he uttered, 'Let there be light.'"[35]

The genius of Wordsworth's poem on the Trosachs is that it appropriates both the imagery and the dogmatic energy of the Christian confessional to achieve a condition of unity that lies at the base of all religious experience. Like the devout Christian who approaches the latticed confessional in the hope of cleansing the self to become worthy of God, so Wordsworth comes to the confessional nooks of the surrounding landscape in the implicate hope of achieving some relief from the burden of mortality attending the self's perception of change. But unlike the conventional Christian who brings with her the sense of a separate soul available to God's embrace as a safe, sure haven in a moving world, Wordsworth brings with him a conviction of his own mutability, confessing not to the representative of a stable absolute or unmoved mover but to the changing and changeable forms of an eternally changing and changeable reality.[36]

The "old felicities" of nature—"Rocks, rivers, and smooth lakes"—work their compensatory magic from within the condition of change as the central absolute of a universe "untouched, unbreathed upon" by the self's need for stability, for perchings or resting places outside the flow of consciousness undifferentiated from the world. "There is only one world," writes Carter, "only experience flowing."[37] Writing from within the viewpoint of change, thus as the viewpoint of change, of impermanence as impermanence, Wordsworth, as change, confesses to change. The result, as in the interchange of the natural and the artificial ferns of Roslin Chapel, is the mutual appropriation of self and world as moving, interanimative aspects of each other. "The world is not something that opposes the self but something that envelops it," says Masao Abe. "And this actual and concrete world is the dialectical world, for within it our knowledge is the self-consciousness of the world and our expression is the self-expression of the world."[38]

The intuitive understanding of self and world as mutually appropriative of each other is, according to Nishida, a "religious" awareness, "the apprehension of that profound unity which lies at the foundation of intelligence and the will, namely a kind of intellectual intuition, a deep grasp of life."[39] By viewing nature as a moving confessional in which one both loses the ego and appropriates the world as the larger self, Wordsworth, like Nishida, reveals his understanding that the perception of such unity is fundamentally religious and that *aware*, the sadness that comes with change, is inseparable from, indeed necessary for, the high joy of *yugen*, the wisdom of stillness or restfulness that accompanies the sense of the depth of things—the subject of the next chapter.

CHAPTER NINE

YUGEN: THE SPIRIT OF DEPTH

Yugen, what I am translating loosely as "the spirit of depth and tranquillity," is perhaps best understood as that point of wisdom comprising both a culmination and a gathering together of the other three moods of Zen. It combines the solitude and disinterestedness of *sabi* with the poverty and humility of *wabi* and the gentle sadness of *aware* to form a still point of oceanic calm and penetrating insight. In *yugen*, the individual looks not only through the surfaces of things and events to the characterless depths of all being but also as the very things and events that comprise ordinary quotidian existence. *Yugen*, then, like enlightenment, is both a mood, that is, a psychological state or condition of being, and an epistemological field; it is both a means of knowing and the ambient arena of all knowing, an environment that we both inhabit and carry about with us as the center of our being. So far as we experience *yugen*, it is not as something we achieve; it is, rather, as an eternally extant ground or field of wisdom to which we admit ourselves and which, in turn, emerges as the defining characteristic of our being.

Aligned traditionally with the aesthetic qualities of beauty, gentleness, tranquillity, and elegance, *yugen* is so subtle a condition that Zen writers frequently resist extensive efforts to define it. Daisetz T. Suzuki, for example, while acknowledging that for some critics "all great works of art embody in them *yūgen* whereby we attain a glimpse of things eternal in the world of constant changes," affirms nevertheless that the term evokes such hazy meanings—"cloudy impenetrability," "obscurity," "unknowability," "mystery"—that we cannot discuss it intellectually: "An object so designated is not subject to dialectical analysis or to a clear-cut definition."[1] Part of the problem is that the term *yugen* corresponds closely with the enlightened Zennist's general sense of the depth of things, a field of vision that resists locus. "There is a 'cosmic resonance' (*kanno-doko*) thundering in the grass-roots of each living thing," writes Hakan Eilert in a recent commentary on Keiji Nishitani's understanding of emptiness, "but still we are unable to locate it anywhere."[2] What Eilert calls "cosmic resonance," a term he borrows from Dōgen, who employs it to describe the enlightened mind's perception of reality, Shin'ichi Hisamatsu identifies as the quality of "endless reverberation" in Zen paintings: "Though, ordinarily, a single thing is no more than a single thing, in these paintings a single thing, even one speck of dust, contains everything, and the 'not a single thing' is inexhaustible."[3] This sense of "endless reverberation" explains the prevalence of what Hisamatsu calls the "unpainted content" of many Zen paintings, a kind of contentless content that conveys "the quality of Deep Reserve," as "when a man does not baldly confront us with his abilities, but keeps them within, as if they were not there."[4] Accurately apprehended, the painting should produce in its audience a correspondent reserve, an understandably contemplative, rather than analytic, frame of mind.[5]

Turning from painting to literature, we sense this contemplative reserve in Lucien Stryk's definition of *yugen* as evoked by Zen poetry. Asserting that *yugen* marks both "the sense of a mysterious depth in all that makes up nature" and "the sense of the mystic calm in things . . . which is always there, below the surface, but which reveals itself only to the 'ready,' " Stryk offers two examples of the term. One, a poem by the seventeenth-century Japanese master Manan, suggests the depth of all things by comparing freedom from the need for specific place to the absolute sourcelessness of the individual Zen life lived beyond the barrier of a constraining selfhood:

> Unfettered at last, a traveling monk,
> I pass the old Zen barrier.
> Mine is a traceless stream-and-cloud life.
> Of those mountains, which shall be my home?[6]

Stryk's second example, a famous work by the thirteenth-century Zen philosopher Dōgen, turns on the contrast between the shallow illusoriness of conventional life, with its implicit pursuit of fame, wealth, and distraction, and the awakened state of the Zen seer aware of the bottomless depths of the most common of things in life:

> This slowly drifting cloud is pitiful;
> What dreamwalkers men become.
> Awakened, I hear the one true thing—
> Black rain on the roof of Fukakusa Temple.[7]

Like Suzuki and Hisamatsu, however, Stryk studiously avoids a lengthy explication of the poems. Of Manan's work he says only that it "suggests the sense of a strong communion with nature, a descent into depths." Of Dōgen, he remarks simply that "To hear that 'black rain' . . . is to enter the realm of *Yugen*" and that "Not to hear it . . . is to remain a 'dreamwalker,' blind not only to the beauty of the world but to its reality."[8]

Suzuki's reticence and Stryk's brevity, commendable in themselves, underscore both the high esteem in which *yugen* is held and Zen's unwillingness to reduce the deepest subtleties of its praxis to the level of an intellectual and cultural problem. Predicated, as we have seen elsewhere, on the four maxims composed early in the sect's history—

1. *Transmission outside scriptures*
2. *Not relying on letters*
3. *Pointing directly to one's Mind*
4. *Attainment of Buddhahood by seeing into one's Nature*[9]—

Zen is naturally suspicious of words, particularly as they convey analytic procedures that rely on conceptual frames of reference. As the eighteenth-century Zen master Hakuin writes in his "Zazen Wasan" (Song of Zazen), those who look deeply "within themselves" during the process of *zazen* "Testify to the truth of Self-nature, / To the truth that Self-nature is no-nature." Such individuals, according to Hakuin, "have really gone beyond the ken of sophistry."[10] Commenting on Hakuin's lines, Shibayama remarks that "No verbal expression can fully describe the fact of 'testifying to the truth of Self-nature.'"[11] The experience of *yugen*, like that of enlightenment, carries with it such a fundamental change in the individual's perception of himself and his world, what Stryk calls a "state of readiness," that

his perception of his own depth and of the profound stillness at the
heart of his own being is virtually inseparable from his sense of his
perfect identity with the things around him. "If I scoop the water, the
moon is in my hands," writes one Zen master.[12] To see the water and
the reflected moon as this master sees them is to be those things. "If
I scoop the water, I myself am the water and reflect the moon," writes
Shibayama.[13]   To view this line only as a literary trope, as a
metaphorical complication, is, for the Zennist, to be trapped in a linguistic and conceptual frame built around the fundamental dualism
of self and other. It is not until we identify completely with what we
encounter through the senses and move beyond both the tropic and
the analytical configurations of language that we can understand the
Zennist's experience of the depth of things.

The difficulty of achieving and relating such experience
emerges with superlative poignancy in the well-known story of
Hsiang-yen Chih-hsien (Japanese, Kyōgen Chikan). Hsiang-yen, a
scholar with comprehensive knowledge of Buddhist texts, was asked
by his teacher to describe his original face before the birth of his parents. Unable to find an answer in the *sutras* and in other Buddhist
commentaries, Hsiang-yen burned his books, resolved to give up
Buddhism, and retired to a hermitage at Nan-yang, intending to
spend the remainder of his life caring for the grave of Hui-chung.
One day, as he was sweeping the ground, his broom hurled a pebble
against the trunk of a nearby tree. We are told that "At the sound of
the pebble striking the trunk Hsiang-yen experienced enlightenment."[14] Shibayama comments that upon hearing the sound of the
pebble, Hsiang-yen was himself "resounding throughout the universe
as the rap of the stone."[15] Like the Zen master who experiences himself as the water and the moon while scooping water in which the
moon is reflected, so Hsiang-yen experiences no bottom, no end, as it
were, to his own hearing as it marks the absolute dimensionlessness
and continuity of cosmic existence manifest in and through individual beings and particular acts. To his students, Hsiang-yen remarks:

> The way is realized through one's own inner awakening; that
> is not dependent on words. If you look at the invisible and
> limitless, where is there a gap there? How could you reach it
> through an effort of conceptual mind? [The Way] is simply a

reflection of enlightenment, and that is also your entire daily task. Only the ignorant go in the opposite direction.[16]

In the wake of such experiences, to which *yugen*, if not identical, is so deeply related as to render nugatory our efforts to distinguish it from enlightenment, one can understand the Zennist's reluctance to enter upon an extended explication of the poems or texts that both reflect and embody the dynamics of engaged depth.

There is, however, a downside to such hermeneutic reluctance. Despite warnings of intellectual reductionism, whether explicit, as in Shibayama's claim that "all literary expressions or cultural activities are of secondary importance,"[17] or implicit, as in Suzuki's and Stryk's evasion of extensive critical analysis, the Zennist's legendary reticence regales such terms as *yugen* in a mysteriousness that tends to detract from their suchness, what Suzuki, as we saw in the last chapter, calls the "just-so-ness" of things and events. An example of such simplicity and matter-of-factness as it relates to *satori*, the experience of enlightenment, surfaces forcefully in the story of Chao-pien, a government officer and lay disciple of Fach'uan of Chiang-shan. One day, while sitting leisurely in his office, he was startled by a clap of thunder and experienced a moment of *kensho* or "breakthrough." He wrote the following poem in response to the experience:

> Devoid of all thought, I sat quietly by the desk in my
>   official room,
> With my fountain-mind undisturbed, as serene as water;
> A sudden clash of thunder, the mind-doors burst open,
> And lo, there sitteth the old man in all his homeliness.[18]

In that moment of awakening, when the doors of the "fountain-mind"—the absorptive, all-embracing consciousness unpreoccupied with concerns of the self—opened as if to admit the world, Chao-pien was the thunder. He was not simply a being who heard thunder. Nor was he one who had become thunder, as if in response to the presence of an indwelling Hegelian-like process that moves things to become something else, to proceed, as it were, from the dualism of thesis in the form of individual percipient and antithesis in the form of external nature to the synthesis of individual and thunder as a higher third. Rather, Chao-pien was the thunder from the very beginning;

or, if you will, the thunder, even before its eruption, was Chao-pien himself in the absolute nothingness of the eternal present.

As thunder itself emerges from the inexplicable and unmapped depths of the universe, is the expression of the universe in the instant of its eruption, so Chao-pien, experiencing the thunder within his own consciousness, is in the moment of hearing made aware that he is, as he has always been, perfectly identical with the very same universe or, as it were, with the eternally abiding, yet ever-changing, nothingness out of which the universe itself comes and of which it is essentially composed. The final line of the poem, which depicts the Buddha-nature as a homely old man, prohibits our thinking of Chao-pien's experience as anything other than the perfectly ordinary, perfectly commonplace reality of things and events as perceived in the realm of the everyday.

Another example of suchness as the determining attribute of one's seeing the depth of things, their limitlessness, occurs in a famous death poem by the Chinese master Etsuzan:

> Light dies in the eyes, hearing
> Fades. Once back to the Source,
> There's no special meaning—
> Today, tomorrow.[19]

Though Etsuzan's fading senses contrast sharply with Chao-pien's poignant hearing, both men perceive the depth of things and find in that bottomlessness nothing special. There is no sense of a natural supernaturalism, no religious exaltation that might in any way hinder the "just-so-ness" of enlightened hearing and seeing. "Indeed a certain enthusiasm can help us in the conquest of the mirages we have created," says Robert Linssen, while contrasting Buddhist homeliness with Christian glorification, "but we should have to rid ourselves absolutely of the exaltation so that there would only remain existential felicity which is sufficient unto itself."[20] Etsuzan's return to the source through death can have "no special meaning," for we are this source; we carry it with us at all times, "Today, tomorrow." So far as we live in the unborn Buddha-mind, we experience neither birth nor death. "If anyone confirms that this unborn, illuminative wisdom is in fact the Buddha-mind and straight away lives, as he is, in the Buddha-mind," says Bankei, "he becomes at that moment a living

Tathagata, and he remains one for infinite kalpas in the future."[21] The term *tathagata* translates from both Sanskrit and Pali as "the thus-gone" or as the "thus-come" or "thus-perfected one," one who has realized her essential oneness with all things as they exist in a state of perfect suchness. To exalt this state through ecstacy is to endow it with emotional qualities it does not in its naturalness require, and to omit speaking of it altogether as somehow too precious or too mysterious for ordinary discourse is to assign it a specialness it does not want. Both approaches soil enlightenment with the "dust" of an unnecessary religiosity or a misleading mysticism.

Given the force of such considerations, then, it is not surprising that Yomyo-Enju, a Chinese master, writes so matter-of-factly, though nevertheless paradoxically, about the world-shattering experience of his awakening at the instant of hearing a pile of wood toppling over:

> Toppling over is none other than THAT:
> Nowhere is found an atom of dust.
> Mountains, rivers, plain—
> All reveal the Buddha-body.[22]

To hear the toppling of this woodpile in *wu-shih* (Japanese, *buji*), the condition of "nothing special," is to see a new world and yet to know that we have always been and always will be at the point of the depth we long to achieve.

By evading efforts to explicate the poetry relating such experiences of depth, we risk exalting the very experience of insight that requires, for its final effect, our acceptance of its ordinariness. When Hsiang-yen, for example, heard the pebble that sounded the depth of things as the lived experience of his own being, he knew that he could not remain aloof, so to speak, in an exalted quietude beyond words, for to do so would be to undermine the unassuming suchness of the spirituality he had achieved. Thus he writes:

> One stroke has made me forget all my previous knowledge.
> No artificial discipline is at all needed;
>> In every movement I uphold the ancient way
>> And never fall into the rut of mere quietism;
> Wherever I walk no traces are left,
>> And my senses are not fettered by rules of conduct. . . . [23]

In Zen, as in other spiritual practices, it is easy to confuse art and religion and to place such stress on literature that aesthetic experience becomes an end in itself, an "artificial discipline" that brings joy and high ecstasy but that, if unexamined, may lead the percipient away from the very ordinariness of the world that yields such experience. Takashi Ikemoto, a modern poet and practicing Zennist, reminds us that the "five-temple literature" of the Japanese medieval period fell into just such a trap. Quoting the medieval poet Keian, for example, who wrote that " 'The finer poetry is, the more matured Zen is,' " Ikemoto warns against the related and well-known postulate, " 'Poetry and Zen are of a savor,' " and declares: "To a poet-monk absorbed in versification, satori will remain a sealed book. Or if he has already gained a measure of satori, it will never mature."[24] What Ikemoto says of *satori* can also be said of *yugen*. To see the mood as too mysterious or too mystical to be explicated is to approach the "rut of quietism" Hsiang-yen disparages and to risk making it into one of the artificial disciplines he finds it necessary to abandon; it is to be trapped in the form of the experience, held hostage, as it were, to the psychological and the aesthetic.

By associating *yugen* with wisdom in the spirit of suchness as the functional ground of the mood, I wish to claim for the experience a genuine spiritual poignancy beyond the specialness of its presentation in art yet accessible through the ordinary practices of poetry. *Yugen*, as I will try to show, is rooted neither in the entirely psychological nor in the purely aesthetic but in the spirituality of ordinary experience, which includes literary experience. It is the point at which moods pass beyond moods or, if you will, the point at which the psychological and the aesthetic pass over into the epistemological and the spiritual. Wordsworth's "The Ruined Cottage," composed 1797–99, is particularly helpful here because it shows the English poet struggling at a relatively early point in his career with questions of poetic form and spiritual content as they articulate an evolving Buddhistic-like perception of the bottomless depth of things.

"The Ruined Cottage" centers upon a young man's progress from a condition of restless agitation in the face of natural processes to a state of wisdom that enables him to see into the moving form of things and to accept as an end in itself the deep tranquillity at the heart of eternal change. The setting of the poem is midpoint in a summer's day when "the sun was mounted high" (1) and the surfaces of things were dappled with the shadows of "deep embattled clouds" (6).[25] Reflecting the aerial strife above, the narrator enters the poem toiling "With languid feet" (20) and fretted with an "insect host which gathered round my face / And joined their murmurs to the tedious noise / Of seeds of bursting gorse that crackled round" (24–26). Turning for relief from what he can only experience as the tedium of nature, he comes upon "a ruined house, four naked walls / That stared upon each other" (31–32) and an old man, a peddler, "Alone, and stretched upon the cottage bench" (34). The peddler, unlike the narrator, appears at rest in the world—not simply content, but rather one with the moving conditions of nature itself. Aligning him with the mottled surfaces at the beginning of the poem, "The shadows of the breezy elms above / Dappled his face" (47–48) in such a way as to leave him almost invisible in nature, more an extension of the things around him, including the empty house, than a specific figure in the landscape. The dialogue between these two will form the central action of the poem, the means by which the narrator will awaken to a new sense of the depth and beauty of things and of his relation with them.

The contrast between the two figures is worth exploring momentarily, for it mirrors the student-teacher relationship we see in Zen. Like the narrator in Wordsworth's poem, the Zen student enters the relationship with his teacher from the dualistic perspective of self and world, frequently bearing with him some "bitter disappointment in life," as one anecdote puts it, and seeking relief or freedom in the form of enlightenment or awakening.[26] Like the partly invisible peddler, the Zen master confronts the student more in the capacity of a trackless wave than as a pedagogue armed with specific knowledge. "All I am talking about is only medicine appropriate for curing specific ailments," says Master Rinzai (Chinese, Lin-chi) to his students. "In my talks there is nothing absolutely real."[27] Elsewhere, he tells his students: "If you meet a buddha, kill the buddha. If you meet a patriarch, kill the patriarch."[28] Joshu similarly advises a departing student: "Do not stay where the Buddha is! And pass quickly through a place where there is no Buddha!"[29] What the Zen master gives the student, whether in the form of a *koan* or of direct advice or sometimes only as instruction in quiet sitting (Japanese, *shikantaza*), is an opportunity so to focus the mind as to enable the individual to move completely beyond the limits of a dualistic world of self and other to the trackless depths of an oceanic experience. "The further one breaks into the region of the origin," as one Zen saying puts it, "the deeper the region becomes."[30]

In Wordsworth's poem, the symbol and analogue of this region of bottomless depth is a well "Half-choked [with willow flowers and weeds]" (63), situated in a "damp cold nook" (62) of the abandoned "plot / Of garden-ground, now wild" (54–55) beside the ruined cottage. The narrator slakes his thirst at the well and returns to the "shady bench" to sit beside the old man whom he has met elsewhere in his travels. Perceiving the younger man's continuing discomfiture, a condition unrelieved by this "cheerless spot" (60), as the narrator calls it, the peddler remarks, "I see around me here / Things which you cannot see" (67–68). The basis of his seeing, the old man explains, is his knowledge that although all beings and things die or undergo change, and though poets—by calling "upon the hills and streams to mourn"—evoke the "creative power / Of human passion" in partial compensation for loss, there are nevertheless "Sympathies . . . More tranquil, yet perhaps of kindred birth, / That steal upon the meditative mind / And grow with thought" (68–82).

In asserting the presence of unifying sympathies and deep tranquillities beneath the creative force of human passions, sympathies that "grow with thought" and that exist, therefore, within what he calls the "meditative mind," the peddler affirms in true Zen fashion the unity of consciousness and nature, a unity mirrored outwardly in his own visible oneness with his surroundings. The meditative mind that enables the deeper sympathies among things to emerge and to grow with thought is of the nature of reality, one with reality in what Zen understands as the mutual identity of self and other. "There is always a certain unchanging reality at the base of the mind," writes Kitarō Nishida. But, like the peddler of Wordsworth's poem, Nishida understands that this "reality" is a state of "continuous change of the unifying center."[31] This eternally changing center cannot be understood as in any way apart from the individual as unifier:

> The world we can know and understand is established by a unifying power identical to that of our consciousness. . . . Although the self as unifier is regarded in psychology as separate from that which is unified, such a self is simply an abstract concept. In fact, there is no self apart from things— our self is the very unifier of the universe.[32]

For the Zennist, as Nishida writes elsewhere, "there are no distinctions between subjectivity and objectivity or spirit and matter."[33] What the individual perceives as sympathies among things in a state of continual motion is the result of the unifying power of his own consciousness functioning as both a fold within and an embodying agent of the consciousness of reality itself.

The emotional configuration of this mind-state is one of deep and abiding tranquillity and stillness, a condition inclusive of yet beyond both sorrow and joy. Nishida describes this region of depth in terms that resonate well with the peaceableness of the peddler's countenance:

> There's something bottomless
> Within me I feel.
> However disturbing are the waves
> Of joy and sorrow,
> They fail to reach it.[34]

For Zennists, this experience of bottomlessness occurs most visibly in moments of *satori*, of deep meditation. "Going further and further down," writes William Johnston in his commentary on Nishida's poem, "one reaches a still point where peace reigns even while above there may be storm."[35] It is important to understand that the peacefulness Nishida and Johnston describe adumbrates or lines, if you will, a mind-state that does not disperse the "storm" of thought and feeling that constitutes the individual's psychic life. Nor is it a condition that resolves tensions into a third state of lesser intensity. It is, rather, a species of what Johnston elsewhere calls "vertical thinking, a process in which the mind goes silently down into its own center, revealing cavernous depths ordinarily latent and untouched by the flow of images and concepts that pass across the surface of the mind."[36]

For the Zennist, access to this deep meditative ground proceeds not from the rejection or the displacement of disturbing thoughts or discomforting emotions but from a sincere opening to all that bubbles up in the course of human existence. The modern Zen master Kōshō Uchiyama refers to this process as "opening the hand of thought." Uchiyama explains that "When we try to put everything in order using only our brains, we never succeed." Like the narrator who, in drinking at the well beside the ruined cottage, quenches his thirst but fails to achieve peace of mind and acceptance of his surroundings, the individual who attempts to resolve his problems through the application of analytic thought or conventional understanding succeeds only in aggravating an already uncomfortable situation. It is not until we encounter the meditative mind, the sitting mind of *zazen*, that we experience the peacefulness of a free state in which thoughts are simply allowed to come and go as they will. "When we are sitting," Uchiyama continues, "we open the hand of thought and let all our thoughts come and go freely." This process of opening, Uchiyama explains, is the state of "No gaining, no knowing," a state in which the mind is compared to an "expansive sky" that does not hinder the floating clouds.[37]

In "The Ruined Cottage," access to the expansive sky of vertical consciousness, to what the peddler calls the "meditative mind," accrues through the individual's opening to sadness as the emotional lining of the state of change that comprises reality. And again, the well or spring beside the cottage forms the central analogue of the individual's understanding. "Beside yon spring I stood / And eyed its waters till we seemed to feel / One sadness, they and I" (82–84), says the peddler. In approaching the well through the meditative mind, that is, in looking beneath the willow flowers and weeds that threaten to choke it and, concurrently, beyond its ability simply to relieve thirst and so to provide respite from the pain of life, the old man accepts the very discomfiture the narrator tries to elude. By thus accepting the conditions of the well and its surroundings, the old man encounters a compensatory unity of being that allows discomfiture its proper place in the evolving scheme of things, a field of play that deflates the authority of pain and its power to overwhelm the visible cheerfulness and mildness that form what the narrator later, in line 201, describes as the underlying features of the peddler's face and, implicitly, as the true emotional ground of human existence.

In this unity of sadness, what we might describe more accurately, perhaps, as an ambient field of sadness that eliminates all sense of barrier between human individual and natural form, between the act of perception and the thing perceived, the old man proceeds to tell the story of Margaret, the former inhabitant of the cottage, of how her husband, afflicted with poverty and illness, abandoned her and their children, leaving her to cope as best she could.

Before going very far, however, the old man interrupts his narrative
with a question about the purpose of intruding thoughts of suffering
upon an otherwise cheerful and harmonious condition of natural wisdom and comfort. Indicating that " 'Tis now the hour of deepest
noon," a time that marks a "still season of repose and peace"
(187–88), the peddler asks:

> Why should a tear be in an old man's eye?
> Why should we thus with an untoward mind
> And in the weakness of humanity
> From natural wisdom turn our hearts away,
> To natural comfort shut our eyes and ears,
> And feeding on disquiet thus disturb
> The calm of Nature with our restless thoughts? (192–98)

The old man's question reminds us that he is concerned not with suffering and pain but with natural wisdom and comfort. He does not,
after all, question the fact of suffering. He questions only why we
obtrude our perception of it on what is otherwise a peaceful, even a
blissful, state.

The answer comes in the opening lines to the second part of the
poem and has nothing to do with the conventional mind's quest for
explanations and justifications. Describing the peddler, the narrator
remarks:

> He spake with somewhat of a solemn tone:
> But when he ended there was in his face
> Such easy chearfulness, a look so mild
> That for a little time it stole away
> All recollection, and that simple tale
> Passed from my mind like a forgotten sound. (199–204)

The answer to the peddler's question resides in his countenance, not
in his words. In fact, the tale itself as an aesthetic object disappears
momentarily for the narrator. It is the peddler's manner that
attracts the narrator. And the peddler's manner, expressed through
the features of his countenance, contrasts sharply with his stated
feelings. He is cheerful despite the sadness he feels, and he wears the
face of mildness despite the intensity of the grief implicit in the tale
he has begun.

From a Buddhist perspective, the peddler understands that "there is suffering, but none who suffers." The lesson emerges with special force in the popular fifth-century Pali text, *The Path of Purification* (Visuddhimagga), composed by the Indian philosopher Buddhaghosa:

> For there is suffering, but none who suffers;
> Doing exists although there is no doer;
> Extinction is but no extinguished person;
> Although there is a path, there is no goer.[38]

The Buddhist understands that one cannot avoid suffering and that the way to deal with suffering is to open to it completely. The principle is especially visible in an anecdote about the Zen master Shaku Soen. One day, while out for a stroll, he heard loud lamentations from a nearby house that had just suffered the loss of one of its members. Entering the house, he sat down and cried with the mourners. An old man, startled at seeing the famous master crying, remarked: "I would have thought that you at least were beyond such things." Master Soen replied: "But it is this which puts me beyond it. . . ."[39]

The Buddhist understands that suffering is a function, not an end, of reality and that by opening to pain in the absence of a self that would bend the flow of the eternal present to fit the expectations of a private ego, she opens as well to the vividness and preciousness of life as a moving process with no abiding center and no place for an abiding selfhood. "We are here," writes Nolan Pliny Jacobson, "not to bring the universe under our human designs, but to celebrate the vividness and preciousness of life in the passing *now*."[40] The narrator of Wordsworth's poem cannot see what the peddler sees, cannot see the vivid beauty and preciousness of the abandoned cottage and of the weeds that choke the well from which he drinks because he views reality from the dualistic perspective of self and other. "The duality of all things," according to Seng-t'san, "Issues from false discriminations."[41] Significantly, Seng-t'san does not proscribe discrimination, only what he calls "false discriminations." To escape the realm of false discrimination, one must, according to Seng-t'san, "Develop a mind of equanimity," a mind that does not "pick and choose" and that "does not exert itself," a mind whose environment "is not a place of thinking."[42] Seng-t'san is not objecting to thought itself, no more than he is trying to eliminate discrimination. These are, after all, functions of the mind and cannot be discarded. Rather, in the words of Shido Bunan, he is saying: "No-thought does not mean 'without thought,' but 'no defiled thought.'"[43]   Shibayama explains that "no defiled thought" is "the state of mind free from the defilement of dualistic discrimination."[44]

This pure mind, which Shibayama says "is fair, impartial and is absolutely free,"[45] simply cannot surface from within the arena of individual ego, even though it encompasses the self and makes possible the very ego that frequently obscures it. The individual trapped in selfhood, in the perception of himself as in some essential way separate from or other than the surrounding conditions of the moment, must of necessity project that very sense of selfhood onto all he sees and hears and so aggravate suffering by clinging to such distinctions as beauty and ugliness, cheerfulness and melancholy, presence and absence. "The major source of suffering is the illusion of an indestructible, unitary, self-identical, not-further-analyzable self," writes Jacobson. In the absence of such a self-oriented perspective, however, the individual discovers a process that is, Jacobson continues, always "with us, moving out of the past already vanished into the future yet to come, nourishing the present with the transient qualities the organisms are marvelously created to enjoy." Access to this enjoyment requires our acceptance of existence as itself a forever-emerging act of opening, what the Buddhist calls the "vital nothingness" or the active Void available only to the meditative mind. "Elsewhere in the world blank walls are really considered empty spaces to be filled in," says Jacobson, concluding his treatise on nothingness and self-emptying. "In Buddhist meditation the blank walls and empty spaces are already full. "[46]

The narrator of Wordsworth's poem encounters these blank walls and empty spaces in the "four naked walls" (31) of the abandoned cottage open to the sky and in the meditative countenance of the peddler's dappled face, a countenance surprisingly full despite its owner's earlier admission that the loss of Margaret was like the loss of a daughter. Attracted by the old man's "easy chearfulness"—a manner that, paradoxically, both draws upon and deflates the solemnity of his tone while conveying, as well, a deep warmth that contrasts sharply with the "heartfelt chillness" the narrator claims to experience in response to the story of Margaret's suffering—the younger man begs the peddler to resume his tale. The old man consents, but not before warning the narrator that the enjoyment his story may inspire should not be construed as a "vain dalliance with the misery / Even of the dead . . . A momentary pleasure never marked / By reason, barren of all future good" (223–26). The caveat recalls the peddler's earlier concern with natural wisdom and reminds us that the narrative, if effective, must move us from the purely emotional to the realm of thought that marks the prevalence of the "meditative mind." Having provided both a cautionary and a meditative frame for his story, the peddler tells of how Margaret languishes following the departure of her husband, of how she falls into poverty and despair, and finally into the oblivion of negligence:

> But for her Babe
> And for her little friendless Boy, she said,
> She had no wish to live, that she must die
> Of sorrow. (428–31)

Eventually, however, even the children die. With their loss, yet "Expecting still to learn her husband's fate" (467), Margaret lapses into a "reckless" solitude (481) until, weakened by sorrow and longing, she dies, "Last human tenant of these ruined walls" (492).

Margaret's death, viewed in response to the evolving meditative context of the poem, that is, to the unfolding wisdom the peddler seeks to make available to his younger interlocutor, is an analogue of the death of the self which the individual must experience on the path to spiritual awakening. For the narrator, the early stages of this process of self-emptying produce feelings of weakness and passivity. He speaks of being "mov'd" by the tale, of "rising instinctively," of turning "aside in weakness," and finally of blessing Margaret "in the impotence of grief" (493–500). His sadness corresponds remarkably to the liberative tears the Zen meditator frequently experiences as he encounters the region of selfless compassion accompanying moments of spiritual breakthrough. "What do these tears mean?" asks a recent student of Zen in a meditation diary. "They're a sign of my helplessness," he responds, "a tacit admission that my intellect, my ego, has reached the limit of its power."[47] But if one finds oneself helpless, trapped, as it were, like Hakuin in a field of ice with no place to go, one also finds release from the ego, freedom to let the very sadness revealed by tears cleanse the ego of its reliance on specific emotional conditions and on the need for abiding perspectives and explanations so that one may engage the larger "sympathies" the peddler had described earlier in Wordsworth's poem. "Yes, tears are nature's benediction," continues the modern Zen diarist in a further entry that could, perhaps, have been written by the peddler, "her attempt to wash away the grime of ego and soften the harsh outlines of our personalities made arid and tense through an egotistic reliance on the invincibility of reason."[48]

Like the Zen meditator pushed to the edge of emotional and intellectual trauma, to the region of doubt the Zen master Hakuin describes as an "ice sheet extending tens of thousands of miles,"[49] the younger man of Wordsworth's poem, who speaks paradoxically of being comforted by the very tale that brings him so much grief, has effectively yielded the opposing self of the earlier lines. He experiences now a moment of egolessness in which concern for himself is eclipsed by concern for another.

Expressed through what he calls "the impotence of grief," however, the narrator's concern for Margaret, together with his blessing, signals that the process of self-emptying is incomplete: the compassion he experiences, while certainly commendable in its brotherly affection and reflective of a progress from the alienating cheerlessness of his initial reaction to the ruined cottage, is not the vital, active compassion of life itself, what Buddhists call the "*tathāgata-garbha*." The term combines the Buddhist concept of 'suchness', the commonplace and unremarkable "thus-gone" or "thus-come" nature of the "perfected one," with the notion of "germ" or "womb" as source, an approximation to that which contains the *tathāgata*.[50] Gishin Tokiwa, a modern Zen philosopher and student of ethics, relies on the translation of *tathāgata-garbha* as "womb of the Buddha." For Tokiwa, the *tathāgata-garbha* is a state of compassion in which the individual, emptied of self, lives the life of suffering in a state that is yet free of suffering: "Here suffering is empty, and emptiness as the True Self can, does, and will suffer. . . . It is the emancipated who can say and go through what suffering is."[51] The "True Self" that Tokiwa mentions here is known also as the Formless Self, the condition of cosmic selfhood redolent of and immanent in all form, yet itself subject to no form, to no particular state of emotional and intellectual being. Access to this high selfhood accrues through a process of ego-dispersal that results in a mode of wisdom which allows one to experience suffering while yet remaining free of suffering and so to engage the highest compassion—the compassion that exists beyond all notions of reward, of right and wrong, of principle, the compassion that is, for all practical purposes, of the nature of reality itself as the liberated individual embodies and expresses that reality in the lived experience of the passing moment. Commenting on Tokiwa's notion of the relationship between such compassion and the wisdom of liberative suffering, Donald Mitchell, who sees parallels between the Buddhist *tathāgata-garbha* and the Christian experience of kenotic benevolence, the self-emptying compassion for which Mary is the model, writes that

> the paradox is that with wisdom, one is, as Formless Self, free from suffering (Nirvana). And at the same time with compassion, one is an ordinary being that "goes through suffering" (*samsara*) for the sake of others. This is truly living the Bodhisattva Ideal as an "empty being." It is the True Life of the Formless Self born from the *tathāgata's* womb, full of the compassion of that womb, for the benefit of all sentient beings.[52]

Unlike the peddler, the narrator of "The Ruined Cottage," though he experiences a brotherly sympathy for Margaret, cannot yet enter the region of *tathāgata-garbha*, the realm of wise suffering or of suffering-nonsuffering compassion, for he is bound by grief and still thinks in dualistic terms. Though he has purged the self through suffering and now accepts the weeds and flowers and "silent overgrowings" that occupy the ruined cottage in Margaret's absence, he nevertheless traces the new life to what he calls "That secret spirit of humanity":

> At length [towards] the [Cottage I returned]
> Fondly, and traced with milder interest
> That secret spirit of humanity
> Which, 'mid the calm oblivious tendencies
> Of nature, 'mid her plants, her weeds, and flowers,
> And silent overgrowings, still survived. (501–6)

The *tathāgata-garbha* that Tokiwa celebrates as the true compassion available to the Formless Self of empty being cannot be traced to a separately existing humanistic principle or spirit, however indwelling it appears among things. To do so would be to affirm a panhumanism at the ground of existence and to give way to a fundamental dualism that sees the forms of things as in some way separate from that which causes them and to which they point as a power which is basically other. In seizing upon grief and in allowing it to define the presence of an underlying "secret spirit" of humanity, the narrator simply affirms in another form the principle of abstraction that bound Margaret to the perception that the only world she could inhabit was one that included her husband: "She loved this wretched spot, nor would for worlds / Have parted hence" (487–88).

The humanism which the narrator celebrates is, for the spiritualist, a delimiting principle, an abstraction that prolongs suffering and prevents access to the empty mind of true compassion and liberation. *"We suffer because we are human,"* writes Albert Low, a modern Buddhist thinker. But the source of our suffering is not, as Low explains, our humanity. It is our ignorance of "our true nature," Low continues, a nature which lies completely outside or beyond derived intellectual principles and which is obscured by the human tendency to theorize, to find what Low calls a "ghost in the machine" (a phrase belonging originally to the British philosopher Gilbert Ryle). Such ignorance, according to Low, separates knowledge and being: "Our true nature is knowing that is being, being that is knowing. It is precisely the illusory separation of knowing and being that is at the root of our woe."[53] The *tathāgata-garbha* that Tokiwa sees as the true compassion in wisdom is predicated not on the presence of an indwelling humanistic principle of causation among things but on the identity of all things, all forms, as "the true oneness or unity of all beings—the original, true formless Self of all of us."[54]

Seeing that the younger man has not made the final leap, so to speak, into the "formless Self" that defines the true depth of things and that contains the wisdom which moves beyond grief to an understanding of the community of oneness we share with all things and beings in the cosmic groundlessness of life, the peddler resumes:

My Friend, enough to sorrow have you given,
The purposes of wisdom ask no more;

Be wise and chearful, and no longer read
The forms of things with an unworthy eye.
She sleeps in the calm earth, and peace is here. (508–12)

Like the Zen master, the peddler understands that the wisdom to see
the forms of things with a worthy eye requires that we yield all perspectives grounded in theory and that we see things from the viewpoint of formlessness itself. To cling to sorrow would be to exalt the
human over other forms, to resist the fundamental openness or
emptiness at the ground of our being, and, finally, to deny ourselves
access to the knowing-being wisdom that comes with the egoless
apprehension of reality; it would be to deny the emptiness at the core
of all being. The *Heart Sutra*, as we have seen, reminds us that form
is emptiness. But our understanding is not complete unless we can
see that emptiness, as the second line of the sutra affirms, is also
form. We can understand how form is emptiness because we can see
that all things undergo change. But the assertion that emptiness is
form presents difficulties, for we must approach the region of understanding from the realm of emptiness itself. To do this, we must put
the ego to sleep. We must see that from the very beginning, separate
selfhood, with its attendant or projected notions of separate forms, is
illusory. Such seeing can occur only when we enter what Buddhists
call the "region of Mind," where form and formlessness interact or
fold upon each other in an amorphous unity beyond all notions of a
secret causal spring. Zen thinkers like to convey this understanding
of Mind through question-answer constructs like the following:

Now, Mind itself has no form. What is it, then, that hears and
works and moves about? Delve into yourself deeper and deeper until you are no longer aware of a single object. Then
beyond a shadow of a doubt you will perceive your True-
nature, like a man awakening from a dream.[55]

The peddler, like any Zen thinker, understands that access to
such "Mind" or "True-nature," what he calls "wisdom," accrues
through the process of laying the self to rest and viewing the moving
panorama of existence from the depths of a powerful and abiding
peacefulness. Hence, his reference to Margaret as asleep rather than

dead and his subsequent equating of tranquillity with depth of insight and with cheerful meditative wisdom:

> I well remember that those very plumes,
> Those weeds, and the high spear-grass on that wall,
> By mist and silent rain-drops silver'd o'er,
> As once I passed did to my heart convey
> So still an image of tranquillity,
> So calm and still, and looked so beautiful
> Amid the uneasy thoughts which filled my mind,
> That what we feel of sorrow and despair
> From ruin and from change, and all the grief
> The passing shews of being leave behind,
> Appeared an idle dream that could not live
> Where meditation was. I turned away
> And walked along my road in happiness. (513–25)

Unlike the younger man, the peddler does not trace the deep, still unity of life to anything outside the meditative mind, to any indwelling "secret spirit" that causes things and events to occur. The meditative state implied by line 512 acknowledges the grief accompanying change and ruin but views such a condition as "an idle dream," a passing emotional form that emerges upon the surface of the oceanic mind only to collapse again into the formless tranquillity that is ours in our sense of our inherent oneness with all things. For the peddler, as for the student of Zen, the oceanic mind, no matter how rippled its surface appears with waves of grief and despair, remains tranquil in its bottomless depths, a place of rest for the individual buffeted by the force of change. "When we rest in Formless Mind," writes the twentieth-century Zen philosopher Sokei-an, "the mind is like the bottomless ocean—all potentiality. It is in a state of omnipotence."[56]

The mark of the omnipotence of this mind-state is a deep happiness predicated, not on the intellectual gratification that comes with the sense of having discovered an answer or of having arrived at a concluding explanation, but on the enlightened peaceableness that comes with the courage to accept, to open to, the simple, unadorned, unremarkable suchness of things. "The only true enlightenment is awareness of the vivid reality of life, moment by moment," says Kōshō Uchiyama. "Enlightenment is not like a sudden realization of something mysterious. Enlightenment is nothing but awakening from illusions and returning to the reality of life."[57] In such a state, one has no choice but to be happy. Explaining that "Buddhism teaches the transience of all things, a certain calm detachment from others and from oneself," a Tibetan monk tells Andrew Harvey:

> We are taught not to take ourselves too seriously, and we are taught to believe that there is little ultimate truth in grief or misery. The real wisdom is joy. The real wisdom is happiness. . . . It takes a great courage when you are suffering to see beyond your suffering to the clear relations between things, to the laws that cause and govern your suffering; it takes great courage to be ruthless with one's griefs.[58]

The peddler's abruptness in telling the narrator that he has given enough to sorrow and that he sees the forms of things with an "unworthy eye" contains an element of the ruthlessness Buddhism expounds. It is not the ruthlessness of indifference, what the narrator perceives as "the calm oblivious tendencies / Of nature." It is, rather, a mark of the strength, of the "omnipotence," to use Sokei-an's vocabulary, that comes with the sense of our inherent community with all things in the formless yet creative depths of an endless process of change. "Beginning in the sixth century B.C.," writes Jacobson, "Buddhism has perceived reality as the inexhaustible process of energy flowing out of the depths of things, quite apart from any conscious effort to bring the process about."[59] The weeds the narrator sees as choking the well and covering its depths emerge for the peddler from those very depths, are those depths of creativity come forth in such natural form. They are not a sign of the oblivion of natural process. They are natural process, as is Margaret herself. We cannot encounter the happiness of this perception so long as we think of reality as harboring a secret spring of humanistic resistance beneath the flow of events. Rather, the weeds convey to the peddler an image of tranquillity and happiness because he knows, from the moving perspective of the Formless Self, that he and they are one and the same, that their peace is his peace, that their abiding is his abiding. To ask more of life is to ask for a happiness grounded in the ego and therefore unworthy of the very eye that sees.

To what extent the narrator of "The Ruined Cottage" accepts the peddler's teaching remains obscure. The poem ends with the two going off to a "rustic inn" down the road, to an "evening resting-place" (538). The suggestion here is that the younger man has learned something of the depth of things and of the happy availability of an abiding tranquillity at the heart of life, a condition Wordsworth celebrates throughout his work. In poem after poem he returns to the theme of tranquillity and formless depth as the natural accompaniment to a life lived beyond the demands of a constricting ego. Most of these works find this deep sense of peace in natural settings. In "Animal Tranquillity and Decay" (*PW* 4:247), for example, a poem that, like "The Ruined Cottage," appeared early in his career, between 1797 and 1798, Wordsworth presents the figure of an old man so spiritualized with age that he "moves / With thought . . . insensibly subdued" (6–7) to such a "settled quiet" (8) that "He is by nature led / To peace so perfect that the young behold / With envy, what the Old Man hardly feels" (12–14). Even "The little hedgerow birds," we are told at the beginning of the poem, "regard him not" (1–2). There is no sense here of a motivating self separate from the things and processes of nature.

In "A Slumber Did My Spirit Seal" (*PW* 2:216), composed in 1799, the death or the laying to rest of the human spirit in nature results not in fears for the individual selfhood but in a condition of immortality defined as freedom from "The touch of earthly years"—a freedom predicated on the innate oneness of the human and the natural as the two merge in the motionless motion of cosmic process:

> A slumber did my spirit seal;
> I had no human fears:
> She seemed a thing that could not feel
> The touch of earthly years.
>
> No motion has she now, no force;
> She neither hears nor sees;
> Rolled round in earth's diurnal course,
> With rocks and stones and trees. (1–8)

Like the peddler of "The Ruined Cottage," who understands that in the cosmic depth of things, he is one with the weeds that overgrow Margaret's well, so the human spirit, sealed here in sleep, enables the individual to escape time, not by residing outside it, but, in Zen fashion, by realizing that as natural process, one is, like rocks and stones and trees, time itself. "Rats are time. . . . So are tigers," writes the Zen master Dōgen in images even more startling than Wordsworth's. "Sentient beings are time, and buddhas are too."[60] Dōgen is anxious to show that time is being, that being is time, and that forms are both empty and full, both absolute and in motion, undergoing change. "There is no universal form, time. There is no time without all beings," writes Joan Stambaugh in explication of Dōgen. "Time is simply the way these beings take place or presence; they are nothing over and above and beyond this taking place and presencing. There is no substance and no duration."[61] In his depiction of the human spirit at rest in the depths of natural process, Wordsworth understands, like Dōgen, the essential unity of being and time and the necessity of accepting this unity to achieve peace.[62]

In line with the universality of his vision, however, and with its freedom from specific form, including the forms of nature, Wordsworth celebrates this cosmic peace as the bedrock of city life as well. The most famous example is, perhaps, "Composed upon Westminster Bridge, September 3, 1802" (*PW* 3:38). Viewing the city in the deep morning calm prior to its awakening to human activity, Wordsworth describes London as "silent, bare"; its "Ships, towers, domes, theatres, and temples lie / Open unto the fields, and to the sky; / All bright and glittering in the smokeless air" (5–8). In its openness to field and sky, London is a metaphor of the human soul open to a "calm so deep," as Wordsworth writes near the end of the poem, that all things seem to move paradoxically in a motionless motion that cuts beneath all human efforts to grasp the processes of being as either alive or dead:

> Ne'er saw I, never felt, a calm so deep!
> The river glideth at his own sweet will:
> Dear God! the very houses seem asleep;
> And all that mighty heart is lying still! (11–14)

Focusing on the last line of the poem, while viewing nature and consciousness as separate, J. Hillis Miller writes that the force behind this sonnet is death, that Wordsworth is trying to transform London, "what is 'really there' into emblem, that is, into a corpse." Unable to view the stillness at the heart of the poem as a vital, active flowing aligned with the motions of a stable cosmic process, Miller argues that Wordsworth in "Westminster Bridge" imposes on London the rural preoccupations of his own self-nature:

> It [the poet's imagination] creates out of the dislocations of literal language a rural scene and figure, sleeping or dead, where there was only London on a September morning. In this verbalized transformation the poet stamps his image on nature, inscribes himself on it, makes nature into emblem.[63]

However, reading "Westminster Bridge" in the context of *yugen*, that is, in the context of the simple, unadorned depth of things in all conditions, whether rural or urban, we see that the central mood of the poem is not London's calm, which could be construed as death, but the openness that allows for such calm. London's availability to field and sky is the openness of all things and beings to the bottomless depths of reality. In such openness, there is no abiding image, say an urban form that confines cityscapes to one identity, nor is there a separately existing force, say the human imagination, that converts things into emblems of its own preoccupation. The human imagination, viewed as part of the process by which all things open to moving depths empty of abiding form, does not stamp the poet's image on nature so much as reveal the elemental continuity of mind and what it perceives initially as other. The spirit does not sleep in the conventional sense. Nor is it dead. Empty of abiding form, it is open to depths art can suggest but never confine.

In the next chapter, we will explore the relationship between these depths and the art that suggests them. We will see that in the moment of awakening, language, conventionally regarded as a human phenomenon, puts itself to sleep, displacing itself to reveal the fundamental continuity of observer and observed. At the deepest levels of prelingual consciousness, a state both prior to and inclusive of the symbol-making powers of the mind, the work of art, especially Wordsworth's art, leads, like London, beyond itself, emptying itself into the formless, decentralized interbeing of all things.

CHAPTER TEN

THE LESSON OF
THE CONCH

In his lectures, Masao Abe has a memorable way of showing the difficulty with understanding and expressing the mind emptied of self and of the self's need for perspective. Pointing to the floor at his feet, Abe says that if asked to show the ground on which he is standing, he could reveal it by stepping back and pointing to it. But that would not be the ground on which he is presently standing. "To show the ground on which I *am standing now*," Abe remarks, "I may again step back and point to it. Again, however, it is only the ground where I was standing before. How can I show the *ground on which I am standing now*?"[1] Recalling Huang Po's famous claim that "You cannot use Mind to seek Mind," Abe's tactic of stepping back to see the ground on which he is standing implies the endless regressiveness of conceptual thinking and the accompanying impossibility of apprehending transpersonal consciousness through mental faculties attaching to the individual self. Such faculties are restricted to the pursuit of conceptual knowledge that must, in the presence of the nondual mind Zennists seek, give way to what Huang Po calls "wisdom": "You must use that wisdom which comes from nondualism to destroy your concept-forming, dualistic mentality."[2] For the student of Zen, wisdom, as we saw in the last chapter, is a matter of seeing into one's real nature by experiencing the essential identity of subject and object, of perceiving and perceived, as the very ground of one's existence. Thus, to the question "What is implied by 'seeing into the real Nature'?" Huang Po responds: "That Nature and your perception of it are one."[3]

175

In looking to a realm of wisdom beyond conceptual knowledge, Zen tends, as well, to eschew reliance on language and on the written word. "The Dharma [the cosmic law or great norm underlying the world] cannot be explained, because it is beyond spoken language and written words,"[4] says the thirteenth-century master Shiqi Xinyue, also known as "Mind-Moon of Stone River." Stone River's assertion about the limits of the written and spoken word accords well with the seventh-century maxim, cited earlier, which claims that Zen is a transmission outside the scriptures, a form of wisdom that employs but does not rely on letters. Commenting on this maxim in an effort to show that Zen is more praxis than spiritual philosophy, J. C. Cleary remarks that "Zen points directly to the human mind, without establishing any verbal formulations as sacred, in order to enable people to see their real identity and become enlightened."[5] Language, as Burton Watson puts it, "is grievously inadequate to describe the true Way, or the wonderful freedom of the man who has realized his identity with it."[6] Similarly, Takashi Ikemoto, describing the sense of fullness or wholeness that accompanies the Zen experience of oneness, writes: "There is, fundamentally, no room for words and letters."[7]

Though "grievously inadequate," however, language can be used to point to the intuitive mind. Indicating the best way to read Chuang Tzu, the early Taoist master roughly contemporaneous with Lao Tzu, Watson asserts that one should not "attempt to subject his thought to rational and systematic analysis, but to read and reread his words until one has ceased to think of what he is saying and instead has developed an intuitive sense of the mind moving behind the words, and of the world in which it moves."[8] In like manner, Takashi Ikemoto, qualifying his earlier claim that in Zen "There is, fundamentally, no room for words and letters," writes elsewhere that "No one can shut his eyes to the conspicuous role letters and words have played in Zen discipline." Aware of the many occasions on which poems, prayers, anecdotes, and sermons have inspired moments of breakthrough into *satori* (awakening), Ikemoto asserts that "in Zen one must fathom more than the ordinary dualistic meaning of letters and words; that is, one must intuit Nothingness or Buddhahood, identifying oneself with it."[9] Such an approach to reading implies that language is not an end in itself, a *biblos* or text to be cherished or exalted, but a kind of net, something that can be used but discarded in the very act of being used once the meaning is caught. "The fish trap exists because of the fish," says Chuang Tzu; "once you've gotten the fish, you can forget the trap. . . . Words exist because of meaning; once you've gotten the meaning, you can forget the words. Where can I find a man who has forgotten words so I can have a word with him?"[10]

Chuang Tzu's question "Where can I find a man who has forgotten words so I can have a word with him?" corresponds remarkably with Abe's question, "How can I show the *ground on which I am standing now?*" The early Taoist sage and the latter-day Zen philosopher both understand the limitations of language and yet the need to use language to express the way in which transpersonal consciousness manifests. Both writers understand that the intuitive mind, though essentially beyond language, need not be apprehended in a linguistic vacuum, as it were, outside the ordinary discursive efforts of humankind. "The Tao is originally without words, but we use words to reveal the Tao," writes Yuanwu (1063–1135), author of the famous Zen *koan* collection *The Blue Cliff Record.* "People who truly embody the Tao penetrate it in the mind and clarify it at its very basis."[11]

The ground of this understanding of the contradictory uses of language inheres in the perception that the mind which Zennists and Taoists alike seek is not really apart from the ordinary mind of everyday life. Explaining that for Buddhists "the word 'mind' is used in two basic senses," J. C. Cleary writes, "There is no ontological separation between the human mind and the Buddha-mind, because the Buddha-mind is the ground of being for all phenomena, including the perceptual worlds of unenlightened human beings."[12] The same both-and structure of thought attaches to the Zen understanding of selfhood. " 'Person' has two aspects," says Masao Abe, explaining D. T. Suzuki's work on Lin-chi's theory of "Cosmic Unconsciousness"; "one exists as a finite individual, and at the same time, one is a 'bottomless abyss.' "[13] The Zen mind or the mind of Tao cannot exist apart from the ordinary individual phenomena that both embody and manifest it. Hence, Abe's continuing effort to express it in some way. Hence, Chuang Tzu's request to "have a word" with the individual "who has forgotten words." Both philosophers recognize that emptiness manifests itself through a dynamic enfoldment of individual and universal. "The supra-individual

Emptiness or Cosmic Unconsciousness cannot manifest itself directly unless it materializes in an individual existence," writes Abe. "On
the other hand, an individual existence is really individual only inso-
far as the supra-individual Emptiness or Cosmic Unconsciousness
manifests itself in and through it."[14]

For many students of Zen, the mutual enfoldment of the individual and the supra-individual emerges most poignantly through
language in the form of poetry. As Taigan Takayama writes, "despite
the Zen sect's negation of letters, there seems to lie the possibility of
Zen experience necessarily taking the form of verse when it gives
itself literary expression."[15] Poetry, perhaps more than any other discipline, enables the participant to voice as writer and to perceive as
reader that which is beyond words. "Zen literature is an expression
of the Inexpressible," writes Takashi Ikemoto, "and Zen poetry is a
typical example."[16] What enables the Zennist to express the inexpressible through poetry is his understanding that art is grounded in
experience, not in the individual's experience of something conceived
as in some way different from himself, but in his perception of formless being as creative cosmic impulse expressing itself through him
as the very ground of his own existence. To understand such a paradoxical expression of the mutual enfoldment of individual and supra-
individual, we must know something of experience as Zennists
understand the term. The modern philosopher Kitarō Nishida is
very helpful here. Proclaiming that early in his career he "wanted to
explain all things on the basis of pure experience as the sole reality,"
Nishida says: "Over time I came to realize that it is not that experience exists because there is an individual, but that an individual
exists because there is experience. I thus arrived at the idea that
experience is more fundamental than individual differences."[17] By
"pure experience," Nishida means "to know in accordance with facts
by completely relinquishing one's own fabrications" and to encounter
life "just as it is without the least addition of deliberative discrimination."[18] It is a question not of what the individual experiences but
of what experiences itself through the individual.

Later in his life, however, Nishida came to realize that the concept of 'pure experience' was inadequate to explain the totally interanimative nature of all things and events in the world. That which he
had earlier called "the world of direct or pure experience" he came
eventually to regard as the realm of "action-intuition" (kōiteki-
chokkan): "The world of action-intuition—the world of poiesis—is

none other than the world of pure experience."[19]   Nishida did not reject pure experience. Rather, as Thomas Kasulis explains, he "realized his earlier Jamesian view to be overly subjectivistic."[20] To escape this psychologistic standpoint, Nishida redefined the relationship between self and world on the grounds of paradoxicality: "I hold that the self is consciously active when it is interactive, and its interactivity is constituted in a dialectic of mutual negation and affirmation of self and other," he writes near the end of his career. Affirming that this dialectical relationship of self and world is rooted in "the absolutely contradictory identity of the many and the one," Nishida asserts that "Our conscious worlds are the places in which we express the world in ourselves as the contradictory identity of the transcendent and the immanent, of space and time. . . . we are only active as formative positions in the world's own calculus of self-expression."[21]

The calculus Nishida here affirms does not deny individuals distinction and volition. "We express the world as the world's individual acts," Nishida continues; "and each individual act has its own unique position as a self-forming individual."[22] The self's consciousness as Buddha-mind emerges from, contains in the sense of expressing, and functions within the transpersonal logic of a creative matrix comprising absolute nothingness, what Nishida more clearly defines as "place" (Japanese, *basho*). This place is an act, not a separately existing spatiotemporal phenomenon. Like the nothingness Abe describes as forever emptying itself to become true fullness, the place of nothingness entails for Nishida "the self-negation of the absolute at the very ground of the existence of our individual selves, our personal selves."[23] As we move within ourselves to the bottomless depths of the individual, we discover the true absolute, which is, paradoxically, forever negating itself through us in a self-emptying matrix of eternal creativity. "Creation, real creativity, entails that the world, the contradictory identity of the one and the many, express itself within itself," says Nishida; "it is its own self transforming process in the form of a movement from the created to the creating."[24] To awaken to, which is to say to open to, the depths of our own nature is to lose the ego and to become one with creativity itself: "We act as creative elements of the creative world, as the self-determinations of the absolute present."[25]

As a thinker preoccupied with the nature of creativity, Nishida came to understand that we occupy and express, both in ourselves and through our culture, a formative, self-contradictory arena of creativity larger than a discourse grounded in individual experience, however pure, could articulate. Like Zen philosophers before and after him, he understands that in emptying the self and losing the ego, one encounters pure experience. But to reside only in pure experience, as the mystic does, is to risk limiting the absolute to its expression through the individual or to affirm that nothingness is a separately existing transcendental realm unto itself. Indicating, therefore, that "Zen has nothing to do with mysticism," Nishida writes:

> Kenshō, seeing one's nature, means to penetrate to the roots of one's own self. The self exists as the absolute's own self-nega-tion. . . . The very process of self-realization, in which the self knows itself, is self-contradictory. Hence we always possess ourselves in something that transcends ourselves in our own bottomless depths; we affirm ourselves through our own self-negation. . . . Zen's principle of the absurd must be grasped as this paradox.[26]

For Nishida, the person who best expresses this principle of the absurd as it focuses on the contradictory identity of self and other, of the transcendent and the immanent, is the fourteenth-century Zen master Myōchō (Daitō Kokushi):

> Buddha and I, distinct through a billion kalpas of time,
> Yet not separate for one instant;
> Facing each other the whole day through,
> Yet not facing each other for an instant.[27]

Commenting on Nishida's understanding of paradox as it serves to define the individual's sense of identity in the place of nothingness, Carter writes: "A is A, and yet A is not-A, therefore A is A. . . . It is here, in the individual as the place (basho) of paradox, where contra-dictories meet, that identity is achieved as well."[28]

To avoid viewing nothingness as a self-formative substance either within the self or as an ambient field outside the self, we must leave behind all notions of subjectivity and objectivity, all perceptions grounded in dualistic ways of thinking, and enter upon the realm of paradoxicality. "Empty 'pure experience' once more, and empty the 'self' as well," writes Carter in explication of Nishida's departure from pure experience as adequate to express the field of emptiness. "Empty emptiness itself, and keep everything nonsubstantial and in the flow of movement in being-time."[29] The flow that Carter affirms is not movement from one point to another but the flow of creativity that emerges through and as all things in an endless cosmic process of absolute self-emptying. Paradoxicality preserves the flow. "Not to speak paradoxically is to fix the focus, to stop the flow, to carve out a discrete time and event, and to privilege oneself or some-thing as the center from which all else is distinguished and located."[30] It is only through paradoxicality that one enters the realm of true creative suchness and becomes transparent. "The self, the I, is never 'there,'" writes Carter, "but is at each moment in the process of transforma- tion, now losing every trace of itself in nothingness, now blooming selflessly with the flowers and like one of them, now meeting anoth- er and making the encounter into its own self."[31] Nishida himself expresses this point more succinctly in claiming simply that "Truth arises in the concrete dimension where we open our eyes and see the world and open our ears and hear the world."[32] The entire enterprise is simply to get us to awaken to what is right here.

The problem Nishida encounters as a philosopher trying both to express and to explain the world through the contradictory identity of self and other assails the artist as well. It is not what the indi- vidual artist expresses as a response to reality but what reality expresses through the individual when it takes the form of poetry— or of any art, for that matter. And like the philosopher, the Zen artist is driven to a form of expression grounded in paradox, a mode of statement that undermines all sense of a separate formative source that distinguishes language from things and things from each other. A good example of the form occurs in the work of Hyobong, a twenti- eth-century Korean master who writes the following lines in cele- bration of his awakening:

At the bottom of the ocean, a deer hatches an egg in a
    swallow's nest.
In the heart of a fire, a fish boils tea in a spider's web.
Who knows what is happening in this house?
White clouds float westward; the moon rises in the east.[33]

Hyobong's blending of images reflects his understanding that all things in the universe penetrate one another freely and without obstruction. His acceptance of reality as a creative matrix of totally interwoven objects and events surfaces in the unremarkable, matter-of-fact statement that "clouds float westward" and that "the moon rises in the east." In its pointing to the perfect suchness of the events it records, the poem both reflects and expresses the *tathāgata-garbha* or the thus-come, thus-gone nature of all things and all conditions, celebrating the wonder of life while eschewing concurrently all appeals to an exalted mysticism beyond the ordinary events of quotidian life available to the individual who has seen his own nature.

Equally significant for our purposes, however, is the way in which the language of Hyobong's poem employs paradox both to convey the contradictory identity of deer and swallow, of fish and spider, and to reveal how art dies to itself as a separately existing form of expression. In shifting its viewpoint from ocean to fire, thereby calling into doubt the presence of a stable central consciousness that might respond to the question posed in line three, and in accepting the absurdity of a deer's hatching an egg, of a fish's boiling tea, the poem itself appears to come from nowhere, emerging both as the voice of individual things and as itself the self-emptying embodiment of the processes of a totally moving, interactive world predicated on the nonabiding, essenceless nature of the very things it expresses. Hyobong's poem does not simply point to the endless process of interanimation that comprises Zen reality. In the absence of a specifiable psychological and conventional intellectual center, it is that process. By decentering itself through its use of paradox, the poem thus reenacts the endless means by which things die to themselves, empty themselves of abiding form, in order to live in the greater unity of interbeing that comprises the moving center of existence. As the act of consciousness, according to Nishida, "lives to die and dies to live,"[34] so the poem dies to itself as the expression of a separate consciousness by opening to the denial of perspective and to the truth of absurdity: in its paradoxicality, it is both the expression of the world and an individual cultural artifact pointing to that expression.

It is owing to the structureless structure of poems such as Hyobong's that Taigan Takayama can insist that Zen poetry is not the product of a separate individual but the form that Zen experience takes when it emerges as literary expression. Just as the individual, while remaining yet an individual, inhabits an ambient, prior field of experience both inclusive of and emergent through his own existence, a field that requires paradoxically the death of the individual as a separate being in order that he may live completely in the eternal moment of the absolute self-emptying nothingness of pure being, so the poet inhabits an ambient field of expression that both calls forth and reveals itself through the individual voice but that must eventually destroy or empty itself of the very voice it employs in order to remain the creative, fluid continuum of its own existence. Similarly, as the individual must undergo a process of self-emptying in order to emerge as the absolute at the ground of his own existence, so poetry, indeed art in general, must empty itself of any claims to authority, permanence, and ideologic rationality if it is to retain its power as a spiritual praxis based in freedom from all dualistic concerns with selfhood.

Among Wordsworth's poems, the theme of art as a self-emptying process coextensive with the effluent forces of nature emerges most conspicuously in book 5 of *The Prelude*. And here, as in Zen poetry, the key to our apprehension of these processes as they shape both the artifact and our response to the artifact is a contemplative state, what Wordsworth calls "the steadiest mood of reason," that looks beyond the conventional woes of humankind to the suffering caused by high achievement:

> Even in the steadiest mood of reason, when
> All sorrow for thy transitory pains
> Goes out, it grieves me for thy state, O Man,
> Thou paramount Creature! and thy race, while ye
> Shall sojourn on this planet; not for woes
> Which thou endur'st; that weight, albeit huge,
> I charm away; but for those palms achieved,
> Through length of time, by study and hard thought,
> The honours of thy high endowments; there
> My sadness finds its fuel. (1805-6 *Prelude* 5.1–10)

Normally, we think of mood and reason as occupying separate realms. The one is emotional; the other intellectual. By collapsing the distinction between the two, Wordsworth suggests a holistic condition of being beyond, yet inclusive of, the dualisms that normally drive the psyche. In later versions of the poem, Wordsworth substitutes the more abstract term "Contemplation" for "steadiest mood of reason" but adds a level of explanation by comparing the state to "the night-calm felt / Through earth and sky," a calm that "spreads widely, and sends deep / Into the soul its tranquillizing power" (1850 *Prelude* 5.1–3). It is in this egoless realm of stellar calm that Wordsworth confronts the melancholy vanity of high achievement.

Wordsworth's later description of the "steadiest mood of reason" as a contemplative "night-calm felt / Through earth and sky" resonates closely with Zen depictions of the enlightened mind as a state of exceeding clarity and serenity that obliterates notions of external and internal. Explaining that "The essence lies in being empty inside and having free space" and that "in the midst of floods of tumult" the enlightened individual "will naturally stand serene above it all," the Chan master Hongzhi writes of the Zen mind: "Clean, pure, perfectly clear; the power of the eye cannot reach its bounds. Still, silent, empty and vast—the ken of the mind cannot find its edges."[35] Similarly, the modern Zen master Kōshō Uchiyama compares the depthless mind of Zen enlightenment to a "sky without clouds or mist."[36] Master Chōsa Shōken of the Sung Dynasty is even more explicit:

> The entire world is reflected by the eye of a monk, the entire world is contained in everyday conversation, the entire world is throughout your body, the entire world is your own Divine Light, the entire world is within your Divine Light and the entire world is inseparable from yourself.[37]

In more modern philosophical terms, Wordsworth's "steadiest mood of reason" corresponds to Nishida's "*basho*" and Nishitani's notion of Zen-mind as the realm of "circuminsessional interpenetration." It is the place where the human and the natural, the immanent and the transcendent, the internal and the external intersect, what Masao Abe defines as a "completely unobjectifiable, an all-embracing ultimate Reality identical with 'Absolute Nothingness.'"[38] In terms of its effect, this *basho* enables the poet to embrace the sorrow of the human condition on an open ground that deflects the power of sadness to overwhelm, thereby permitting him to see, perhaps more clearly than on other occasions, the true source of human suffering. The sadness Wordsworth feels in this meditative state is for those closest to him and his audience, possibly the most anguished of all humans—those whose accomplishments have evoked in them not the desired sense of wellbeing and honor that comes with "palms achieved" and "high endowments" but an exalted sense of self and its accompanying sense of human frailty and alienation from the universe. "Oh! why hath not the Mind / Some element to stamp her image on / In nature somewhat nearer to her own?" (5.44–46), he asks; "Why, gifted with such powers to send abroad / Her spirit, must it lodge in shrines so frail?" (5.47–48).

The plaintive force of this question belies the unique power of the mind that states it. The predicative strength of the question lies in the paradoxical or contradictory identity of the embracive cosmic mind suggested initially as "the steadiest mood of reason" and the egotistical mind that would seek through its own cultural achievements to imprint itself on nature. The relation between "the steadiest mood of reason," which is essentially universal and indwelling among all things as their ground, and the mind that would imprint itself on nature mirrors the paradoxical relationship of world and self in Zen terminology. "Our selves, existential monads of the world, mirror the world, and, at the same time, are the world's own creative expressions," writes Nishida. "The self exists in this paradox, reflecting the absolute's own self-affirmation through self-negation."[39] As the monadic reconstruction of the cosmic in the individual requires the contradictory identity of the two and their concurrent self-negation, so the expression of "the steadiest mood of reason" requires its own self-negation through the very force of the individual mind that threatens to replace the moving universal with elegiac impulses designed to preserve the self as a persisting other. The interrogative force of the query, coming, as it does, out of a kind of grand cosmic immensity associated with the night-sky, invites us to address the question directly and look away from the creative transhuman field in which it issues. If we take up the invitation outside the "steadiest mood of reason" introduced at the beginning of book 5, we privilege the self and risk viewing the awakening that lies potentially in high cultural achievement as an effort to preserve the human rather than as an opportunity to open to the bottomless depths of nature as the ground of all being.

This privileging of the individual human self is exactly the mistake made by the nameless interlocutor Wordsworth introduces immediately following his question about the mind's need for a natural element on which to stamp itself. " 'Twas going far to seek disquietude" (5.52), says the friend. He does not understand, or understands only partially, what the spiritually liberated individual knows—that the breakthrough into total freedom from the self and the apprehension of one's own unique depths require a departure from the secure stillness of high contemplation. "Do not immediately settle down in peaceful stillness," advises Zen master Ta Hui. Warning that such stillness (called in Zen the "Deep Pit of Liberation") is "much to be feared," Ta Hui tells his students that "You must make yourself turn freely, like a gourd floating on the water, independent and free, not subject to restraints, entering purity and impurity without being obstructed or sinking down."[40] To rest in stillness, in the restfulness of meditative calm, is to misperceive the most important of all Zen principles—the contradictory identity of samsara, the phenomenal world of ordinary existence, and nirvana, the enlightened state of freedom from desire, hatred and delusion.[41] "Samsara and Nirvana are originally not two," writes Kusan Sunim shortly before his death; "As the sun rises in the sky / It illuminates the three thousand worlds."[42] The peacefulness, the "steadiest mood of reason," the spiritualist encounters in her moments of deepest meditation cannot be apprehended as a separate state. Like the sun of Kusan Sunim's poem, it must, rather, illuminate all circumstances. "A Zen man is at peace in both favorable and adverse conditions, and his mind is not disturbed under any circumstances," writes Shibayama. "Is there anything you dislike? Is there anything you have to hold fast to?"[43] To settle down in stillness is to preserve the very ego one must transcend in order to open to the clear reality at the ground of all being.

Unable to understand the process of such opening as it relates to cultural achievement, the nameless friend of Wordsworth's poem relates a dream he once experienced while contemplating the nature and effect of the arts and sciences.[44] The friend explains that he had been reading Cervantes "in a rocky cave / By the sea-side" and that "The famous history of the errant knight" had provoked thoughts of "poetry and geometric truth," which he calls "The knowledge that endures." He is compelled by the "high privilege of lasting life, /

Exempt from all internal injury." Falling asleep over the open book, the friend dreams that he is sitting in a wide Arabian "wilderness / Alone, upon the sands" when suddenly a Bedouin horseman appears carrying a stone and a shell. The stone, we are told, represents "'Euclid's elements.'" The shell is a book, "'something of more worth,'" according to the horseman. Holding the shell to his ear, the dreamer hears "An Ode, in passion uttered, which foretold / Destruction to the children of the earth / By deluge, now at hand." Wishing in his fear "To cleave unto this man," the dreamer joins the Arab in his mission to "bury those two books." Before long, however, the Arab, moving in haste "With the fleet waters of the drowning world / In chase of him," abandons the dreamer, leaving him to wake "in terror" before the sea, Cervantes's book at his side (5.55–139).

The Arab Dream episode, as it is called, when viewed in relation to the developing thrust of book 5 of *The Prelude*, is put forth not so much in counterpoint to as in extension of the mood in which Wordsworth asks why the mind has not in nature "Some element to stamp her image on." In terms of its effect on Wordsworth, the friend's dream, though offered initially as a critique of the poet's questions, acts much in the manner of a Zen *koan*. The *koan*, according to William Johnston, fosters a state of frustration and neurosis by trapping the mind with an illogical problem that brings on a condition of "intolerable anguish." Release from this anguish creates what Johnston calls a "burst of spiritual energy that gives enlightenment."[45] The release that Johnston affirms cannot occur unless the individual is willing to abandon the ego and give himself entirely to the anguish of the *koan*, a process that parallels the act of giving oneself to the changing conditions of life. "*Security and changelessness are fabricated by the ego-dominated mind and do not exist in nature*," write Stewart W. Holmes and Chimyo Horioka in an effort to reveal the cognation of Zen art and meditation. "*To accept insecurity and commit oneself to the unknown creates a relaxing faith in the universe*" (italics Holmes's and Horioka's).[46] Other Zen thinkers view the acceptance of anguish as a form of grace: "Receiving trouble is receiving grace: / Receiving happiness is receiving a trial."[47] In this condition of grace, one awakens to what T. P. Kasulis calls the "presence of things as they are." It is a condition of being in which one cannot identify a delimiting standpoint or perspective. Relating Hakuin's experience of hearing a bell in a state of self-loss, a condition of "pure without-thinking" brought on by wrestling with a *koan*, Kasulis writes:

> When that last residual sense of the self is finally abandoned . . . one no longer takes any intentional standpoint at all. As pure without-thinking, one's formerly empty consciousness is suddenly filled by the simple sounding-of-the-bell. There is no I and no bell but rather the hearing of the bell. . . .[48]

But if the *koan*—which can be taken as an analogue of the work of art or, in this instance, as an analogue of the Arab Dream episode—is pursued with a view to preserving the self or the conditions that provide security for the self, it fails to bring the meditator to the desired state of release. This is exactly what happens to Wordsworth's friend, who awakens, not to an enlightened sense of his oneness with the world, but in terror, in fear for the very self he had an opportunity to abandon momentarily in the act of reading Cervantes. The source of the dreamer's terror, as of the Arab's, is his belief that anything, including the arts and sciences, can have the "high privilege of lasting life, / Exempt from all internal injury."

Wordsworth, presenting the whole incident in the "steadiest mood of reason" announced at the head of book 5, has an entirely different response to the dream. Instead of terror at the thought of annihilation as conveyed by the conch and through the diluvial images at the end of the dream, Wordsworth experiences a detached compassion for the "Arab phantom," as he calls him, a calmative, liberating compassion emerging from a disinterested perception of his own anxiety in the face of encroaching mortality. Explaining that he "Could share that maniac's anxiousness, could go / Upon like errand," the poet admits that "Oftentimes at least / Me hath such deep entrancement half-possessed, / When I have held a volume in my hand" (5.160–63). The conditional "could" joins with the poet's sense of being "half-possessed" to underscore the high state of reason and freedom in which he regards the entire incident: Wordsworth is free of the phantom that enthralls him, free of the very being with whom he identifies.

The source of this paradoxical alignment of freedom and identity in compassion, what in the last chapter we saw as the *tathāgata-garbha*, is the poet's disarmingly simple acceptance, announced early

in book 5, of the "transitory woes" of humankind. As the transitoriness of all things is the message of the conch, of art proper, so also is
it for the Zennist the message of the universe. "The universe is forever falling apart," writes the Zen poet Shinkichi Takahashi; "No
need to push the button, / It collapses at a finger's touch: / Why, it
barely hangs on the tail of a sparrow's eye."[49] For the individual
whose perceptions lie outside the conjoined region of poetry and
nature, however, reality is "so much eye secretion" (5). Such an individual is confined by the conceptual, which offers itself in opposition
to the moving dynamic of nature. Asserting that the conceptual universe is "A paltry thing" (10), Takahashi counsels his readers to seek
oneness with nature, in this case, oneness with the sparrow, to
engage that very destructiveness and so to conquer its power to
frighten us: "You and the sparrow are one / And, should he wish, he
can crush you. / The universe trembles before him" (12–14).
Commenting on this poem, Lucien Stryk says that

> man, unlike the sparrow, has created forms which confine and
> frustrate, and until he sees that they have no reality, are pal-
> try, "so much eye secretion," he will continue to tremble before
> them, their prisoner. He must live freely as the sparrow who
> can, should he wish, crush the universe and its creator.[50]

What Takahashi's awakened individual achieves through his
joining with the sparrow Wordsworth accomplishes by accepting the
message of the conch, thereby identifying with the very world the
Arab seeks to escape. This identity yields him both freedom from the
Arab's mission and compassion for individuals set upon such
"errands." To accept the transitoriness of life as the homeground one
shares with all beings, then, is to encounter all beings on what Keiji
Nishitani, as we have seen elsewhere, calls the "field" or "horizon" of
nihility. But predicated though it is in nihility, in the recognition that
there is no abiding selfhood, that all things are empty, this field produces, as well, or shall we say makes possible, a dynamic sense of
unity as the interwoven identity of all things. "In short," says
Nishitani, "it is only on a field where the being of all things is a being
at one with emptiness that it is possible for all things to gather into
one, even while each retains its reality as an absolutely unique
being."[51] In such a field, communication *between* gives way to the

implosive communication of one thing *in* or *as* another. Commenting on Nishitani's field of nihility, Robert E. Carter sees such identity-based communication as the very ground of what he calls "cosmic compassion":

> Individual and whole, birth and death are but aspects of the same reality, and the one is inextricably connected with the other because each is the other. Each interpenetrates each. . . . I care about another as I care about myself because I am, in fact, the other. The result is clearly a *cosmic compassion*.[52]

Wordsworth's compassion for the Arab, his sense of being half-possessed by the maniacal Bedouin, is not the result of an innate sympathy for the Arab's mission but the universal imperative of the self-emptying, interanimative process of communication that unfolds as the living profile of *basho*. It is the very complexion of *basho*, the field of eternally emergent nihility. In the absence of self, Wordsworth asks for no messages, seeks no answers from the retreating Bedouin. Rather, he becomes the Arab, shares his fears for human culture, and yet, in the final analysis, remains free of the very compulsion that lends the moment dramatic irony and aesthetic force. The destructiveness the conch proclaims to the sleeping ear of the friend is for Wordsworth, immersed already in the Zen-like "night-calm" of "steadiest reason," the functional mode of the self-emptying creativity of the world. To join with rather than to run from the diluvial oblivion of nature is to act, in the words of Nishida, as "creative elements of a creative world."

From the very beginning of book 5, then, we see that Wordsworth has no compelling interest in what culture can do for the self. His concern, rather, is for those high achievers whose studious efforts impel them to expectations of lasting fame or to the hope that through involvement with that which is perceived as eternal, they will at least touch immortality and so be spared the pain attendant upon awakening to the passing nature of life.

Viewed in the contemplative field offered by the "steadiest mood of reason" and by the contrasting responses of the friend and the poet, the Arab Dream episode forms a vital commentary on the distinction between sleep and wakefulness and on the role that art, in this instance storytelling, plays in arousing individuals to their innate spirituality. Like the Buddhist, Wordsworth records the episode in the awakened understanding that nothing endures. The friend, however, is already in a state of sleep before he falls asleep; he awakens not to the brave compassion that governs Wordsworth's response but to nightmare and terror. From the Buddhist perspective, the entire longing for continuance, for that which endures, conduces to dream, is dream. Spiritual wakefulness, however, is based in the knowledge that all, including art, is a passing phenomenon— the message the conch offers the friend's sleeping ear but that he cannot, in the absence of an egoless contemplativeness, accept.

It is altogether appropriate, therefore, that the friend fall asleep before the ocean, the perfect symbol of an encompassing and liberative consciousness he carries within himself and that he inhabits as an ambient field but that he cannot see. That he falls asleep before a work of art that should awaken rather than simply distract him as a pleasant amusement for a summer's afternoon furthers our sense of his intractable torpor. Unlike the poet, the friend is essentially ignorant of his own nature, pursuing the horseman of his dreams for answers that, in the Buddhist perspective, lie within. "Because of our ignorance we are unable to appreciate the great bliss of being embraced in the Absolute Being, and are unaware of the thoroughly pure and immaculately white Mind-Ox, which is within ourselves," writes Zenkei Shibayama. "Thus we fancy that the Truth is something that is to be sought after outside of ourselves."[53] Were he in an awakened state, the dreamer would understand, to recall Chōsa's words, that "the entire world is throughout your body," that he is the very flood, the diluvial oblivion, he seeks to escape.

What enables Wordsworth to accept the very transitoriness the Arab and the dreamer fear is the understanding, buried deep in his own childhood, that art and nature, properly conceived and experienced, are extensions of each other, not opposing forces. Presenting himself later in book 5 as one "who in his youth / A wanderer among the woods and fields / With living Nature hath been intimate," Wordsworth claims that he was as a child able to "Receive enduring touches of deep joy / From the great Nature that exists in works / Of mighty Poets" (610–19). Significantly, it is nature, not the extended voice of a specific poet, that speaks through poetry to the receptive child. Concurrently, it is the absence of a demanding selfhood in the child that permits nature to speak to him through works of art. The dual absence that Wordsworth here implies corresponds remarkably with the enabling emptiness at the heart of Buddhist poetry. Commenting, for example, on the eighth-century Chinese poet Wang Wei, Tony and Willis Barnstone write:

> The transcendental sign that unifies nature for Wang Wei is distinguished from the Western sign in that in Buddhism the sign implies an absence, not a presence. Through the contemplation of the unity of all things, we may revert to that primordial absence, particularly in nature, which is viewed as closer to the absent center than is the dusty busy world of people. The knowledge that all is illusion is a step toward escape from the mutable world to the emptiness and perfect stillness of nirvana. . . . The poem then is a pure text of nature, worthy of contemplation . . . the poem is nature, the word is its object, and at the moment of contemplation there is no distinction between them.[54]

Wang Wei's poetic techniques, according to the Barnstones, "produce an artifact whose proper contemplation can itself be the catalyst, a Zen koan, for entering a state of *ekstasis*."[55]

The *"ekstasis"* the Barnstones here indicate as a possible response to Buddhist poems surfaced for Wordsworth in his youthful engagement with texts that drew him out of himself, indeed rendered the self nugatory:

> Oh! give us once again the wishing cap
> Of Fortunatus, and the invisible coat
> Of Jack the Giant-killer, Robin Hood,
> And Sabra in the forest with St. George!
> The child, whose love is here, at least, doth reap
> One precious gain, that he forgets himself. (5.364-69)

The child of these lines contrasts poignantly with the studious youth, a "monster birth" and "dwarf man," as the poet calls him, "Engendered by these too industrious times" (5.293–96). Recalling his depiction of the frightened dreamer and the crazed Bedouin, Wordsworth's picture of the industrious child of his own day evokes the impression of a being who studies culture for selfish reasons:

"Vanity," the poet tells us of this youth, "That is his soul, there lives he, and there moves; / It is the soul of every thing he seeks; / That gone, nothing is left which he can love" (5.354–57).

Appalled by the industrious "monster" who engages art for the sake of preserving and swelling the self, Wordsworth asks when "the tutors of our youth" will "be taught / That in the unreasoning progress of the world / A wiser spirit is at work for us" (5.376–85). The "wiser spirit" Wordsworth here proclaims emerges in the Boy of Winander episode of book 5 not as a separate entity or force but as the composite figuration of that moment in which the self disappears into pure action, what Nishida calls "action-intuition" or "poeisis." "There was a boy," Wordsworth tells us, who "Blew mimic hootings to the silent owls, / That they might answer him" (5.389, 398–99). But the boy moves beyond mimesis and its attendant dualisms to become in the moment of the birds' response the variant voice of the owls or, if you will, a variant voice of the one nature that speaks through both the boy and the creatures with whom he communicates. In this con- dition of superlative unity or oneness with nature,

> when it chanced
> That pauses of deep silence mocked his skill,
> Then sometimes, in that silence while he hung
> Listening, a gentle shock of mild surprise
> Has carried far into his heart the voice
> Of mountain torrents; or the visible scene
> Would enter unawares into his mind,
> With all its solemn imagery, its rocks,
> Its woods, and that uncertain heaven, received
> Into the bosom of the steady lake.   (5.404–13)

The lines that record how "a gentle shock of mild surprise / Has carried far into his heart the voice / Of mountain torrents" evoke a notably Zenlike image of the boy's selfhood as an aural space rather than as a recipient object. It is the boy's largeness of soul, if you will, his emptiness, his capaciousness, that enables him to accept the "voice" of the surrounding world to be the place, the *basho*, as Nishida might say, through which that world experiences its own self-emptying. The peculiar syntax of lines 409–10, which depict the "visible scene" entering "unawares into his mind," conveys a radical dislocation of consciousness that combines with the uncertainty mirrored in the lake's reception of heaven to present all things and events, including both aural and visual events, as blending into one. The absence of a central focusing artifice undermines any sense of self and other and resonates closely with the transcendental absence Tony and Willis Barnstone identify as the functional essence of Zen poetry.

For Wordsworth, as for the Zennist, this transcendent, yet refulgent and dynamic, absence forms the context in which books should be read—not as vain sepulchres for the self, but as passing, eternally deconstructing forms that carry deep into the empty yet vital stillness at the heart of our being and of all being. In the power and contentment of such moods, there can be no terror, for all is somehow good, is somehow part of the emerging aesthetic of the moment. The field in which this aesthetic emerges cannot be restricted to the human. It is, rather, one in which the human and the natural coincide in such a way as to be extensions of each other, a continuity poignantly depicted in the following passage from book 5, where Wordsworth recalls a childhood incident in which he saw a drowned man being pulled from Esthwaite lake:

> At length, the dead man, 'mid that beauteous scene
> Of trees and hills and water, bolt upright
> Rose, with his ghastly face, a spectre shape
> Of terror even; and yet no vulgar fear,
> Young as I was, a child not nine years old,
> Possessed me, for my inner eye had seen
> Such sights before, among the shining streams
> Of faery land, the forests of romance.
> Thence came a spirit hallowing what I saw
> With decoration and ideal grace;
> A dignity, a smoothness, like the works
> Of Grecian art, and purest poesy. (5.470–81)

Like the "wiser spirit" that informs the Boy of Winander episode, the "hallowing" spirit of these lines accepts the destructiveness of nature as the bittersweet requisite of an indwelling and encompassing aesthetic aligned with the moving, flowing way of things. This is a world in which there can be no death in any absolute sense because there

is no birth. There is only the ebb and flow of an eternally creative
destructiveness.

In a poem that recalls Wordsworth's use of the conch in the
Arab Dream episode, Takahashi writes:

> Nothing, nothing at all
>   is born,
> dies, the shell says again
>   and again
> from the depth of hollowness.
>   Its body
> swept off by tide—so what?
>   It sleeps
> in sand, drying in sunlight,
>   bathing
> in moonlight. Nothing to do
>   with sea
> Or anything else. Over
>   and over
> it vanishes with the wave.[56]

The eternal hollowness of Takahashi's shell resonates closely with
the conch's message of endless destructiveness in the Arab Dream
passage and with the message of abiding beauty in the human corpse
rising out of Esthwaite. The shell, the conch, and the corpse can
never really be buried. The Arab's mission is as futile as the ocean's
ebb and flow in Takahashi's "Shell," for the ocean and the shell, like
the conch and the flood, are of the same moving nature of all things.
As the conch and the shell are the voice of the very destructiveness
that preserves all of us in the abiding emptiness of life, and as the
interanimative hootings of the Boy of Winander and of the owls he
mimics create the silence in which mountain torrents voice themselves and in which rocks and woods image forth their forms, so the
corpse is the sign of the very nonbeing that comprises the ground of
our immortality. Viewed in the light of an absent selfhood, art, empty
itself of abiding form, celebrates death as emergent life, prepares us
to receive death as part of the entire aesthetic movement of life merg-
ing into and emerging from ever new variants of itself. Forever
aware of its own refulgent hollowness, art, like the shell and the

conch, thus undermines its own claims to immortality by giving itself to life, much as the corpse, though whispering death, gives itself to the brave vision of the child.   In this way, and paradoxically, art achieves the only immortality worth having—that which is of the endlessly passing, unborn nature of life itself.

The poet who speaks thus in the voice of emptiness is the poet who, to recall Chuang Tzu's question, has forgotten words. Wordsworth reveals this perception of language as the functional base of his practice when, near the end of book 5, he writes:

> Visionary power
> Attends upon the motions of the winds,
> Embodied in the mystery of words:
> There, darkness makes abode, and all the host
> Of shadowy things do work their changes there,
> As in a mansion like their proper home.
> Even forms and substances are circumfused
> By that transparent veil with light divine,
> And, through the turnings intricate of verse,
> Present themselves as objects recognized,
> In flashes, and with a glory scarce their own. (5.619–29)

Wind is a perfect image of the refulgent nihility that makes for visionary power. We see its effects, but not itself, for it is all the things it plays upon, containing that which it uses, but limited to none and therefore empty of abiding form. Poetry offers a similarly contradictory realm that both reveals and hides its source. As wind emerges from a totality of being that is at once the ever-emergent manifestation of nihility, so poetry, as the embodiment of visionary power, emerges from an active mystery that functions both as a projective energy to reveal things and as a place, a "mansion," in which the "host / Of shadowy things do work their changes."

Evoked, as it were, by the very things it reveals, much as wind is revealed by that which it plays upon, poetry, then, is also a moving place, like Nishida's *basho*, like the hollowness of the conch, which voices and is voiced by the self-emptying absolute that produces and comprises that which it yields. In language that resonates closely with Nishitani's description of the field of emptiness as a mode of "circuminsessional interpenetration," Wordsworth speaks of poetry as a "mansion" in which "forms and substances are circumfused" with a transparent "light divine" that both veils and unveils. In the place where all things are eternally changing, therefore disappearing even as they move into the unveiling light by which they are made visible, we experience a unity predicated on the contradictory identity of the one and the many, of light and form, of the divine and the mundane— even as "that uncertain heaven" is "received / Into the bosom of the steady lake." For Wordsworth, poetry evokes what Nishitani calls "an absolute self-identity in which the one and the other are yet truly themselves, at once abolutely [sic] broken apart and absolutely joined together."[57]

Like Chuang Tzu, Wordsworth realizes that the very language he cherishes so conspicuously as a practicing poet is after all but a net that, to be thoroughly effective, must, like the wind, like the visionariness attendant upon the wind, disperse, empty itself, into that which it reveals, allowing the very things it illuminates and momentarily houses to change, to disappear, to empty themselves into the eternal flow at the heart of their being, of all being. As a poet of nature, a poet whose voice surfaces as an extension of nature itself, Wordsworth, like the Zen poet, understands that there is nothing to cling to, neither book nor man, that "when reading a poem," as Albert Low says of Zen texts, "one constantly has to dwell in that domain in which there is no certainty."[58] Wordsworth's response to the Arab Dream is an analogue of his response to the entire phenomenon of culture. As the dream must be apprehended within a "steadiest mood of reason," a "steady lake" that eschews all modes of selfhood and all appeals to an abiding self, so culture must be apprehended in a liberative field of consciousness that accepts destructiveness as identical with creativeness. Wordsworth knows from the very beginning of book 5 that in the honors attendant upon producing and engaging culture, there is, like the visionariness attendant upon "the motions of the winds," nothing enduring, that the purpose of art is not simply to remind us of our mortality but to open us to the cosmic flow of change as the lived and living reality of our being. Only in this way can art save us from the very diluvium that comprises our deepest ground. Art cannot save us from nature. It must, rather, be nature itself and return us to the condition of our own being as a conscious extension of the world rather than as a dreaming opponent of its endless ebb and flow.

CONCLUSION:
FORGETTING THE MIND

At the end of *The Prelude*, while speaking of what he hopes to give his readers, Wordsworth describes himself and his friend Coleridge as "joint labourers in a work . . . Of their [the readers'] redemption" (13.439–41). Wordsworth wants literally to redeem his readers, to buy them back to a lost divinity. The inspiration for this redemptive process will be a new perception of mind:

> Prophets of Nature, we to them will speak
> A lasting inspiration, sanctified
> By reason and by truth: what we have loved,
> Others will love, and we may teach them how;
> Instruct them how the mind of man becomes
> A thousand times more beautiful than the earth
> On which he dwells, above this frame of things
> (Which, 'mid all revolutions in the hopes
> And fears of men, doth still remain unchanged)
> In beauty exalted, as it is itself
> Of substance and of fabric more divine. (13.442–52)

Though human consciousness becomes, under the influence of poetry, "A thousand times more beautiful than the earth" on which humankind dwells, it is not separate from that earth. It is, after all, as a prophet of nature that Wordsworth makes his claim about mind, suggesting that the consciousness he exalts as dwelling "above this frame of things" requires the forms and energies of this very "frame" for its expression. We cannot, therefore, think of the Wordsworthian mind as inherently separate from the world on which it dwells.

Zen thought and art, as I have tried to show in this study, provide us with an especially articulate and vital context for understanding the deeply collusive and coadunative intermingling of mind

199

and nature in Wordsworth's poetry. The consciousness Wordsworth affirms here and throughout his poetry corresponds to the meditative mind of Zen practice, emerging paradoxically as both product and container of the earth on which its human exponents dwell. "Whenever we see form, it is just seeing the mind," says the eighteenth-century Zen master Ma-tsu. "The mind does not exist by itself; its existence is due to form."[1] The ascendancy Wordsworth claims for the mind of man at the end of *The Prelude*, like the high privilege Zennists assert for the Buddha-mind, results not from a process of exclusionary human transcendence but from an inclusive opening to the sourceless depths of existence as manifested in the self-emptying nature of all things, including poetry.

Nowhere in Wordsworth's poetry are these depths, together with the ascendancy of mind as the parallactic identity of human consciousness and nature, depicted more vigorously and memorably than in the opening passages to book 13 of *The Prelude*. Returning to an incident that occurred early in his career, in 1791, Wordsworth describes himself ascending Mount Snowdon through "a huge sea of mist, / Which, meek and silent, rested at my feet" (13.43–44). Suddenly, as he breaks out of the cloud-cover at his feet, "A hundred hills their dusky backs upheaved / All over this still ocean" (13.45–46). Significantly, the poet's ascendancy occurs within a cloudy setting that conflates depth and height, real and illusory, such that "the real sea" in the distance "seemed / To dwindle, and give up its majesty, / Usurped upon as far as sight could reach" (13.49–51). In this state of perceptual displacement, as it were, Wordsworth spies, "not the third part of a mile" from him, "a blue chasm" (13.55–56), what he further adumbrates as

> a fracture in the vapour,
> A deep and gloomy breathing-place through which
> Mounted the roar of waters, torrents, streams
> Innumerable, roaring with one voice!

Arrested by the unitary power and aural grandeur of the scene before him, the poet asserts that

> The universal spectacle throughout
> Was shaped for admiration and delight,

Grand in itself alone, but in that breach
Through which the homeless voice of waters rose,
That dark deep thoroughfare, had Nature lodged
The soul, the imagination of the whole. (13.56–65)

The passage is important not so much in what it reveals as in what it prevents our seeing. As the voice of the waters is itself "homeless," yet coming from all nature, so the unitary and unifying mind Wordsworth identifies as "The soul, the imagination of the whole," cannot be fixed either in the human individual or in a particular object external to the individual. Nor can one see mind and nature here as simple analogues of each other or as sharing what one reader calls a "reciprocation."[2]   Rather, mind and nature, like the roaring of the one voice of the waters, are so conjoined as to be indistinguishable. In this suprarational, parallactic condition of implosive unity, Wordsworth perceives a oneness in which all distinctions between the human soul and the soul of nature, the human imagination and the "imagination of the whole," fall inward on each other.

Contemplating the event a few hours later, the poet encounters a meditative state revealing a brooding mind of infinite proportions:

A meditation rose in me that night
Upon the lonely mountain when the scene
Had passed away, and it appeared to me
The perfect image of a mighty mind,
Of one that feeds upon infinity,
That is exalted by an underpresence,
The sense of God, or whatsoe'er is dim
Or vast in its own being. . . . (13.66–73)

The "meditation," he tells us, "rose in me," as if it had a will of its own, using him, displacing him as separate individual, yet perfectly identified with him. Like the univocal waters of the "blue chasm," the vision and the product of that vision, the poet's mind and the cosmic mind he envisions, are indistinguishable, and neither can be separated from the surrounding landscape out of which they emerge.

From a Buddhist perspective, Wordsworth's syntax indicates an intuitive understanding that mind cannot, in the words of Kenneth K. Inada, "mediate between the self and reality." Explaining that the mind cannot in Buddhist terms be one thing and reality something else, Inada asserts that

> The mind may be a "cleaver" of the passage of reality, but in the final analysis the "cleaver" does not or cannot "cleave" itself, nor does it leave its marks on reality by the "cleaving" process: that is, reality is not divided by the mind, nor is it manipulated and transformed into new realities. . . . Paradoxically, but inextricably, the mind is part and parcel of the very reality that it attempts to understand.[3]

Like the Buddhist meditator who comes to understand that *kensho*, the experience of enlightenment, includes the interposition of nirvanic and samsaric mind-states, so Wordsworth understands that the mind which broods upon infinity is both visionary and naturalistic, encompassing both synoptic energies and discriminatory functions, what Inada would term its ability to "cleave" reality: the poet can, after all, distinguish the "real sea" in the distance from the "sea of mist" at his feet. Aligned with a godhead identified later with "whatsoe'r is dim / Or vast in its own being" (71–73), its capaciousness, which is also its ability to inhabit that upon which it broods, is predicated on a self-emptying process that precludes its being identified with any quality of existence other than infinity and that mirrors the emptiness of all things. As a moving phenomenon of nature surfacing through the individual thing as well as through the individual observer, it includes both the visionary and the nonvisionary and functions in such a way as to

> make one object so impress itself
> Upon all others, and pervade them so
> That even the grossest minds must see and hear
> And cannot choose but feel. (13.81–84)

As the objects of its own efforts are themselves empty of abiding identity, infinitely permeable by all other objects, thus empty participants in a continually moving web of interanimative, self-contradictory identities, so the mind is itself empty of abiding form, "dim / Or vast" and eternally immanent in all that it perceives. What even the "grossest minds" see and hear under the influence of such consciousness is what Buddhists identify as the true self. It is the very coming forth of nature and has no particular form. Explaining, for example, that the true self "is the self which exists before everything is born and which does not die," the Zen master Takuan Soho (1573–1645) asserts that "Man, the birds, beasts, and plants, all possess this self within them. . . . This self has no shadow, no form, no life, and no death."[4]

Particularly intriguing for readers of Wordsworth, as well as for Zennists, is the role of the human imagination in this process of mutual self-creation and self-emptying. The power of the meditative mind Wordsworth encounters on Snowdon makes "one object so impress itself / Upon all others, and pervade them" that we see all things as empty of self-existence, capable of being pervaded and so of achieving identity with each other. The source of this power is the emptiness of the very mind that employs it. For Wordsworth, the human imagination functions in such a way as to provide the individual with a similar or parallel ability. The human imagination, what Wordsworth further on calls "a genuine counterpart / And brother of the glorious faculty / Which higher minds bear with them as their own" (13.88–90), is the power to drop the self and to see with or through that which one at first perceives as other. For Zennists, this mode of seeing is itself the spiritual life, the godhead come forth in the formless form of what Wordsworth describes as the "dim" and the "vast" in our own being. "It is extremely rare for us so to 'fix our attention' on things as to 'lose ourselves' in them . . . to *become* the very things we are looking at," writes Nishitani in terms remarkably close to those of Wordsworth. "To see through them directly to 'God's world,' or to the universe in its infinitude, is even rarer."[5] What Nishitani describes as "God's world" Thomas Merton identifies as "the 'pure consciousness' of Zen":

> The pure consciousness . . . does not look *at* things, and does not ignore them, annihilate them, negate them. It accepts them fully, in complete oneness with them. It looks "out of them," as though fulfilling the role of consciousness not for itself only but *for them also*.[6]

For Wordsworth as well, minds that employ imagination, the counterpart of nature's transformative power, to send from themselves "like transformations" (94)—that is, so to impress one object on all others as to pervade them, hence, to see their mutual interpenetration on a field of moving interanimative identities—are minds which, like the brooding intellect that feeds upon infinity, recognize themselves as of the nature of infinity itself. They both contain all things and perceive the mutual solution of all things in each other.

Zen helps us to understand the meditative paradox of mind as that which it beholds. "This reality is regarded as one's most immediate and true nature which is beyond any objectification and mediacy," writes Urs App; "thus there can neither be access to it nor departure from it."[7] Describing this "reality" in relation to the Soto practice of *zazen* (sitting, and in a larger sense dwelling always, in a state of thought-free, alertly wakeful attention), the modern Zen master Dainen Katagiri writes: "Zazen is not a way to reach the peak; zazen is exactly that we are buddha, we are already on the peak." The defining, certainly the most visible, characteristic of this meditative experience is a dynamic imperturbability and tranquillity: "Zazen is to adjust our body and mind to exactly fit this imperturbability, so it naturally comes up. Zazen is exactly identical with the original nature of existence, which is called tranquillity, imperturbability."[8] In such a condition of quiet focus, we cannot look to defining conceptual systems or even to the mind itself as a sanctuary for the self. Explaining that we cannot "examine a situation or system without altering the system by the very act of examination," a principle of observation resonating closely with Wordsworth's perception that mind is innately transformative in its functioning, Mu Soeng Sunim remarks that "in the deepest experience of meditation, the object of consciousness is embedded in the observing consciousness; the two are fused together by the energy or *sunyata* out of which both emerge."[9]

But if Zen meditation helps us to understand the paradox of mind as that which it beholds, Zen as a total spiritual practice requires that we forget mind. Comparing mind to the water that contains a fish, the first patriarch Bodhidharma writes:

Whoever wants to see a fish sees the water before he sees the fish. And whoever wants to see a buddha sees the mind before he sees the buddha. Once you've seen the fish, you forget about the water. And once you've seen the buddha, you forget about the mind. If you don't forget about the mind, the mind will confuse you, just as the water will confuse you if you don't forget about it.[10]

We cannot experience fully the richness of meditative consciousness in a context that continually draws attention to mind, for we risk conceiving mind, however disseminative we understand it to be, as separate from the moving, changing world that comprises its being. "Self-nature is empty of all characteristics, including emptiness," says Red Pine in his commentary on Bodhidharma's water metaphor; "and yet it defines reality."[11] The Zennist understands that the true expression of mind must accrue through a moving continuum of the one and the many, of the individual and the whole, evolving in such a way as to call attention to the sheer majesty and mystery of individual things and beings. Quoting Joseph Wood Krutch's famous claim that what he is "after is less to meet God face to face than really to take in a beetle, a frog, or a mountain when I meet one," Michael Adam writes:

> Zen is what shows when we leave aside all concepts, all the appurtenances of philosophy and religion, to see what is before us—a Buddha, a flower, a beggar, a fly in the eye of a cow. . . . Zen is simply seeing simply. . . . To see any one thing is to see all, for *seeing is all*. . . . Seeing any one thing, one loses oneself to find oneself *as* all things.[12]

For Wordsworth as well, the work of "clearest insight, amplitude of mind, / And Reason in her most exalted mood," the work of imagination, what he calls the "faculty" that "hath been the moving soul / Of our long labour" (13.169–72), requires a radical independence that leaves aside all reliance on anything outside the human individual:

> Here must thou be, O Man!
> Strength to thyself; no Helper hast thou here;
> Here keepest thou thy individual state:
> No other can divide with thee this work:
> No secondary hand can intervene
> To fashion this ability; 'tis thine,
> The prime and vital principle is thine

> In the recesses of thy nature, far
> From any reach of outward fellowship,
> Else 'tis not thine at all. (13.188–97)

The high autonomy Wordsworth here celebrates is not predicated, as I have tried to show in this study, on separation from or transcendence of nature. It is not, in other words, an egotistical sublime. To achieve the work of spiritual amplitude Wordsworth exalts, the individual must be great nature itself come forth through what Takuan Soho calls the "extremity" of the individual to take possession of itself.[13] The individual must yield all reliances, all dependencies, including reliance on the capacious intellect that is itself the brooding mind of infinity. Perhaps this is why Wordsworth suppressed publication of *The Prelude* in his own lifetime. He understood, as well as the Zen spiritualist, that the true expression of mind must accrue through a moving continuum, a "moving soul," which forgets mind and calls attention to individual things, beings, and events as absolute in themselves.

For Wordsworth, the sign and seal of this liberative continuum is an abundant literary productivity arranged in such a way as to employ motion itself as an organizing principle and as a guarantor of the self-emptying process by which all things emerge as absolute in themselves and as expressions of the individual observer. In 1815, Wordsworth began to arrange his poems categorically. Some of these groups, like *Poems Referring to the Period of Childhood*, call attention to a specific time in a representative human life. Others, like *Poems of the Fancy* and *Poems of the Imagination*, explore a predominant mood or an aesthetic state. Such categories as *Poems Dedicated to National Independence and Liberty* and *Ecclesiastical Sonnets* focus on subject and genre, while collections like *The River Duddon* and the *Memorials* of various tours call attention to specific events. By arranging his poems categorically, frequently juxtaposing early and late works and placing under one heading pieces written for different occasions, Wordsworth undermines our preoccupation with the particular form of his own individual achievement, inviting us instead to move among his poems much as a traveler journeying down a river moves from object to object, from perspective to perspective, taking in all, becoming all that he sees and hears. This motion makes possible our appreciation of all objects of eye, ear, and mind by preventing our consciousness from being snagged on any one object, poem, or condition of being. To confront the body of Wordsworth's poetry in this way is to see the Formless Mind itself emergent through the sheer moving immensity of a production that returns us to the absolute uniqueness and mutual solution of all things.[14]

The River Duddon (PW 3:244–61), a series of sonnets composed between 1806 and 1820, provides a specially good example of how categorical motion based in continually shifting perspectives and identities supports and manifests the self-emptying process behind all vital spiritual creativity. In the first poem of the sequence, Wordsworth, claiming that he seeks "the birthplace of a native Stream," associates his own poetry with the flow of the river itself: "Pure flow the verse, pure, vigorous, free, and bright, / For Duddon, long-loved Duddon, is my theme" (13–14). But the source he seeks cannot be found in a particular location or even in a specific image, for all is motion and change, a moving birthplace that is continually with us, of us, requiring for its emergent purity that we yield all sense of a separate self. Thus, concluding sonnet 6, a tribute to the flowers of Duddon, with the claim that "All kinds alike seemed favourites of Heaven," Wordsworth, in the next poem, yields even the desire for abiding perspective, asking through the voice of a youthful persona that he be changed into all that he sees:

"Change me, some God, into that breathing rose!"
The love-sick Stripling fancifully sighs,
The envied flower beholding, as it lies
On Laura's breast, in exquisite repose;
Or he would pass into her bird, that throws
The darts of song from out its wiry cage;
Enraptured,—could he for himself engage
The thousandth part of what the Nymph bestows;
And what the little careless innocent
Ungraciously receives. Too daring choice!
There are whose calmer mind it would content
To be an unculled floweret of the glen,
Fearless of plough and scythe; or darkling wren
That tunes on Duddon's banks her slender voice. (1–14)

The rose and the bird into which the child longs to be changed are not simply iconic reproductions of an embryonic self but temporary perchings for the empty locus, the creative potential, at the heart of the stripling's being, at the heart of all being. In this view, the child's love-sickness is also his liberation, for it enables him to communicate not *with* his surroundings, as if he were one thing and the world something else, but *as* those very surroundings. Free of an abiding self at the heart of his being, the child is free of a defining metaphor, of a categorical form that confines the metamorphic creativity of his interaction with the world. At the heart of his being is motion, change, the potential for identity with all things rather than a hard core of selfhood planted over and against the world, seeking to communicate through conventional lines that only preserve the individual's separateness from his milieu. Whatever selfhood can be said to exist in this realm of change must exist, like the source of Duddon, as the event of its own flowing.

The Arcadian conventions of the poem contribute to this psychic flexibility by balancing the intensity of the child's emotion against the suggestion of Elysian grandeur and stability, contributing a lightness of being that frees both poet and reader from the need for conceptual, as well as psychological, schemas. The calmer mind that consents to be an "unculled floweret of the glen" differs from the mind of the stripling's only in degree, not in kind, employing Arcadian imagery much as the persona of book 5 of *The Prelude*, as we saw in the last chapter, employs the "steadiest mood of reason" to confront and accept the dark irrationalities of life. The Arcadian images, indicative of the more conventional formalities of much of Wordsworth's later poetry, thus stabilize without confining, leaving both writer and reader free to wander among a variety of experiences that become the temporary locus of individual being.[15] It is little wonder that those of "calmer mind" are "fearless of plough and scythe." The individual who lives always in the potential to change, to abide in all forms, embodies in herself the root of all existence. To understand the flow of life in this context is to be deathless, infinitely transformative and transforming.

In applauding the "calmer mind" that would be "content / To be an unculled floweret of the glen," Wordsworth associates the spirit of Duddon with the absence of self, including the self's need for answers. Asking, thus, in the next poem (sonnet 8) "What aspect bore the Man who roved or fled, / First of his tribe, to this dark dell—who first / In this pellucid Current slaked his thirst?" (1–3), the poet remarks:

> No voice replies;—both air and earth are mute;
> And Thou, blue Streamlet, murmuring yield'st no more
> Than a soft record, that, whatever fruit
> Of ignorance thou might'st witness heretofore,
> Thy function was to heal and to restore,
> To soothe and cleanse, not madden and pollute! (9–14)

The purity of Wordsworth's verse, like the purity of Zen conscious-ness, follows the purity of Duddon's continual self-emptying. The stream, like the pure verse of the sequence, like the Zen *koan* to which it is comparable, answers no questions. Rather, it heals and restores, not by rejecting human record, including institutional record, but by displacing it from its authority over the human indi-vidual's need for a conceptual home for the ego.

In the Duddon poems, as in so much of Wordsworth's poetry when read categorically, that to which we are restored is motion itself. "On, loitering Muse—the swift Stream chides us—on," the poet writes in sonnet 12. Nothing is allowed to become a resting place for eye and mind. "Niagaras, Alpine passes," the "Abodes of Naiads," oak trees, palaces, towers, all "are crumbled into dust," Wordsworth asserts. To be sure, "The Bard who walks with Duddon for his guide, / Shall find such toys of fancy thickly set," but "Turn from the sight, enamoured Muse—we must," the poet continues; "And, if thou cans't, leave them without regret!" (1–14). One sees that Wordsworth's leave-taking, here and throughout his poetry, marks not so much a refusal to abide as an opening to all conditions, an acceptance so com-plete that the very experience of the alternating joy and sorrow attending the continual arrival and departure of objects of the sens-es sets the poet beyond those very senses. Wordsworth has, in effect, reached what the fifteenth-century Zen monk Gidō Shūshin calls "the point of doing away with happiness and sadness."[16] Happiness and sadness do not cease to exist for such an individual. Such emo-tions cease, rather, to hold him. The "Bard who walks with Duddon" is one who, like the Zennist stripped of all concern for the individual self, has yielded the desire for permanence and safety, finding instead

a quiet faith in the very permanence of impermanence. *"Security and changelessness are fabricated by the ego-dominated mind and do not exist in nature,"* to recall Holmes's and Horioka's explication of the Zen artist's meditative mind. *"To accept insecurity and commit oneself to the unknown creates a relaxing faith in the universe."*[17]
In the act of giving himself to all that he sees and hears in the onward flow of life, the poet accepts Duddon as more than just a guide. It becomes an analogue of the self-emptying, self-forgetting mind whose capaciousness is the act of opening onto the depths of its own nature. "Not hurled precipitous from steep to steep" (1), writes the poet in sonnet 32,

> but in radiant progress toward the Deep
> Where mightiest rivers into powerless sleep
> Sink, and forget their nature—*now* expands
> Majestic Duddon. . . . (4-7)

In its own continual opening, Duddon produces a graceful milieu in which the landscape itself appears to open and view the river: "Beneath an ampler sky a region wide / Is opened round him:—hamlets, towers, and towns, / And blue-topped hills, behold him from afar" (9–11). Opening begets opening, and vision is a function of all things, not of an abiding eye located in the separate mind of a *spectator ab extra*. Duddon's movement toward and eventual disappearance in "the Deep" of the oceanic Thames is, like the Zen process Abe remarks as the emptying of emptiness itself, an opening onto its own cosmic nature.
For Wordsworth, then, as for the Zennist, the proper cast of mind, so far as we can speak of mind as having a proper cast at all, is a radical humility (*wabi*), a self-forgetting before the eternally expanding dimensions of its own vastness. "But here no cannon thunders to the gale; / Upon the wave no haughty pendants cast / A crimson splendour," writes Wordsworth in the opening lines of his "Conclusion" to the sequence (sonnet 33). We cannot sail this river in a proud vessel, for to do so would be to restrict to the ego the very freedom (*sabi*) of movement that lines the expansive walls of the mind's capaciousness. Asserting, thus, that "lowly is the mast / That rises here, and humbly spread, the sail" (3–4), Wordsworth declares that "The Wanderer seeks that receptacle vast / Where all his unambitious

functions fail" (7–8). The only ambition worth pursuing is the freedom from self that enables the individual to live the eternity of his
own nature:

> And may thy Poet, cloud-born Stream! be free—
> The sweets of earth contentedly resigned,
> And each tumultuous working left behind
> At seemly distance—to advance like Thee;
> Prepared, in peace of heart, in calm of mind
> And soul, to mingle with Eternity! (9–14)

Unable to conclude the sequence at this point, however,
Wordsworth returns in his final poem, "After-thought" (sonnet 34), to
the theme of form. The mingling Wordsworth exalts in his
"Conclusion" cannot, he seems to be saying in a final gesture to his
reader, be understood along conventional lines. It must, rather,
include a deep and abiding conflation of movement and stillness, of
change and permanence, as interactive aspects of the same cosmic
unity. Looking back on Duddon in a glance that folds the dimensions
of time and space into an eternally moving unity of the now and the
here, Wordsworth asserts: *"I see what was, and is, and will abide; /*
Still glides the Stream, and shall for ever glide; / The Form remains,
the Function never dies" (4–6; italics Wordsworth's). Zen helps us
understand that the coadunation of form and function in
Wordsworth's poetry is itself the manifestation of the form of the
formless mind of cosmic unity, that, in the words of Mu Soeng Sunim,
"form . . . is an 'event,' existing momentarily in time and space."[18] To
understand his poetry, Wordsworth seems to be saying in "After-
thought," we must understand that form is not a paradigm and that
function is not a separate predicate of that paradigm, but that form
and function comingle and interact as aspects of each other in an
eternal self-emptying that is itself the cosmic mind or what Sokei-
An, writing as one among many Zennists, calls the "Formless Mind":

> Formless Mind means you are not fixed in mind. Mind is
> always fluctuating; it does not reside in one place. It is in a
> true sense "formless." Mind passes like a mirage, like images
> before a mirror. Knowing it is ephemeral, you do not cherish
> it. When you do not cherish it, you are on the ground of
> Formless Mind.[19]

If the community of Zen thought and art provides a context for understanding the formless form of the Wordsworthian mind and the radical freedom at the heart of his spirituality, Wordsworth contributes to the Zen community and to the world an abiding sense of human greatness as the ability to serve the future in a love, hope, and faith predicated on the joyous, yet humble, acceptance of human mortality:

> *While we, the brave, the mighty, and the wise,*
> *We Men, who in our morn of youth defied*
> *The elements, must vanish;—be it so!*
> *Enough, if something from our hands have power*
> *To live, and act, and serve the future hour;*
> *And if, as toward the silent tomb we go,*
> *Through love, through hope, and faith's transcendent dower,*
> *We feel that we are greater than we know.* (7–14; italics
> Wordsworth's)

NOTES

INTRODUCTION THE PURER MIND

1. William Wordsworth, *The Poetical Works of William Wordsworth*, 5 vols., ed. Ernest de Selincourt, 2d ed., rev. Helen Darbishire (Oxford: Clarendon Press, 1952–59), 5:4, lines 35–41 (hereafter cited as *PW*). Unless otherwise noted, citations of the poetry identify line numbers from this edition.

2. John Milton, *Complete Poems and Major Prose*, ed. Merritt Y. Hughes (Indianapolis: Odyssey Press, 1957), 217; lines 254–55.

3. William Wordsworth, *The Prelude: A Parallel Text*, ed. J. C. Maxwell (New Haven: Yale University Press, 1971), 92. Unless otherwise noted, subsequent references are to the book and lines of the 1805 version given in this edition of *The Prelude*.

4. Recent commentaries view Wordsworth's turning to Dorothy as an evasion of political and social responsibility in his headlong attempt to ground the self in a subjective individualism. See especially Jerome McGann, *The Romantic Ideology: A Critical Investigation* (Chicago: University of Chicago Press, 1983), 87–88; Heather Glen, *Vision and Disenchantment: Blake's "Songs" and Wordsworth's "Lyrical Ballads"* (Cambridge: Cambridge University Press, 1983), 257–58; Marjorie Levinson, *Wordsworth's Great Period Poems: Four Essays* (Cambridge: Cambridge University Press, 1986), 37–38, 45–46, 49; and David Simpson, *Wordsworth's Historical Imagination: The Poetry of Displacement* (New York and London: Methuen, 1987), 110. Though M. H. Abrams, in *Doing Things with Texts: Essays in Criticism and Critical Theory*, ed. Michael Fischer (New York: Norton, 1989), attempts to counter the negative force of these studies by arguing that "Dorothy is both a real and crucially functional 'other,'" he asserts nevertheless that "'Tintern Abbey' is 'subjective' or 'private' in its point of view; inescapably so, because the first-person lyric establishes the lyric speaker as its center of consciousness" (387). A particularly insightful essay on Dorothy's continuing ability to "see into the life of

213

things" appears in Beth Darlington, "Reclaiming Dorothy Wordsworth's Legacy," in *The Age of William Wordsworth: Critical Essays on the Romantic Tradition*, ed. Kenneth R. Johnston and Gene W. Ruoff (New Brunswick, NJ: Rutgers University Press, 1987), 160–72. All these views hover, with only slight variations, around the thesis that "Tintern Abbey" is concerned primarily with self-establishment rather than with self-dispersal. An alternative perspective, one closer to my own, appears in James B. Twitchell, "Romanticism and Cosmic Consciousness," *The Centennial Review* 19 (1975): 287–307. Twitchell asserts that "Tintern Abbey" entails "a loss of selfhood" resulting in a "'mystic' experience." Like most readers, however, Twitchell views the earlier "serene and blessed mood" of "Tintern Abbey" as a prerequisite for the later "sense sublime / Of something far more deeply interfused" rather than as an experiential cosmic ground that continues in various forms throughout the poet's life. As a result, Twitchell complains that Wordsworth "left no prescriptive patterns of spiritual ascent, no intellectual system of theological and metaphysical synthesis . . . " (295). Twitchell raises a centrally important concern I hope to resolve in my study.

5. M. H. Abrams, *Natural Supernaturalism: Tradition and Revolution in Romantic Literature* (New York: Norton, 1971), 28.

6. Kenneth R. Johnston, "The Idiom of Vision," in *New Perspectives on Coleridge and Wordsworth: Selected Papers from the English Institute*, ed. Geoffrey H. Hartman (New York: Columbia University Press, 1972), 8.

7. Frederick Garber, *The Autonomy of the Self from Richardson to Huysmans* (Princeton: Princeton University Press, 1982), 92–93.

8. Barbara Schapiro, "Wordsworth's Visionary Imagination: A New Critical Context," *The Wordsworth Circle* 18 (1987): 137. Similarly, Mervyn Nicholson, "The New Cosmology in Romantic Poetry," *The Wordsworth Circle* 20 (1989): 123–31, invokes modern quantum physics, together with Hume, to argue that romantic "Consciousness is a mirror that reflects objects in space sequentially, randomly" (123). But he views this "Object Cosmology" (125) as essentially nihilistic and atheistic.

9. David Perkins, *The Quest for Permanence: The Symbolism of Wordsworth, Shelley, and Keats* (Cambridge: Harvard University Press, 1959), 12.

10. Geoffrey Hartman, *Wordsworth's Poetry, 1787–1814* (New Haven: Yale University Press, 1971), 17–18, 225–26.

11. Charles J. Rzepka, *The Self as Mind: Vision and Identity in Wordsworth, Coleridge, and Keats* (Cambridge: Harvard University Press, 1986), 9. Similarly, David Simpson, *Wordsworth and the Figurings of the*

Real (Atlantic Highlands, NJ: Humanities Press, 1982), asserting that "the mind itself is a composite identity open to the refractions of passion and feeling, interest and inclination," argues that "The mind, if it does not completely 'project' itself into the world, selects and composes such sense data as it receives into particular codes of significance, elements of meaning" (xi). Paul de Man, *Romanticism and Contemporary Criticism: The Gauss Seminar and Other Papers*, ed. E. S. Burt, Kevin Newmark, and Andrzej Warminski (Baltimore: Johns Hopkins University Press, 1993), also rejects the marriage metaphor as particularly inadequate to express the self's confrontation with time (see especially 145–46).

12. John Jones, *The Egotistical Sublime: A History of Wordsworth's Imagination* (London: Chatto and Windus, 1970), 32–33.

13. Based on a reading of "Home at Grasmere," for example, Anthony J. Harding, "Forgetfulness and the Poetic Self in 'Home at Grasmere,'" *The Wordsworth Circle* 22 (1991): 109–18, argues that Wordsworth's poetry embodies "two *contradictory* ways" of relating mind and nature—the one neoclassical and conveying an "appeal for poetic inspiration to a power above and around the self," the other "a Christian desire to 'save' fallen nature by treating it as textual, as a book, in which the individual may 'read.'" Harding acknowledges, however, that "Both models of the mind-nature relationship assume the separation of man from nature . . . " (110). Quoting a version of the Prospectus, John A. Hodgson, *Wordsworth's Philosophical Poetry, 1797–1814* (Lincoln: University of Nebraska Press, 1980), demonstrates that "Wordsworth's constant metaphysical concern was with how the individual 'consists / With being limitless the one great Life'" (xiv). Hodgson reveals that Wordsworth's understanding of the one power of the universe changed over the years, but his study does not break through the dualistic pattern of viewing Wordsworth's understanding as grounded in the relational notion that ultimate "Power" is one thing, the individual mind something else—a perceiving agent essentially other. Keith G. Thomas, *Wordsworth and Philosophy: Empiricism and Transcendentalism in the Poetry* (Ann Arbor, MI: UMI Research Press, 1989), sees Wordsworth's philosophical development as "oscillating. . . between that hard-won transcendentalism and a reemergent, reenergized, almost atavistic empiricism" (15). John O. Hayden, *William Wordsworth and the Mind of Man: The Poet as Thinker* (New York: Bibli O'Phile Publishing, 1992), avoids cosmic consciousness altogether, arguing simply that Wordsworth was "an intellectual poet . . . in the true sense of one who is curious about everything he runs across, questions the truth of everything, and thinks constantly about it" (vii). M. H. Abrams, in "Two Roads to Wordsworth," in *The Correspondent Breeze: Essays on English Romanticism*

(New York: Norton, 1984), 145–57, traces the problem to Wordsworth himself, who, he claims, reveals two distinct voices throughout his canon. The one is the voice of the Preface to *Lyrical Ballads*, which associates the quest for unity with what Abrams calls "the essential, the elementary, the simple, the universal, and the permanent" (145). The other is the voice of the later "Essay, Supplementary to the Preface" (1815), which is "complex, paradoxical, problematic," dominated by "a pervasive sense of mortality and an ever-incipient despair of life . . . hostile to temporal man and the world of sense" and inclined essentially "toward another world that transcends biological and temporal limitations" (149). Readers anxious to affirm the poet's commitment to union without undermining the dark complexities of his work must, according to Abrams, resort to a critical approach based on the notion of unity as an achieved "reciprocity between the natural world and the minds of men" (157). Whether this reciprocity is viewed as mediated by the poet's imagination or by his adoption of a cultural tradition like Christianity, or even by a combination of the two, the result is still a critical vision that sees the mind as one thing, the world as something else. Perhaps, as Karl Kroeber remarks in his bibliographical essay, *William Wordsworth*, in *The English Romantic Poets: A Review of Research and Criticism*, 4th ed., ed. Frank Jordan (New York: Modern Language Association of America, 1985), 255–339, the reason for the abiding dualism of Wordsworth studies can be traced to an increasingly modernist "tendency to associate Wordsworth with Blakean antinaturalism," a practice that exalts the individual mind and that tends to view poetry, particularly the lyric, as elegiac—as mourning our lost selves—rather than as celebrating the vital unity of self and other (256–57).

14. Amelie Enns, "The Subject-Object Dichotomy in Heidegger's *A Dialogue on Language* and Nishitani's *Religion and Nothingness*," *Japanese Religions* 15 (January 1988): 38.

15. Winston L. King, foreword to *Religion and Nothingness*, by Keiji Nishitani, trans. Jan Van Bragt (Berkeley and Los Angeles: University of California Press, 1982), xi.

16. M. H. Abrams, foreword to *William Wordsworth and the Age of English Romanticism*, by Jonathan Wordsworth, Michael C. Jaye, and Robert Woof (New Brunswick and London: Rutgers University Press, 1987), ix. For a brief overview of the impact of German philosophy on English romantic thought, see Kevin Hilliard, "German Philosophy and Criticism," in *A Handbook to English Romanticism*, ed. Jean Raimond and J. R. Watson (New York: St. Martin's Press, 1992), 115–18.

17. Albert O. Wlecke, *Wordsworth and the Sublime* (Berkeley and Los Angeles: University of California Press, 1973), 5.

18. Marilyn Gaull, *English Romanticism: The Human Context* (New York: Norton, 1988), 306.

19. Masao Abe, *Zen and Western Thought*, ed. William R. LaFleur (Honolulu: University of Hawaii Press, 1985), xxi.

20. Robert Linssen, *Living Zen*, trans. Diana Abrahams-Curiel (New York: Grove Press, 1958), 52.

21. Lucien Stryk and Takashi Ikemoto, trans. and eds., *Zen: Poems, Prayers, Sermons, Anecdotes, Interviews*, 2d ed. (Athens: Ohio University Press / Swallow Press, 1981), 91.

22. Edward Conze, trans., *Buddhist Wisdom Books: Containing* The Diamond Sutra *and* The Heart Sutra (London: G. Allen & Unwin, 1958), 81.

23. Thich Nhat Hanh, "Commentary on *The Heart Sutra*," *Tricycle: The Buddhist Review* 1 (spring 1992): 27.

24. Ibid.

25. Steve Odin, *Process Metaphysics and Hua-yen Buddhism: A Critical Study of Cumulative Penetration Vs. Interpenetration* (Albany: State University of New York Press, 1982), 26, 21, 5.

26. Masao Abe, "The Problem of Self-Centeredness as the Root-Source of Human Suffering," *Japanese Religions* 15 (July 1989): 24–25.

27. Nolan Pliny Jacobson, *Buddhism and the Contemporary World: Change and Self-Correction* (Carbondale: Southern Illinois University Press, 1983), 8.

28. Sasaki Joshu, *Buddha is the Center of Gravity*, trans. Fusako Akinu (San Cristobal, NM: Lama Foundation, 1974), 22.

29. Sean Dennison, historical introduction to *Lao-tzu's Treatise on the Response of the Tao*, by Li Ying-chang, trans. Eva Wong (San Francisco: HarperCollins, 1994), xv.

30. Daisetz Teitaro Suzuki, *Manual of Zen Buddhism* (New York: Grove Press, 1960), 81.

31. Eihei Dōgen, *Moon in a Dewdrop: Writings of Zen Master Dōgen*, ed. Kazuaki Tanahashi (San Francisco: North Point Press, 1985), 70.

32. Thomas Cleary, trans. and ed., *Zen Essence: The Science of Freedom* (Boston: Shambhala, 1989), xv, 80.

33. Reiho Masunaga, *The Sōtō Approach to Zen* (Tokyo: Layman Buddhist Society Press, 1958), 10.

34. Although Wordsworth would certainly have known something of Buddhism through his long association with his friend and colleague, Samuel Taylor Coleridge, who wrote considerably on Eastern thought in general, there is no evidence to suggest that he was formally influenced by the philosophy. For an account of Coleridge's knowledge of Eastern culture, see especially John Drew, *India and the Romantic Imagination* (Delhi: Oxford University Press, 1987), 183–227. Readers interested in the history of Buddhism in Europe should consult Guy Richard Welbon, *The Buddhist Nirvana and Its Western Interpreters* (Chicago: University of Chicago Press, 1968). The first major effort to see connections between Wordsworth and Buddhism occurs in R. H. Blyth, *Zen in English Literature and Oriental Classics* (Tokyo: Hokuseido Press, 1942), especially 412–25. Blyth's study, though immensely suggestive, is impressionistic and cursory, juxtaposing passages from Wordsworth and Zen with little or no commentary. For a recent essay that forms the basis of the present study, see John G. Rudy, "Wordsworth and the Zen Void," *Thought: A Review of Culture and Idea* 65 (1990): 127–42.

CHAPTER 1   CAPACIOUSNESS AS NATURAL PROCESS

1. Herbert Guenther, "Tasks Ahead," *Journal of the International Association of Buddhist Studies* 4, no. 2 (1981): 120.

2. Nolan Pliny Jacobson, *Understanding Buddhism* (Carbondale: Southern Illinois University Press, 1986), 78.

3. Ibid., 79.

4. Abe, *Zen and Western Thought*, 167.

5. Michael Adam, *Wandering in Eden: Three Ways to the East within Us* (New York: Knopf, 1976), 45.

6. Dōgen, *Sounds of Valley Streams: Enlightenment in Dōgen's Zen*, trans. Francis H. Cook (Albany: State University of New York Press, 1989), 68.

7. Ibid., 59.

8. Ibid. The Buddhist idea that there is no individual being or existence "apart from the ultimate reality" emerges frequently in the theme that there is no birth, no death. The Buddhist philosopher Nāgārjuna (ca. 150–250 A.D.), for example, writes that "At nowhere and at no time can entities ever exist by originating out of themselves, from others, from both (self-other), or from the lack of causes" (Kenneth K. Inada, trans. and ed.,

Nāgārjuna: A Translation of his Mūlamadhyamakakārikā with an Introductory Essay [Tokyo: Hokuseido Press, 1970], 39). Masao Abe, *A Study of Dōgen: His Philosophy and Religion*, ed. Steven Heine (Albany: State University of New York Press, 1992), writes similarly that "the Buddhist interpretation of human existence as something that undergoes birth-and-death rather than merely as something that must die maintains that all existence, including the human, is without beginning or end. . . . There is also no presupposition of a transcendental principle that gives rise to the beginning or end of humans and history" (171–72).

   9.   Suzuki, *Manual of Zen Buddhism*, 76–77.

   10.   Ingrid Fischer–Schreiber, Franz-Karl Ehrhard, and Michael S. Diener, *The Shambhala Dictionary of Buddhism and Zen*, trans. Michael H. Kohn (Boston: Shambhala, 1991), 221.

   11.   Dennis Genpo Merzel, *The Eye Never Sleeps: Striking to the Heart of Zen*, ed. Stephen Muho Proskauer (Boston: Shambhala, 1991), 3.

   12.   Ibid., 7.

   13.   Cleary, *Zen Essence*, xvi. Explaining that Buddhists see good and evil as "different manifestations of the same dualistic process," Benjamin and Amy Radcliff, *Understanding Zen* (Boston: Tuttle, 1993), assert that "One liberated from socially-defined moral conventions is not one who has no regard for the happiness or security of his fellows. Instead, the liberated person sees such conventions for what they are: artificial, socially-defined rules lacking any necessarily compelling moral force" (158–59).

   14.   Merzel, *The Eye Never Sleeps*, 7.

   15.   Trying to account for such a blending or fusing of terms within the conventional, dualistic perspective of Western linguistics, Donald G. Marshall, in his foreword, "Wordsworth and Post-Enlightenment Culture," in *The Unremarkable Wordsworth*, by Geoffrey H. Hartman (Minneapolis: University of Minnesota Press, 1987), vii–xxiii, says Wordsworth's "referentiality" has a "ghostly quality." Quoting a portion of Hartman's text, Marshall argues that Wordsworth "does not quite refer definitely, so that his 'descriptive' poetry peculiarly blends 'the fallen sublimity of classicizing or poetic diction . . . with the naturalism of elemental speech-acts of wishing, blessing, naming.' And yet any tendency to take leave of the real world for a transcendent or apocalyptic realm is chastized, and natural mediators are re-inserted" (x). My thesis is that at the deepest levels of his spirituality, Wordsworth avoids the "natural mediators" Marshall and other Western readers have come to expect in his poetry.

16. Aldous Huxley, *The Devils of Loudun* (London: Folio Society, 1986), 80.

17. Abe, *Zen and Western Thought*, 167.

CHAPTER 2 CAPACIOUSNESS AS RECEPTACLE

1. Hui Neng, *The Sutra of Hui Neng,* in *The Diamond Sutra and The Sutra of Hui Neng,* trans. A. F. Price and Wong Mou-Lam (Boston: Shambhala, 1985), 26.

2. Huang Po, *The Zen Teaching of Huang Po on the Transmission of Mind,* trans. John Blofeld (New York: Grove Press, 1958), 29.

3. Ibid., 33.

4. Hui Neng, *The Sutra of Hui Neng,* 26.

5. Huang Po, *Zen Teaching on the Transmission of Mind,* 19–20.

6. Ibid., 20. Kenneth K. Inada, in his commentary on Nāgārjuna's *Mūlamadhyamakakārikā,* writes similarly that "Passage or flow of existence means that there is no objectifying or entifying of the mind itself and its objects of perception. Thus any concept . . . viewed abstractly is taken to task and brought to its ultimate idiocy or self-contradiction" (*Nāgārjuna,* 24).

7. Huang Po, *Zen Teaching on the Transmission of Mind,* 17.

8. Robert Aitken, *A Zen Wave: Bashō's Haiku and Zen* (New York: Weatherhill, 1978), 19.

9. Ibid., 30.

10. Ibid., 32.

11. Dōgen, *Moon in a Dewdrop,* 76.

12. Qtd. in Abe, *Zen and Western Thought,* 62.

13. Huang Po, *Zen Teaching on the Transmission of Mind,* 41.

14. Blyth, *Zen in English Literature,* 266.

15. Aitken, *A Zen Wave,* 101.

16. Chang Chung-yuan, *Original Teachings of Ch'an Buddhism: Selected from The Transmission of the Lamp* (New York: Pantheon Books, 1969), 46.

17. Aitken, *A Zen Wave*, 102–3.

18. Nyogen Senzaki and Ruth Strout McCandless, comps., trans., and eds., *Buddhism and Zen* (New York: Wisdom Library, 1953), 77.

19. Hakuin, *The Zen Master Hakuin: Selected Writings*, trans. Philip B. Yampolsky (New York: Columbia University Press, 1971), 118.

20. Zenkei Shibayama, *Zen Comments on the* Mumonkan, trans. Sumiko Kudo (San Francisco: Harper & Row, 1974), 28.

21. Daisetz Teitaro Suzuki, *The Zen Doctrine of No-Mind: The Significance of the Sūtra of Hui-neng (Wei-lang)*, ed. Christmas Humphreys (London: Rider, 1983), 26.

22. Ibid., 28–29.

23. Wei Wu Wei, *Open Secret* (Hong Kong: Hong Kong University Press, 1970), 157.

24. Joel Haefner, "Displacement and the Reading of Romantic Space," *The Wordsworth Circle* 23 (1992): 151–56, argues the opposing thesis that the blind-beggar passage is "representative of a mode of reading which displaces meaning into another plane of signifiers, to 'another world' " (151). Haefner invokes Barthes, Lacan, and Derrida to assert that "Reading may be thought of as entailing some kind of mapping—the encoding of space, the desire to locate Subject (Self, or meaning) within the parameters of Other (the world, society, or text)" (151). My reading of the blind-beggar passage asserts that Wordsworth exalts self-displacement and the annihilation of place as requisite for a fully spiritual existence.

25. Sheng-yen, trans. and ed., *The Poetry of Enlightenment: Poems by Ancient Ch'an Masters* (Elmhurst, NY: Dharma Drum Publications, 1987), 54, lines 138–42.

26. Sheng-yen, *The Sword of Wisdom: Lectures on the Song of Enlightenment*, ed. Christopher Marano (Elmhurst, NY: Dharma Drum Publications, 1990), 142.

27. Suzuki, *Zen Doctrine of No-Mind*, 26.

28. Qtd. in Welbon, *Buddhist Nirvana*, 303.

INTRODUCTION TO PART TWO

1. Chang Chung-yuan, trans., *Tao: A New Way of Thinking* (New York: Harper & Row, 1975), 4.

2. Lao Tzu, *Tao Te Ching*, trans. Stephen Addiss and Stanley Lombardo (Indianapolis: Hackett Publishing, 1993), 25.1–9. The *Tao Te Ching* is a collection of poems. The Addiss-Lombardo translation simply numbers each poem. Subsequent references identify poem number and lines from this edition.

3. Ibid., 25.10–12.

4. Henry Wei, *The Guiding Light of Lao Tzu: A New Translation and Commentary on the* Tao Te Ching (Wheaton, IL: Theosophical Publishing House, 1982), 29–30.

5. Wing-Tsit Chan, trans. and comp., *A Source Book in Chinese Philosophy* (Princeton: Princeton University Press, 1963), 136. A full examination of the parallels between Wordsworthian and Taoist themes is beyond the scope of this paper. A particularly original and suggestive study of the correspondences between Wordsworthian and Taoist visions of nature, however, occurs in Qian-Zhi Wu, "The Wordsworthian Imagination: Seeing Nature as IT IS—A Taoist Reading of Wordsworth" (Ph.D. diss., Columbia University, 1987), abstract in *Dissertation Abstracts International* 49 (1988): 514A.

6. Roger T. Ames, "Putting the *Te* Back into Taoism," in *Nature in Asian Traditions of Thought: Essays in Environmental Philosophy*, ed. J. Baird Callicott and Roger T. Ames (Albany: State University of New York Press, 1989), 132, 135.

7. Lao Tzu, *Tao Te Ching*, 48.1–2.

8. Chang Chung-yuan, *Tao: A New Way of Thinking*, 13.

9. Martin Heidegger, *On the Way to Language*, trans. Peter D. Hertz (New York: Harper & Row, 1971), 13. A particularly good study of the similarities and differences between Zen and Heidegger's thought appears in Michael E. Zimmerman, *Eclipse of the Self: The Development of Heidegger's Concept of Authenticity* (Athens: Ohio University Press, 1981), 255–76.

10. Abrams, *Natural Supernaturalism*, 193, 123, 286. Like Abrams, other readers tend to view Wordsworth's treatment of the journey motif as an attempt to preserve or to enhance the self. Asserting, for example, that "The Romantic movement is from nature to the Imagination's freedom,"

Harold Bloom, "The Internalization of Quest-Romance," in *Romanticism and Consciousness: Essays in Criticism*, ed. Harold Bloom, 3–24 (New York: Norton, 1970), writes: "The quest is to widen consciousness as well as to intensify it, but the quest is shadowed by a spirit that tends to narrow consciousness to an acute preoccupation with self. This shadow of imagination is solipsism" (6). Jeffrey C. Robinson, in "The Structure of Wordsworth's *Memorials of a Tour in Scotland, 1803*," *PLL* 13 (1977): 54–70, relies heavily on Bloom's *The Anxiety of Influence* and *A Map of Misreading* to argue that Wordsworth's journeys were motivated primarily by a desire to preserve his own poetic powers in a perceived climate of literary influence. Robinson's assertion echoes Bernard Blackstone's thesis in *The Lost Travellers: A Romantic Theme with Variations* (London: Longmans, 1962) that romantic travelers are lost in "deserts of Time and Space" (1) and are seeking escape from a fallen world. Similarly, R. F. Brissenden, in *Virtue in Distress: Studies in the Novel of Sentiment from Richardson to Sade* (New York: Harper & Row, 1974), 66–77, maintains that the Wordsworthian traveler is an alienated, impotent figure, unable to alleviate the world's suffering and seeking escape in the contemplation of nature. For a comprehensive review of Wordsworth's reading in travel literature, see Charles N. Coe, *Wordsworth and the Literature of Travel* (New York: Bookman Associates, 1961).

11. Wei, *Guiding Light of Lao Tzu*, 30.

CHAPTER 3 "STEPPING WESTWARD" AND "THE SOLITARY REAPER"

1. T. P. Kasulis, *Zen Action/Zen Person* (Honolulu: University of Hawaii Press, 1981), 33–35.

2. Lao Tzu, *Tao Te Ching*, 11.1–6.

3. Adam, *Wandering in Eden*, 66.

4. Walpola Rahula, *What the Buddha Taught*, rev. ed. (New York: Grove Press, 1974), 26.

5. Kasulis, *Zen Action/Zen Person*, 37.

6. Qtd. in Nancy Wilson Ross, *Three Ways of Asian Wisdom: Hinduism, Buddhism, Zen and Their Significance for the West* (New York: Simon and Schuster, 1966), 145.

7. Shôei Andô, *Zen and American Transcendentalism—An Investigation of One's Self* (Tokyo: Hokuseido Press, 1970), 177.

8.   Hartman, *Wordsworth's Poetry*, 17–18. It should be kept in mind that "The Solitary Reaper" was not a rendering of Wordsworth's personal experience; according to Dorothy, it "was suggested to William by a beautiful sentence in Thomas Wilkinson's *Tour in Scotland*" (*PW* 3:444). Dorothy, however, indicates that she and her brother frequently saw "a single person so employed" (*PW* 3:444).

9.   Jonathan Wordsworth, "The Mind as Lord and Master: Wordsworth and Wallace Stevens," *The Wordsworth Circle* 14 (1983): 183–91.

10.   Lao Tzu, *Tao Te Ching*, 16.1–2, 5–6, 7.

11.   Susan J. Wolfson, *The Questioning Presence: Wordsworth, Keats, and the Interrogative Mode in Romantic Poetry* (Ithaca: Cornell University Press, 1986), offers an opposing point of view, seeing Wordsworth's acceptance of the music as a moment of irresolution that merely "keeps him on the stretch of attention" (183). She argues that the questions in "Stepping Westward" and "The Solitary Reaper" are "a pleasant stimulus to the imagination" rather than deeply probing "interrogative occasions" in which the "poetic 'I'" encounters "critical questions of selfhood" (182). Wolfson views the experiences recorded in both poems as moments of enjoyment in which, as Keats says, an "immediate 'sense of Beauty overcomes every other consideration, or rather obliterates all consideration'" (185). The Zen reader might respond that the reference to beauty as a separate and overpowering element of the experience is an abstraction that inhibits one's realization that self and world are identical.

12.   Huang Po, *Zen Teaching on the Transmission of Mind*, 42.

13.   Mike K. Sayama, *Samadhi: Self-Development in Zen, Swordsmanship, and Psychotherapy* (Albany: State University of New York Press, 1986), 12.

14.   Martin Heidegger, *Discourse on Thinking*, trans. John M. Anderson and E. Hans Freund (New York: Harper & Row, 1959), 66, 86. On Heidegger's concept of regioning as a form of clearing, Geoffrey Hartman, in *The Unremarkable Wordsworth*, writes: "Nothing new is gained, except an indeterminacy as to the locus of meaning, or a sense of the text itself as the place of revelation, a clearing (*Lichtung*) from which language, or Being itself, speaks" (200). Hartman's privileging of the text is typical of Western criticism's preoccupation with language, a condition Wordsworth obviously accepts but seems to want, as well, to transcend.

15. Masao Abe, "Emptiness is Suchness," in *The Buddha Eye: An Anthology of the Kyoto School*, ed. Frederick Franck (New York: Cross Road, 1982), 207.

16. Chang Chung-yuan, *Creativity and Taoism: A Study of Chinese Philosophy, Art, and Poetry* (New York: Harper & Row, 1970), 103.

17. Shibayama, *Zen Comments on the* Mumonkan, 19.

18. Kasulis, *Zen Action / Zen Person*, 11.

19. Thich Nhat Hanh, *The Heart of Understanding: Commentaries on the* Prajñaparamita Heart Sutra, ed. Peter Levitt (Berkeley: Parallax Press, 1988), 21.

20. John Crook, ed., introduction to *Catching a Feather on a Fan: A Zen Retreat with Master Sheng Yen* (Longmead, GB: Element Books, 1991), 10.

21. Thomas Cleary, introduction to *No Barrier: Unlocking the Zen Koan* (New York: Bantam Books, 1993), xii. My discourse on Zen meditation has emphasized the *koan* tradition of the Rinzai sect. The Soto sect, however, tends to emphasize pure sitting or *shikantaza*, as it is called, employing the *koan*, but not to the extent and not quite in the same manner as the Rinzai. For an extensive examination of the *koan* tradition in the Soto sect, see especially Carl Bielefeldt, *Dōgen's Manuals of Zen Meditation* (Berkeley and Los Angeles: University of California Press, 1988) and Steven Heine, *Dōgen and the Kōan Tradition: A Tale of Two Shōbōgenzō Texts* (Albany: State University of New York Press, 1994).

22. Lao Tzu, *Tao Te Ching*, 48.2–4.

23. Qtd. in Abbot Zenkei Shibayama, *A Flower Does Not Talk: Zen Essays*, trans. Sumiko Kudo (Rutland, VT: Tuttle, 1970), 19 20 (italics Shibayama's). Attributed by some scholars to Bodhidharma, the First Patriarch of Chan, this maxim is sometimes recited as a *gatha* or prayer in Zen monasteries.

24. Ibid., 25.

25. Nishida Kitarō, *Fundamental Problems of Philosophy: The World of Action and the Dialectical World*, trans. David A. Dilworth (Tokyo: Sophia University Press, 1970), 45.

26. Nishida Kitarō, *Last Writings: Nothingness and the Religious Worldview*, trans. David A. Dilworth (Honolulu: University of Hawaii Press, 1987), 101, 110.

CHAPTER 4   THE ALPINE CROSSING

1.   Hartman, *Wordsworth's Poetry*, 5. I hope that my treatment of Hartman's criticism does not undermine the complexity of his thoughts on Wordsworth's poetry. Paul de Man, in *Romanticism and Contemporary Criticism*, reminds us that Hartman's "talent for phrasing positions he does not necessarily espouse exposes him to the risk of being quoted misleadingly out of context" (137).

2.   Hartman, *Wordsworth's Poetry*, 39.

3.   E. A. Horseman, "The Design of Wordsworth's *Prelude*," in *Wordsworth's Mind and Art*, comp. and ed. A. W. Thomson (Edinburgh: Oliver and Boyd, 1969), 104, 102.

4.   William Wordsworth, *Literary Criticism of William Wordsworth*, ed. Paul M. Zall (Lincoln: University of Nebraska Press, 1966), 150.

5.   Samuel Taylor Coleridge, *Biographia Literaria*, 2 vols., ed. J. Shawcross (London: Oxford University Press, 1907), 1:202; 2:12.

6.   Thomas Weiskel, *The Romantic Sublime: Studies in the Structure and Psychology of Transcendence* (Baltimore: Johns Hopkins University Press, 1986), 203.

7.   Ibid., 204.

8.   Wordsworth, *Literary Criticism*, 183.

9.   Amakuki Sessan, "Hakuin's 'Song of Meditation,'" in *A First Zen Reader*, comp. and trans. Trevor Leggett (Rutland, VT: Tuttle, 1960), 85.

10.   Ken Wilbur, *The Spectrum of Consciousness* (Wheaton, IL: Theosophical Publishing House, 1977), 299.

11.   Shibayama, *A Flower Does Not Talk*, 43, 45.

12.   Abe, *Zen and Western Thought*, 117.

13.   Shibayama, *A Flower Does Not Talk*, 38.

14.   Ibid.

15.   Jacobson, *Buddhism and the Contemporary World*, 70–71.

16.   Weiskel, *The Romantic Sublime*, 200.

17.   Adam, *Wandering in Eden*, 84.

18.   Ibid., 83.

19. Wordsworth, *Literary Criticism*, 149.

20. Nishida Kitarō, *A Study of Good*, trans. V. H. Viglielmo (New York: Greenwood Press, 1988), 28, 1.

21. Chuang Tzu, *Basic Writings*, trans. Burton Watson (New York: Columbia University Press, 1964), 38–39.

22. Wordsworth, *Literary Criticism*, 40.

23. Blyth, *Zen in English Literature*, 420–21; italics Blyth's.

CHAPTER 5 "THE BLIND HIGHLAND BOY"

1. An especially good study of the 1803 *Memorials* as comprising a journey toward autonomy of imagination occurs in Robinson. For a response to Robinson, see John G. Rudy, "Beyond Vocation and Ego: Self-displacement in Wordsworth's 1803 *Memorials*," *SEL* 29 (1989): 637–53.

2. Wordsworth, *Literary Criticism*, 95–96.

3. Adam, *Wandering in Eden*, 83.

4. Yoshito S. Hakeda, trans., *The Awakening of Faith* (New York: Columbia University Press, 1967), 32. Though attributed to the Indian author Asvaghosha and believed to have been composed originally in Sanskrit, the earliest known version is the Chinese translation by Paramartha in A.D. 550.

5. Ibid., 32.

6. Fischer-Schreiber, Ehrhard, and Diener, *Shambhala Dictionary*, 184.

7. Hakeda, *The Awakening of Faith*, 13.

8. Hakuin, *The Zen Master Hakuin*, 118–20.

9. Urs App, "'Dun': A Chinese Concept as a Key to 'Mysticism' in East and West," *The Eastern Buddhist* 26 (autumn 1993): 49.

10. Richard De Martino, *The Zen Understanding of Man* (Ann Arbor, MI: University Microfilms International, 1969), 176.

11. Sheng-yen, *The Poetry of Enlightenment*, 41, lines 187–90.

12. Stryk and Ikemoto, *Zen: Poems, Prayers, Sermons, Anecdotes, Interviews*, 5.

13. William Wordsworth and Dorothy Wordsworth, *The Letters of William and Dorothy Wordsworth: The Early Years, 1787–1805*, ed. Ernest de Selincourt, rev. Chester L. Shaver (Oxford: Clarendon Press, 1967), 402. For an account of the 1803 tour, see especially Mary Moorman, *William Wordsworth: A Biography. The Early Years, 1770–1803* (Oxford: Clarendon Press, 1957), 589–615.

INTRODUCTION TO PART THREE

1.   Lucien Stryk, *Encounter with Zen: Writings on Poetry and Zen* (Athens: Ohio University Press/Swallow Press, 1981), 57.

2.   Taigan Takayama, forward to *Zen Poems of China and Japan: The Crane's Bill*, trans. and comp. Lucien Stryk and Takashi Ikemoto (New York: Grove Weidenfeld, 1973), xv.

3.   Shin'ichi Hisamatsu, *Zen and the Fine Arts*, trans. Gishin Tokiwa (Tokyo: Kodansha International, 1971), 19.

4.   Takashi Ikemoto, preface to Stryk and Ikemoto, *Zen: Poems, Prayers, Sermons, Anecdotes, Interviews*, xix.

5.   Wordsworth, *Literary Criticism*, 42. Normally, readers interpret Wordsworth's prefatory references to formal considerations as meaning the various formal devices of poetry. See, for example, M. H. Abrams, "The Correspondent Breeze: A Romantic Metaphor," in *The Correspondent Breeze*, 25–43.

6.   Wordsworth, *Literary Criticism*, 52.

7.   Unlike Stryk, whose emphasis on "moods" forms the base of his study of Zen aesthetics, Hisamatsu, focusing primarily on the visual arts, distinguishes seven "characteristics" of the individual Zen art object: "Asymmetry, Simplicity, Austere Sublimity or Lofty Dryness, Naturalness, Subtle Profundity or Profound Subtlety, Freedom from Attachment, and Tranquillity" (29). Although his discussion of these characteristics certainly includes and extends our understanding of the moods Stryk identifies, Hisamatsu's concern with aspects of the individual art object tends to restrict his vision of the potential universality of Zen aesthetics and its accessibility to other cultures. Speaking of the seven characteristics of Zen art as an interrelated or codependent network of aesthetic qualities, Hisamatsu writes: "Japan remains a treasure-house of this cultural complex, and, I can say, almost nowhere else—including the West—does there exist another culture with such characteristics" (37).

CHAPTER 6 *SABI*: THE SPIRIT OF SOLITUDE AND FREEDOM

1. Stryk, *Encounter with Zen*, 57.

2. Stryk and Ikemoto, *Zen: Poems, Prayers, Sermons, Anecdotes, Interviews*, 13.

3. Jacobson, *Buddhism and the Contemporary World*, 37.

4. Kasulis, *Zen Action / Zen Person*, 153.

5. Ibid.

6. Ibid.

7. Nolan Pliny Jacobson, *Buddhism: The Religion of Analysis* (Carbondale: Southern Illinois University Press, 1966), 82–83.

8. Ibid., 83.

9. Qtd. in Abe, *Zen and Western Thought*, 4.

10. Ibid., 10.

11. Ibid., 5.

12. Dōgen, *Moon in a Dewdrop*, 70. Susan Edwards Meisenhelder, in *Wordsworth's Informed Reader: Structures of Experience in His Poetry* (Nashville: Vanderbilt University Press, 1988), likewise associates the cloud with the leech-gatherer but, influenced perhaps by the more traditionally Western dualisms of external and internal, human and nonhuman, sees it as forming an "active resistance to external forces. The integrity of its form in moving 'all together, if it move at all' . . . not only belies its apparent ephemerality but also intimates that an internal rather than an external force causes its movement" (68).

13. Fischer-Schreiber, Ehrhard, and Diener, *Shambhala Dictionary*, 260.

14. Qtd. in Shibayama, *A Flower Does Not Talk*, 80.

15. Ibid.

16. Upāsaka Wen-shu (Richard Hunn), ed., introduction to *Empty Cloud: The Autobiography of the Chinese Zen Master Xu-Yun*, trans. Charles Luk (Longmead: Element Books, 1988), xiii, xvi.

17. Dōgen, *Moon in a Dewdrop*, 77.

18. Joan Stambaugh, *Impermanence Is Buddha-Nature: Dōgen's Understanding of Temporality* (Honolulu: Hawaii University Press, 1990), 28.

19. See Dorothy Wordsworth's note (*PW* 2:510–11).

20. Soyen Shaku, *Zen for Americans*, trans. Daisetz Teitaro Suzuki (La Salle, IL: Open Court, 1974), 109.

21. Stryk and Ikemoto, *Zen: Poems, Prayers, Sermons, Anecdotes, Interviews*, 15.

22. Gyomay M. Kubose, *The Center Within* (Union City, CA: Heian International, 1986), 106.

23. Nishitani, *Religion and Nothingness*, 10. Hegel, in contrast, tends to see the rift between consciousness and self-consciousness healed by thought rather than by being:

> The spiritual is distinguished from the natural . . . in that it does not continue a mere stream of tendency, but sunders itself to self-realization. . . . The principle of restoration is found in thought, and thought only: the hand that inflicts the wound is also the hand that heals it. (Qtd. in Geoffrey Hartman, "Romanticism and 'Anti-Self-Consciousness,'" in *Romanticism and Consciousness: Essays in Criticism*, ed. Harold Bloom [New York: Norton, 1970], 49)

24. Stryk and Ikemoto, *Zen: Poems, Prayers, Sermons, Anecdotes, Interviews*, 142.

25. Katsuki Sekida, *Zen Training: Methods and Philosophy*, ed. A. V. Grimstone (New York: Weatherhill, 1975), 34.

26. Nishitani, *Religion and Nothingness*, 5.

27. Adam, *Wandering in Eden*, 82.

28. Hui Neng, *The Sutra of Hui Neng*, 87.

29. Lucien Stryk and Takashi Ikemoto, trans. and eds., *The Penguin Book of Zen Poetry* (London: Penguin Books, 1981), 106.

30. Hisamatsu, *Zen and the Fine Arts*, 16.

31. Thomas Merton, *Mystics and Zen Masters* (New York: Farrar, Straus and Giroux, 1961), 17.

32. Ibid., 17–18.

33. Other poems readers may wish to consult are "The Brothers" (*PW* 2:1), with its tranquil acceptance of death and change; "There Is an Eminence" (*PW* 2:115), in which "deep quiet" and "loneliness" play to free-

dom and acceptance in the midst of things; "Ruth" (*PW* 2:227), which celebrates freedom from the need for specific place and home; "I Wandered
Lonely as a Cloud" (*PW* 2:216), in which freedom from selfhood leads to the
individual's imagined dancing with a sea of daffodils along the banks of
Ullswater; and "Stanzas" (*PW* 4:25), which deals with the theme of relinquishing fears of mortality as one lets go the self.

CHAPTER 7 *WABI:* THE SPIRIT OF POVERTY

1. Stryk, *Encounter with Zen*, 58. *Wabi* is an immensely suggestive
term in Zen culture. "Poverty" is presented here as an inclusive translation
for such related concepts as simplicity, scantiness, and humility. Hisamatsu
aligns *wabi* in Japanese culture with "the Way of Tea" (26); he combines the
term *wabi*, which he defines as "having a 'poverty surpassing riches,'" with
the term *sabi*, which he interprets humanistically as "being seasoned, being
'ancient and graceful,'" to form a composite unity under the heading
"Sublime Austerity," which "is most thoroughly realized in the manner of
being of the Self Without Form" (57). Thomas Merton, in *Zen and the Birds
of Appetite* (New York: New Directions, 1968), compares Zen's sense of
"Sublime Austerity" with the apophatic tradition in Christianity, relying for
a Western expression of the condition on Meister Eckhart's assertion that
"'A man should be so poor that he is not and has not a place for God to act
in'" (9; italics Eckhart's).

2. Aitken, *A Zen Wave*, 74.

3. D. T. Suzuki, "The Morning Glory," *The Way* 2 (November 1950): 3.

4. Stryk and Ikemoto, *Zen Poems of China and Japan*, 32.

5. Ibid., 109.

6. Miyazawa Kenji, "November 3rd," in *From the Country of the
Eight Islands: An Anthology of Japanese Poetry*, trans. and ed. Hiroaki Sato
and Burton Watson (Seattle: University of Washington Press, 1981), 505–6.

7. Dainin Katagiri, *Returning to Silence: Zen Practice in Daily Life*,
ed. Yūkō Conniff and Willa Hathaway (Boston: Shambhala, 1988), 8.

8. Hisamatsu, *Zen and the Fine Arts*, 30–31.

9. Fischer-Schreiber, Ehrhard, and Diener, *Shambhala Dictionary*, 150.

10. Abe, *Zen and Western Thought*, 94.

11. Lao Tzu, *Tao Te Ching*, 8.1–3, 4–5.

12. Ibid., 34.1–7.

13. Kitarō Nishida, *An Inquiry into the Good*, trans. Masao Abe and Christopher Ives (New Haven: Yale University Press, 1990), 166.

14. Stryk and Ikemoto, *Zen Poems of China and Japan*, 21.

15. Stryk, *Encounter with Zen*, 59.

16. Aitken, *A Zen Wave*, 77.

17. Suzuki, "Morning Glory," 1.

18. F. B. Pinion, *A Wordsworth Companion: Survey and Assessment* (New York: Macmillan, 1984), 80.

19. Wei, *Guiding Light of Lao Tzu*, 22–23.

20. Lao Tzu, *Tao Te Ching*, 42.5–8.

21. Ibid., 22.9–10, 11–12; 81.16–17.

22. Ibid., 15.7–14; Stryk and Ikemoto, *Zen Poems of China and Japan*, 126.

23. Lao Tzu, *Tao Te Ching*, 48.7–9.

24. Nishitani, *Religion and Nothingness*, 4–5.

25. Stryk, preface to Stryk and Ikemoto, *Zen Poems of China and Japan*, xlv.

26. Ibid., 140.

27. Wordsworth, *Literary Criticism*, 51. Paul de Man rejects the pleasurableness of such moments, asserting that for Wordsworth "the analogy between mind and nature is an inauthentic covering up of the barrenness of our condition" (*Romanticism and Contemporary Criticism*, 144). Responding to McFarland's notion that all lyrics are " 'evening lyrics' " and that " 'great poems are monuments to our lost selves,' " Karl Kroeber asserts that "While one doesn't expect a modern 'literary personality' to have sympathy for Wordsworth's faith that the processes of life are intrinsically pleasurable, the contemporary Wordsworthians' gravity discourages, because, when not specious, its superficiality tends to conceal the poet's intense emotionality and tragic vision" (257).

28. Aitken, *A Zen Wave*, 78.

29. Christmas Humphreys, *Studies in the Middle Way: Being Thoughts on Buddhism Applied* (London: Curzon Press; Wheaton, IL: Theosophical Publishing House, 1984), 90.

30. Ibid., 91–92.

31. Qtd. in Donald Richie, *Zen Inklings: Some Stories, Fables, Parables, and Sermons* (New York: Weatherhill, 1982), 16.

32. Aitken, *A Zen Wave*, 80.

33. Ibid., 82.

34. Ibid. Modern Wordsworthian scholars tend to reject the purity of the beggar's motifs. For example, Willard Spiegelman, *Wordsworth's Heroes* (Berkeley and Los Angeles: University of California Press, 1985), sees in the beggar's development a complex reciprocity that mirrors a dyadic perception of the surrounding world. Although the beggar reminds us that "We are all pilgrims, sharing an attachment to an earth that is both sustaining and hostile," the old man is "selfish, but the cause of charity in others" (93).

35. Shibayama, *Zen Comments on the* Mumonkan, 10.

36. Cleary, *Zen Essence*, 84.

37. Nishida, *An Inquiry into the Good*, 126.

38. Ibid., 135.

39. Nishitani, *Religion and Nothingness*, 101.

40. Ibid., 148–49.

41. Ibid., 149, xlviii.

42. See for example Hakuin, *The Zen Master Hakuin*, 80.

CHAPTER 8 *AWARE:* THE SPIRIT OF IMPERMANENCE

1. Stryk, *Encounter with Zen*, 59.

2. Stryk and Ikemoto, *Zen: Poems, Prayers, Sermons, Anecdotes, Interviews*, 6.

3. Qtd. in Stryk, *Encounter with Zen*, 59.

4. Ibid.

5. Alan W. Watts, *The Way of Zen* (New York: Vintage Books, 1957), 186–87. Watts's book, it should be kept in mind, is an introductory text, neither exhaustive in its analyses of Zen nor considered particularly authoritative among many Zennists. Philip Kapleau, for example, in *The Three Pillars of Zen: Teaching, Practice, and Enlightenment*, rev. ed. (New York:

Doubleday / Anchor Books, 1980), argues that Watts's books are both weak and misleading in their treatment of Zen practice, particularly the practice of *zazen*, containing no "more than a smattering of information—and some not even that—on this vital subject" (90). Watts's *The Way of Zen*, however, which I mention here as indicative of a tendency in commentary rather than as authoritative in itself, is one of the few texts that mentions the subtle melancholy beneath Zen's poetic treatment of transience. More conspicuous, and possibly more acceptable among Zennists, is the approach Daisetz T. Suzuki takes toward the theme of transience in his monumental *Zen and Japanese Culture* (Princeton: Princeton University Press, 1970). Commenting, for example, on a famous Zen poem which argues that both the pine tree, which "lives for a thousand years," and the morning-glory, which survives for but a day, nevertheless fulfill their destiny, Suzuki writes: "The worth of this moment is not measured by the one thousand years of the one and the single day of the other, but by the moment itself. For this is absolute in each of them. Therefore, beauty is not to be spoiled by the thought of fatalism or of evanescence" (381–82).

6.   Watts, *The Way of Zen*, 187.

7.   Linssen, *Living Zen*, 50.

8.   Friedrich Schiller, *On the Aesthetic Education of Man: In a Series of Letters*, trans. Reginald Snell (New York: Frederick Ungar, 1965), 61–62.

9.   Nishida, *Fundamental Problems of Philosophy*, 39.

10.   Nishida, *An Inquiry into the Good*, 17, 132.

11.   Robert E. Carter, *The Nothingness beyond God: An Introduction to the Philosophy of Nishida Kitarō*, with a foreword by Thomas Kasulas, (New York: Paragon House, 1989), 59. For a protracted discussion of Nishida's concept of change as it relates to Greek notions of time, see especially 22–32.

12.   Abe, *Zen and Western Thought*, 167.

13.   Ibid.; for Abe's comments on emptiness as a self-emptying process, see especially 8, 10, 14, 128, 129.

14.   Ibid., 52.

15.   In his introduction to Nishida's *An Inquiry into the Good*, Masao, Abe makes the related points that in the cultures of China and Japan, "Communication of thought is often indirect, suggestive, and symbolic rather than descriptive and precise" (ix) and that "Many Japanese thinkers steeped in Confucianism and Buddhism were attracted to the theoretical clarity and

logical consistency of Western thought" (viii–ix). Despite whatever claims we can or cannot make for the "theoretical clarity and logical consistency" of Wordsworth's thought, the general discursiveness of his poetry has something as valuable to offer the Eastern literary community as Western philosophy has to offer Eastern philosophical and theological readers.

16. Emphasizing Wordsworth's stoicism, however, many scholars regard the synoptic vision of growth and decay in Wordsworth's later poetry as a defensive reaction to mortality. Thomas McFarland, for example, in "The Wordsworthian Rigidity," in *William Wordsworth: Modern Critical Views*, ed. Harold Bloom (New York: Chelsea House, 1985), says: "The attitude of defense—the armored attitude of the happy warrior—was one that Wordsworth maintained against the assaults of life for more than seventy years. So constant a posture of defense had as concomitant the rigidity that is so notable a feature of his later period" (151). A defender of Wordsworth's later poems, Rachael Trickett argues that Wordsworth's "later experiences were for the most part a prolonged struggle to accept and understand the inevitability of death" ("The Language of Wordsworth's Later Poems," *The Wordsworth Circle* 21 [1990]: 46). Other readers view the later treatment of mortality as the result of Wordsworth's philosophical principles rather than as the deeply felt response to the harmonies of the moment. See, for example, Perkins, *The Quest for Permanence*, 83–91, and Eugene L. Stelzig, "Mutability, Ageing, and Permanence in Wordsworth's Later Poetry," *SEL* 19 (1979): 623–44 passim. No one, to my knowledge, has made an effort to set Wordsworth's later concern with death and change in the context of the spiritual freedom I am claiming for him in this study, a freedom that gave him a deeper, less intense, but more inclusive joy than the ecstacies of his early verse.

17. Shibayama, *Zen Comments on the* Mumonkan, 209.

18. Ibid.

19. Ibid., 211.

20. See, for example, Kitarō Nishida, *Fundamental Problems of Philosophy*, 252.

21. Huang Po, *Zen Teaching on the Transmission of Mind*, 111.

22. *PW* 3:528n.

23. Ibid.

24. Qtd. in Odin, *Process Metaphysics and Hua-yen Buddhism*, xix.

25. Ibid., 3.

26. Ibid.

27. Daisetz Teitaro Suzuki, "Self the Unattainable," in *The Buddha Eye: An Anthology of the Kyoto School*, ed. Frederick Franck (New York: Crossroad, 1991), 17. Paul de Man sees in Wordsworth a "dizziness, a falling or a threat of falling, a *vertige*," but argues that the poet's "evocations of natural, childlike or apocalyptic states of unity with nature often acquire the curiously barren, dead-obsessed emptiness of non-being" (*Romanticism and Contemporary Criticism*, 79, 84).

28. Suzuki, "Self the Unattainable," 17.

29. Ibid., 20.

30. Robert E. Carter, "Paradox, Language, and Reality," in *God, the Self and Nothingness: Reflections Eastern and Western*, ed. Robert E. Carter, 245–61 (New York: Paragon House, 1990), 259. Subsequent references are to *God, the Self and Nothingness*.

31. Nishitani, *Religion and Nothingness*, 96–97.

32. Carter, *God, the Self and Nothingness*, 255. What I am calling Carter's "logic" is really his explication of Nishida's philosophy of self-contradictory identity, which we shall take up in the next two chapters. It should be noted, however, that some thinkers reject the concept of paradox as an appropriate expression of Buddhist emptiness. Explaining that "Perhaps the most straight-forward way to understand emptiness intellectually is in terms of relativity, interdependence, and impermanence—the non-absoluteness of existence," Thomas Cleary, in *Entry into the Inconceivable: An Introduction to Hua-yen Buddhism* (Honolulu: University of Hawaii Press, 1983), writes: "In Buddhist literature we find statements that appear to say 'X is not X' or 'there is no X,' and by literalist interpretation these are all too easily misconstrued as paradoxical, illogical, or simply nonsensical." Cleary goes on to explain that "scriptures in Buddhism are not intended to present doctrines to be accepted or rejected as dogma but have as an important function the provocation of thought and reflection" (18–19).

33. Carter, *God, the Self and Nothingness*, 255.

34. Nishida, *A Study of Good*, 175.

35. Suzuki, "Self the Unattainable," 17.

36. Wordsworth's exploration of Christian themes, together with his frequent appropriation of Christian imagery and symbolic conventions, especially in his later poetry, has been a source of confusion and debate

among his readers. Raymond Dexter Havens, in his monumental work *The Mind of a Poet: A Study of Wordsworth's Thought with Particular Reference to* The Prelude (Baltimore: Johns Hopkins Press, 1941), asserts that Wordsworth's religious beliefs could not be fixed according to a specific institutional faith and that his response to religion was in his experience of joy, solitude, mystery, and nature (179–200). Similar perspectives appear in W. L. Sperry, *Wordsworth's Anti-Climax* (Cambridge: Harvard University Press, 1935; reprint, New York: Russell & Russell, 1966), 191 and in S. F. Gingerich, *Essays in the Romantic Poets* (New York: Macmillan, 1929), 138–39. Despite these early caveats, however, readers continue to emphasize the impact of orthodox religious thought on Wordsworth's poetry. Geoffrey Hartman, for example, argues the presence of a consciously Protestant and Anglican imagination in the later works (see especially *Wordsworth's Poetry*, 190, 273, and his essay, "Blessing the Torrent: On Wordsworth's Later Style," *PMLA* 93 [1978]: 196–204 passim). Richard E. Brantly, *Wordsworth's "Natural Methodism"* (New Haven: Yale University Press, 1975), asserts that Wordsworth is a distinctly Christian poet whose "literary practice can best be understood in terms of his pervasive Evangelical idiom" (xi). Harold Bloom, in *The Visionary Company: A Reading of English Romantic Poetry*, rev. ed. (Ithaca: Cornell University Press, 1971), argues that Wordsworth's use of Christian themes and images signals defeat, "with the light of imagination dying into the light of another day, in which existing conceptions of the world seemed acceptable" (2). John Jones (*Egotistical Sublime*) claims that the later poetry admits of a duality between nature and spirit (172) and that it opposes the principle of reciprocity which *The Recluse* was intended to demonstrate (155). Seymour Lainoff, "Wordsworth's Final Phase: Glimpses of Eternity," *SEL* 1 (autumn 1961), argues that Wordsworth, as he grew older, became increasingly transcendental, relying on symbols conceived as eternity structures to avoid nature and emotion and to support the dualistic theory that the soul is immortal and that the base of the world is God (66–78). Lainoff's claim parallels Paul de Man's assertion, in "Intentional Structure of the Romantic Image" (in Bloom, *Romanticism and Consciousness*, 65–77), that Wordsworth's creation of symbols is primarily an attempt to avoid solitude. The chief defender of Wordsworth's later poetry and its reliance on Christian conventions is Edith Batho, who argues in *The Later Wordsworth* (Cambridge: Cambridge University Press, 1933) that "The Catholicity, in the general as well as the religious sense, of Wordsworth's thought was an offence to the narrower Evangelical orthodoxy of his time, and it has been the cause of bewilderment and confusion to those of a later generation who have not realized the breadth and largeness of the tradition which he inherited" (292). But even Batho's vigorous defense of the later poetry argues the questionable thesis that Wordsworth remained a pantheist all his life (234–37; 245–48). James D. Boulger, "Coleridge on Imagination Revisited," *The Wordsworth Circle* 4 (1973), declares in a more balanced approach that both Wordsworth and Coleridge "are shy of explicit Christian heritage in literature, even after their allegiance to it became fully apparent to both" (21). Though a full-scale exploration of the Christian elements of Wordsworth's art in relation to Zen thought is beyond the scope of this study, an examination of Kenotic Christology in Wordsworth's poetry may provide fruitful insights into his later writing and form a more synoptic context for understanding how the religious impulse in his work relates to other world faiths. A starting point for such a study would be Donald Mitchell's recent and profoundly suggestive *Spirituality and Emptiness: The Dynamics of Spiritual Life in Buddhism and Christianity* (New York: Paulist Press, 1991).

37. Carter, *God, the Self and Nothingness*, 253.

38. Masao Abe, introduction to Nishida, *An Inquiry into the Good*, xxiv.

39. Nishida, *A Study of Good*, 36.

CHAPTER 9 *YUGEN:* THE SPIRIT OF DEPTH

1. Suzuki, *Zen and Japanese Culture*, 220–21n.

2. Hakan Eilert, "Keiji Nishitani (1900–1990)—A Thinker between East and West," *Japanese Religions* 16 (July 1991): 6.

3. Hisamatsu, *Zen and the Fine Arts*, 34.

4. Ibid., 33.

5. Suzuki insists that the response should be primarily emotional: "The feeling is all in all" (*Zen and Japanese Culture*, 221n).

6. Stryk, *Encounter with Zen*, 60–61; Manan's poem is reprinted in Stryk and Ikemoto, *Zen: Poems, Prayers, Sermons, Anecdotes, Interviews*, 14.

7. Stryk, *Encounter with Zen*, 61.

8. Ibid.

9. Qtd. in Shibayama, *A Flower Does Not Talk*, 19–20 (italics Shibayama's).

10. Suzuki, *Manual of Zen Buddhism*, 152.

11. Shibayama, *A Flower Does Not Talk*, 117.

12. Ibid., 122.

13. Ibid.

14. Fischer-Schreiber, Ehrhard, and Diener, *Shambhala Dictionary*, 89.

15. Shibayama, *A Flower Does Not Talk*, 46.

16. Fischer-Schreiber, Ehrhard, and Diener, *Shambhala Dictionary*, 89–90.

17. Shibayama, *A Flower Does Not Talk*, 71.

18. Qtd. in Linssen, *Living Zen*, 233.

19. Stryk and Ikemoto, *Zen Poems of China and Japan*, 24.

20. Linssen, *Living Zen*, 234.

21. Bankei, *The Unborn: The Life and Teaching of Zen Master Bankei 1622–1693*, trans. Norman Waddell (San Francisco: North Point Press, 1984), 35.

22. Stryk and Ikemoto, *Zen: Poems, Prayers, Sermons, Anecdotes, Interviews*, 141.

23. Qtd. in Aitken, *A Zen Wave*, 28.

24. Takashi Ikemoto, preface to Stryk and Ikemoto, *Zen: Poems, Prayers, Sermons, Anecdotes, Interviews*, xviii.

25. The text of "The Ruined Cottage" is that presented in *The Ruined Cottage and The Pedlar*, ed. James Butler (Ithaca: Cornell University Press, 1979), MS.D, 43–75; citations of text identify line numbers from this edition.

26. Irmgard Schloegl, *The Wisdom of the Zen Masters* (New York: New Directions, 1975), 61.

27. Ibid., 48.

28. Lin-chi, *The Zen Teachings of Master Lin-chi*, trans. Burton Watson (Boston: Shambhala, 1993), 52.

29. Schloegl, *Wisdom of the Zen Masters*, 50.

30. Ibid., 56.

31. Nishida, *An Inquiry into the Good*, 61.

32. Ibid., 62–65.

33. Ibid., 74.

34. Qtd. in William Johnston, *The Still Point: Reflections on Zen and Christian Mysticism* (New York: Fordham University Press, 1970), 50.

35. Ibid.

36. Ibid., 132.

37. Kōshō Uchiyama, *Opening the Hand of Thought: Approach to Zen*, trans. Shōhaku Okumura and Tom Wright, ed. Jishō Cary Warner (New York: Penguin/Arkana, 1993), 154–55.

38. Bhadantācariya Buddhaghosa, *The Path of Purification* (*Visuddhimagga*), 2 vols., trans. Bhikkhu Ñyānamoli (Boulder and London: Shambhala, 1976), 2:587.

39. Schloegl, *Wisdom of the Zen Masters*, 21.

40. Jacobson, *Understanding Buddhism*, 130.

41. Sheng-yen, *The Poetry of Enlightenment*, 27, lines 87–88.

42. Ibid., 25–28, lines 109, 2, 116, 117.

43. Qtd. in Shibayama, *A Flower Does Not Talk*, 120–21.

44. Ibid., 121.

45. Ibid.

46. Jacobson, *Understanding Buddhism*, 61–62, 130, 140.

47. Qtd. in Kapleau, *The Three Pillars of Zen*, 228.

48. Ibid., 228–29.

49. Hakuin, *The Zen Master Hakuin*, 118.

50. See, for example, Fischer-Schreiber, Ehrhard, and Diener, *Shambhala Dictionary*, 220–21.

51. Gishin Tokiwa, "Chan (Zen) View of Suffering," *Buddhist-Christian Studies* 5 (1985): 104, 107.

52. Mitchell, *Spirituality and Emptiness*, 188.

53. Albert Low, *The Butterfly's Dream: In Search of the Roots of Zen* (Boston: Tuttle, 1993), 22 (italics Low's), 23, 66, 131.

54. Tokiwa, "Chan (Zen) View of Suffering," 107.

55. Kapleau, *The Three Pillars of Zen*, 191.

56. Sokei-an, *The Zen Eye: A collection of Zen Talks by Sokei-an*, ed. Mary Farkas (Tokyo and New York: Weatherhill, 1993), 47.

57. Uchiyama, *Opening the Hand of Thought*, 157.

58. Andrew Harvey, *A Journey in Ladakh* (Boston: Houghton Mifflin, 1983), 104.

59. Nolan Pliny Jacobson, *The Heart of Buddhist Philosophy* (Carbondale: Southern Illinois University Press, 1988), 14.

60. Dōgen, "Being-Time: Dōgen's Shōbōgenzō Uji," trans. N.A. Waddell, *The Eastern Buddhist* 12 (May 1979): 121–22.

61. Stambaugh, *Impermanence Is Buddha-Nature*, 51.

62. Meisenhelder takes a traditionally Western point of view, arguing that the "She" of the poem "is seen as part of a cosmic process outside natural time" (128). Though not intended as such, a more oriental approach, or at least an interpretation of Wordsworthian spirituality that resonates more closely with Zen thought, appears in Lionel Trilling, "Wordsworth and the Rabbis," in *The Opposing Self: Nine Essays in Criticism* (New York and London: Harcourt Brace Jovanovich, 1950, 1978):   "Much as he [Wordsworth] loved to affirm the dizzy raptures of sentience, of the ear and the eye and the mind, he also loved to move down the scale of being, to say that when the sentient spirit was sealed by slumber, when it was without motion and force, when it was like a rock or a stone or a tree, not hearing or seeing, and passive in the cosmic motion—that even then, perhaps especially then, existence was blessed" (115).

63. J. Hillis Miller, *The Linguistic Moment: From Wordsworth to Stevens* (Princeton: Princeton University Press, 1985), 74–77.

CHAPTER 10 THE LESSON OF THE CONCH

1. Qtd. in Stephen Morris, "Beyond Christianity: Transcendentalism and Zen," *The Eastern Buddhist* 24 (autumn 1991): 59.

2. Huang Po, *Zen Teaching on the Transmission of Mind*, 115.

3. Ibid., 116.

4. Qtd. in J. C. Cleary, trans. and ed., *A Tune Beyond the Clouds: Zen Teachings From Old China* (Berkeley: Asian Humanities Press, 1990), 70.

5. Ibid., 24.

6. Burton Watson, introduction to Chuang Tzu, *Basic Writings*, 6–7.

7. Takashi Ikemoto, preface to Stryk and Ikemoto, *Zen: Poems, Prayers, Sermons, Anecdotes, Interviews*, xvii.

8.   Chuang Tzu, *Basic Writings*, 7–8.

9.   Takashi Ikemoto, introduction to Stryk and Ikemoto, *Zen Poems of China and Japan*, xix.

10.   Chuang Tzu, *Basic Writings*, 140.

11.   Yuanwu, *Zen Letters: Teachings of Yuanwu*, trans. and ed. J. C. Cleary and Thomas Cleary (Boston: Shambhala, 1994), 72. Yuanwu's reference to Tao, like my own tendency here to articulate similarities between Chuang Tzu and Masao Abe, should not be taken as an assertion of the identity of Taoism and Buddhism. While there are strong similarities between the two systems, individual parallels, as in all comparative studies, can be overstated and lead to reductive synoptic claims. Ray Grigg, for example, in a recent study, *The Tao of Zen* (Boston: Tuttle, 1994), tends, perhaps, to overstate the similarities between Taoism and Zen when he says at the head of his text: "Zen is Taoism disguised as Buddhism" (xiii). J. C. Cleary, in his essay "T'aego's World," a historical introduction to *A Buddha from Korea: The Zen Teachings of T'aego*, trans. J. C. Cleary, 1–77 (Boston: Shambhala, 1988), takes a more balanced approach when he says that "With the rise of Zen to intellectual prominence by the tenth century, both Confucianism and Taoism were reshaped under its influence" (23).

12.   Cleary, *A Tune Beyond the Clouds*, 24.

13.   Abe, *Zen and Western Thought*, 75.

14.   Ibid.

15.   Taigan Takayama, foreword to Stryk and Ikemoto, *Zen Poems of China and Japan*, xiv–xv.

16.   Takashi Ikemoto, preface to Stryk and Ikemoto, *Zen: Poems, Prayers, Sermons, Anecdotes, Interviews*, xix.

17.   Nishida, *An Inquiry into the Good*, xxx.

18.   Ibid., 3.

19.   Ibid., xxxiii.

20.   Thomas Kasulis, foreword to Carter, *The Nothingness beyond God*, xiv.

21.   Nishida, *Last Writings*, 49, 51–52.

22.   Ibid., 53.

23.   Ibid., 78.

24. Ibid., 71.

25. Ibid., 101.

26. Ibid., 108.

27. Ibid., 70.

28. Carter, *The Nothingness beyond God*, 62, 67.

29. Ibid., 146.

30. Ibid.

31. Ibid., 147.

32. Nishida, *Last Writings*, 107.

33. Qtd. in Kusan Sunim, *The Way of Korean Zen*, trans. Martine Fages, ed. Stephen Batchelor (New York: Weatherhill, 1985), 43.

34. Nishida, *Last Writings*, 53.

35. Qtd. in Thomas Cleary, trans. and ed., *Timeless Spring: A Soto Zen Anthology* (Tokyo and New York: Weatherhill/Wheelwright Press, 1980), 67–68.

36. Uchiyama, *Opening the Hand of Thought*, xviii.

37. Qtd. in Dōgen, *Shōbōgenzō: A Complete English Translation of Dōgen Zenji's Shōbōgenzō (The Eye and Treasury of the True Law)*, vol. 1, trans. Kōsen Nishayama and John Stevens (Sendai, Japan: Daihokkaikaku, 1975), 53.

38. Masao Abe, "Nishida's Philosophy of 'Place,'" *International Philosophical Quarterly* 28 (1988): 355n.

39. Nishida, *Last Writings*, 110.

40. Ta Hui, *Swampland Flowers: Letters and Lectures of Zen Master Ta Hui*, trans. Christopher Cleary (New York: Grove Press, 1977), 29.

41. See, for example, Fischer-Schreiber, Ehrhard, and Diener, *Shambhala Dictionary*, 184, 159.

42. Kusan Sunim, *The Way of Korean Zen*, 50.

43. Shibayama, *Zen Comments on the* Mumonkan, 298.

44. In the 1850 version of *The Prelude*, Wordsworth presents the dream as his own. The following summary in the text relates book 5, lines 55–139 of the 1805 *Prelude*.

45. Johnston, *Still Point*, 51.

46. Stewart W. Holmes and Chimyo Horioka, *Zen Art for Meditation* (Tokyo and Rutland, VT: Tuttle, 1973), 77.

47. Qtd. in Blyth, *Zen in English Literature*, 277.

48. Kasulis, *Zen Action / Zen Person*, 88, 115.

49. Shinkichi Takahashi, *Triumph of the Sparrow: Zen Poems of Shinkichi Takahashi*, trans. Lucien Stryk and Takashi Ikemoto (Urbana: University of Illinois Press, 1986), 46, lines 1–4. Subsequent references to Takahashi's poetry identify line numbers from this edition.

50. Ibid., 7–8.

51. Nishitani, *Religion and Nothingness*, 148.

52. Carter, *God, the Self and Nothingness*, xxxi.

53. Shibayama, *A Flower Does Not Talk*, 160. Western deconstructive analyses of the diluvial images in Wordsworth do not effectively alter the perception that the world is one thing, art something else. Tilottama Rajan, for example, *Dark Interpreter: The Discourse of Romanticism* (Ithaca: Cornell University Press, 1980), argues that *The Prelude* "deconstructs its own assumptions by associating nature itself with the cataclysms of historical experience, which are described in natural metaphors of flood and deluge that make chaos and discontinuity at least as primary as organic unity . . . "(16). Rajan still opposes the flood as chaos to the primacy of organic unity, implicitly aligning creativity only with the formative process of the universe and not with what on the surface appears to be the destructive energies of the cosmos. The problem with deconstructive efforts, as David A. Dilworth indicates in his postscript to Nishida's *Last Writings*, is that "Derrida's text can only legitimately operate in a dyadic structure. It is constrained to do so by its own two-voiced logic of *differance*, which situates it at the adversative edge of presence and absence in the play of textual significations" (137). For an opposing view, see Michelle Yeh, "Beyond Negation: Zen as Deconstruction," in *Zen in American Life and Letters*, ed. Robert S. Ellwood, 17–32 (Malibu: Undena Publications, 1987).

54. Tony Barnstone and Willis Barnstone, trans. and eds., "The Ecstasy of Stillness," introduction to *Laughing Lost in the Mountains: Poems of Wang Wei* (Hanover and London: University Press of New England, 1991), xxi.

55. Ibid.

56. Takahashi, *Triumph of the Sparrow*, 115.

57. Nishitani, *Religion and Nothingness*, 102.

58. Low, *The Butterfly's Dream*, 48.

CONCLUSION   FORGETTING THE MIND

1. Cheng Chien Bhikshu, trans., *Sun-Face Buddha: The Teachings of Ma-tsu and the Hung-chou School of Ch'an* (Berkeley: Asian Humanities Press, 1992), 62.

2. See Abrams, *Natural Supernaturalism*, 78.

3. Kenneth K. Inada, "The American Involvement with Śūnyatā: Prospects," in *Buddhism and American Thinkers*, ed. Kenneth K. Inada and Nolan Pliny Jacobson (Albany: State University of New York Press, 1984), 75.

4. Takuan Soho, *Immovable Wisdom: The Art of Zen Strategy; The Teachings of Takuan Soho*, comp. and trans. Nobuko Hirose (Shaftesbury, Dorset, and Rockport, MA: Element Books, 1992), 42.

5. Nishitani, *Religion and Nothingness*, 9.

6. Merton, *Mystics and Zen Masters*, 245.

7. Urs App, "'Dun,'" 55.

8. Katagiri, *Returning to Silence*, 97, 101. It is important to understand that the tranquillity Katagiri exalts is not a mere nonintellectual quietism—"an endemic disease of Chan and Zen so prevalent that Chan and Zen literature abound with warnings against it," writes Thomas Cleary in his introduction to the *Book of Serenity* (Hudson, NY: Lindisfarne Press, 1990), xxxvii. It is, rather, the deep tranquillity we associate with nature or the empty way of things. "I like stillness," says Takuan Soho (1573–1645), "but this is not the stillness of a withered tree and a stone in a thicket. It is the stillness which is ceaselessly moving and yet tranquil" (10).

9. Mu Soeng Sunim, *Heart Sutra: Ancient Buddhist Wisdom in the Light of Quantum Reality* (Cumberland, RI: Primary Point Press, 1991), 22.

10. Bodhidharma, *The Zen Teaching of Bodhidharma*, trans. Red Pine (San Francisco: North Point Press, 1989), 67.

11. Ibid., 117n.

12. Adam, *Wandering in Eden*, 81.

13. Soho, *Immovable Wisdom*, 136.

14. Wordsworth's arrangement of his poems has long been a trouble-some issue for his readers. James Scoggins, in *Imagination and Fancy: Complementary Modes in the Poetry of Wordsworth* (Lincoln: University of Nebraska Press, 1966), maintains that "The classification of poems according to the faculties most active in their creation or according to genre or occasion has not proved to be . . . 'a commentary unostentatiously directing the reader's attention' toward some unified impression and effect" (55). See also Judith B. Herman, "The Poet as Editor: Wordsworth's Edition of 1815," *The Wordsworth Circle* 9 (1978): 82–87; Gene W. Ruoff, "Critical Implications of Wordsworth's 1815 Categorization, with Some Animadversions on Binaristic Commentary," *The Wordsworth Circle* 9 (1978): 75–82; and Frances Ferguson, *Wordsworth: Language as Counter-Spirit* (New Haven: Yale University Press, 1977), 35–95.

15. Here, as in much of Wordsworth's later poetry, which relies frequently on the formal conventions of genre and classical allusion, the dark powers of chaos, confusion, and fear are harmonized, transcended, or incorporated into the totality of the poet's being with a steady, quiet confidence that many readers simply cannot accept. Preferring the drama of confrontation, a quality frequently aligned with Wordsworth's earlier poetry, to the gentle lyrics of acceptance prevalent among the later works, Geoffrey Durrant, *William Wordsworth* (Cambridge: Cambridge University Press, 1969), writes: "The readiness to look at the destructive forces of the world and record their power over men's lives is an essential part of Wordsworth's genius. With its fading after 1805 Wordsworth became what the Victorians valued him for—an official comforter and reassurer. With the fading of the tragic vision, the power of joy which is its counterpart also vanishes" (159). Critics applying the dualisms of Blake's terminology to Wordsworth's quest for peace—for a "Perfect Contentment, Unity entire," as he said in 1800 in "Home at Grasmere" (*PW* 5:313–39), an early concern reflected throughout his life—view the poet's hard-won serenity as a potential trap of Beulah. M. H. Abrams, for example, calls this longing for contentment "an habitual refuge from 'intellectual war' " (*Natural Supernaturalism*, 261). Richard Gravil, "Wordsworth's Last Retreat," *Charles Lamb Bulletin* 43 (1983), refers to it as an "embowerment," a retreat from what he regards as the quintessentially Romantic discovery that humankind's proper "realm is that of Becoming" (61, 60).

16. David Pollack, trans. and ed., *Zen Poems of the Five Mountains* (New York: Crossroad Publishing and Scholars Press, 1985), 47.

17. Holmes and Horioka, *Zen Art for Meditation*, 77.

18. Mu Soeng, *Heart Sutra*, 20.

19. Sokei-an, *The Zen Eye*, 47.

BIBLIOGRAPHY

Abe Masao. "Emptiness is Suchness." In *The Buddha Eye: An Anthology of the Kyoto School*, ed. Frederick Franck, 203–7. New York: Cross Road, 1982.

———. "Nishida's Philosophy of 'Place.'" *International Philosophical Quarterly* 28 (1988): 355–71.

———. "The Problem of Self-Centeredness as the Root-Source of Human Suffering." *Japanese Religions* 15 (July 1989): 15–25.

———. *A Study of Dōgen: His Philosophy and Religion*. Ed. Steven Heine. Albany: State University of New York Press, 1992.

———. *Zen and Western Thought*. Ed. William R. LaFleur. Honolulu: University of Hawaii Press, 1985.

Abrams, M. H. *The Correspondent Breeze: Essays on English Romanticism*. New York: Norton, 1984.

———. *Doing Things with Texts: Essays in Criticism and Critical Theory*. Ed. with a foreword by Michael Fischer. New York: Norton, 1989.

———. Foreword to *William Wordsworth and the Age of English Romanticism*, by Jonathan Wordsworth, Michael C. Jaye, and Robert Woof, vii–xi. New Brunswick: Rutgers University Press, 1987.

———. *Natural Supernaturalism: Tradition and Revolution in Romantic Literature*. New York: Norton, 1971.

Adam, Michael. *Wandering in Eden: Three Ways to the East within Us*. New York: Knopf, 1976.

Aitken, Robert. *A Zen Wave: Bashō's Haiku and Zen*. New York: Weatherhill, 1978.

Ames, Roger T. "Putting the *Te* Back into Taoism." In *Nature in Asian Traditions of Thought: Essays in Environmental Philosophy*, ed. J. Baird Callicott and Roger T. Ames, 113–44. Albany: State University of New York Press, 1989.

Andô Shôei. *Zen and American Transcendentalism—An Investigation of One's Self*. Tokyo: Hokuseido Press, 1970.

App, Urs. "'Dun': A Chinese Concept as a Key to 'Mysticism' in East and West." *The Eastern Buddhist* 26 (autumn 1993): 31–72.

Bankei. *The Unborn: The Life and Teaching of Zen Master Bankei 1622–1693*. Trans. Norman Waddell. San Francisco: North Point Press, 1984.

Barnstone, Tony, and Willis Barnstone, trans. "The Ecstasy of Stillness." Introduction to *Laughing Lost in the Mountains: Poems of Wang Wei*, xv–lxii. Hanover and London: University Press of New England, 1991.

Batho, Edith C. *The Later Wordsworth*. Cambridge: Cambridge University Press, 1933.

Bielefeldt, Carl. *Dōgen's Manuals of Zen Meditation*. Berkeley and Los Angeles: University of California Press, 1988.

Blackstone, Bernard. *The Lost Travellers: A Romantic Theme with Variations*. London: Longmans, 1962.

Bloom, Harold. *The Visionary Company: A Reading of English Romantic Poetry*. Rev. ed. Ithaca: Cornell University Press, 1971.

———, ed. *Romanticism and Consciousness: Essays in Criticism*. New York: Norton, 1970.

Blyth, R. H. *Zen in English Literature and Oriental Classics*. Tokyo: Hokuseido Press, 1942.

Bodhidharma. *The Zen Teaching of Bodhidharma*. Trans. Red Pine. San Francisco: North Point Press, 1989.

Boulger, James D. "Coleridge on Imagination Revisited." *The Wordsworth Circle* 4 (1973): 13–24.

Brantly, Richard E. *Wordsworth's "Natural Methodism."* New Haven: Yale University Press, 1975.

Brissenden, R. F. *Virtue in Distress: Studies in the Novel of Sentiment from Richardson to Sade*. New York: Harper & Row, 1974.

Buddhaghosa, Bhadantācariya. *The Path of Purification (Visuddhimagga)*. 2 vols. Trans. Bhikkhu Ñyānamoli. Boulder and London: Shambala, 1976.

Carter, Robert E. *The Nothingness beyond God: An Introduction to the Philosophy of Nishida Kitarō*. With a foreword by Thomas Kasulis. New York: Paragon House, 1989.

———, ed. *God, the Self and Nothingness: Reflections Eastern and Western*. New York: Paragon House, 1990.

Chan Wing-Tsit, trans. and comp. *A Source Book in Chinese Philosophy*. Princeton: Princeton University Press, 1963.

Chang Chung-yuan. *Creativity and Taoism: A Study of Chinese Philosophy, Art, and Poetry*. New York: Harper & Row, 1970.

———, trans. *Original Teachings of Ch'an Buddhism: Selected from The Transmission of the Lamp*. New York: Pantheon Books, 1969.

———, trans. *Tao: A New Way of Thinking*. New York: Harper & Row, 1975.

Cheng Chien Bhikshu, trans. *Sun-Face Buddha: The Teachings of Ma-tsu and the Hung chou School of Ch'an.* Berkeley: Asian Humanities Press, 1992.

Chuang Tzu. *Basic Writings.* Trans. Burton Watson. New York: Columbia University Press, 1964.

Cleary, J. C., trans. "T'aego's World." In *A Buddha from Korea: The Zen Teachings of T'aego,* 1–77. Boston; Shambhala, 1988.

———, trans. and ed. *A Tune Beyond the Clouds: Zen Teachings From Old China.* Berkeley: Asian Humanities Press, 1990.

Cleary, Thomas. *Entry into the Inconceivable: An Introduction to Hua-yen Buddhism.* Honolulu: University of Hawaii Press, 1983.

———, trans. *Book of Serenity.* Hudson, NY: Lindisfarne Press, 1990.

———, trans. *No Barrier: Unlocking the Zen Koan.* New York: Bantam Books, 1993.

———, trans. and ed. *Timeless Spring: A Soto Zen Anthology.* Tokyo and New York: Weatherhill/Wheelwright Press, 1980.

———, trans. and ed. *Zen Essence: The Science of Freedom.* Boston: Shambhala, 1989.

Coe, Charles N. *Wordsworth and the Literature of Travel.* New York: Bookman Associates, 1961.

Coleridge, Samuel Taylor. *Biographia Literaria.* 2 vols. Ed. J. Shawcross. London: Oxford University Press, 1907.

Conze, Edward, trans. *Buddhist Wisdom Books: Containing* The Diamond Sutra *and* The Heart Sutra. London: G. Allen & Unwin, 1958.

Crook, John, ed. Introduction to *Catching a Feather on a Fan: A Zen Retreat with Master Sheng Yen,* 1–20. Longmead, GB: Element Books, 1991.

Darlington, Beth. "Reclaiming Dorothy Wordsworth's Legacy." In *The Age of William Wordsworth: Critical Essays on the Romantic Tradition,* ed. Kenneth R. Johnston and Gene W. Ruoff, 160–72. New Brunswick: Rutgers University Press, 1987.

de Man, Paul. "Intentional Structure of the Romantic Image." In *Romanticism and Consciousness: Essays in Criticism,* ed. Harold Bloom, 65–77. New York: Norton, 1970.

———. *Romanticism and Contemporary Criticism: The Gauss Seminar and Other Papers.* Ed. E. S. Burt, Kevin Newmark, and Andrzej Warminski. Baltimore: Johns Hopkins University Press, 1993.

De Martino, Richard. *The Zen Understanding of Man.* Ann Arbor, MI: University Microfilms International, 1969.

Dennison, Sean. Historical Introduction to *Lao-tzu's Treatise on The Response of the Tao.* By Li Ying-chang. Trans. Eva Wong, xv–xxv. San Francisco: HarperCollins, 1994.

Dōgen. "Being-Time: Dōgen's Shōbōgenzō Uji." Trans. N. A. Waddell. *The Eastern Buddhist* 12 (May 1979): 114–29.

———. *Moon in a Dewdrop: Writings of Zen Master Dōgen.* Ed. Kazuaki Tanahashi. San Francisco: North Point Press, 1985.

———. *Shōbōgenzō: A Complete English Translation of Dōgen Zenji's Shōbōgenzō (The Eye and Treasury of the True Law).* vol. 1. Trans. Kōsen Nishiyama and John Stevens. Sendai, Japan: Daihokkaikaku Publishing Co., 1975.

———. *Sounds of Valley Streams: Enlightenment in Dōgen's Zen.* Trans. Francis H. Cook. Albany: State University of New York Press, 1989.

Drew, John. *India and the Romantic Imagination.* Delhi: Oxford University Press, 1987.

Durrant, Geoffrey. *William Wordsworth.* Cambridge: Cambridge University Press, 1969.

Eilert, Hakan. "Keiji Nishitani (1900–1990)—A Thinker between East and West." *Japanese Religions* 16 (July 1991): 1–13.

Enns, Amelie. "The Subject-Object Dichotomy in Heidegger's *A Dialogue on Language* and Nishitani's *Religion and Nothingness.*" *Japanese Religions* 15 (January 1988): 38–48.

Ferguson, Frances. *Wordsworth: Language as Counter-Spirit.* New Haven: Yale University Press, 1977.

Fischer-Schreiber, Ingrid, Franz-Karl Ehrhard, and Michael S. Diener. *The Shambhala Dictionary of Buddhism and Zen.* Trans. Michael H. Kohn. Boston: Shambhala, 1991.

Garber, Frederick. *The Autonomy of the Self from Richardson to Huysmans.* Princeton: Princeton University Press, 1982.

Gaull, Marilyn. *English Romanticism: The Human Context.* New York: Norton, 1988.

Gingerich, S. F. *Essays in the Romantic Poets.* New York: Macmillan, 1929.

Glen, Heather. *Vision and Disenchantment: Blake's "Songs" and Wordsworth's "Lyrical Ballads".* Cambridge: Cambridge University Press, 1983.

Gravil, Richard. "Wordsworth's Last Retreat." *Charles Lamb Bulletin* 43 (1983): 54–67.

Grigg, Ray. *The Tao of Zen.* Boston: Tuttle, 1994.

Guenther, Herbert. "Tasks Ahead." *Journal of the International Association of Buddhist Studies* 4, no. 2 (1981): 115–23.

Haefner, Joel. "Displacement and the Reading of Romantic Space." *The Wordsworth Circle* 23 (1992): 151–56.

Hakeda Yoshito S., trans. *The Awakening of Faith.* New York: Columbia University Press, 1967.

Hakuin. *The Zen Master Hakuin: Selected Writings*. Trans. Philip B. Yampolsky. New York: Columbia University Press, 1971.

Hanh, Thich Nhat. "Commentary on *The Heart Sutra*." *Tricycle: The Buddhist Review* 1 (spring 1992): 26–27.

———. *The Heart of Understanding: Commentaries on the* Prajñaparamita Heart Sutra. Ed. Peter Levitt. Berkeley: Parallax Press, 1988.

Harding, Anthony J. "Forgetfulness and the Poetic Self in 'Home at Grasmere.'" *The Wordsworth Circle* 22 (1991): 109–18.

Hartman, Geoffrey. "Blessing the Torrent: On Wordsworth's Later Style." *PMLA* 93 (1978): 196–204.

———. "Romanticism and 'Anti-Self-Consciousness.'" In *Romanticism and Consciousness: Essays in Criticism*, ed. Harold Bloom, 46–56. New York: Norton, 1970.

———. *The Unremarkable Wordsworth*. With a foreword by Donald G. Marshall. Minneapolis: University of Minnesota Press, 1987.

———. *Wordsworth's Poetry, 1787–1814*. New Haven: Yale University Press, 1971.

Harvey, Andrew. *A Journey in Ladakh*. Boston: Houghton Mifflin, 1983.

Havens, Raymond Dexter. *The Mind of a Poet: A Study of Wordsworth's Thought with Particular Reference to* The Prelude. Baltimore: Johns Hopkins University Press, 1941.

Hayden, John O. *William Wordsworth and the Mind of Man: The Poet as Thinker*. New York: Bibli O'Phile Publishing, 1992.

Heidegger, Martin. *Discourse on Thinking*. Trans. John M. Anderson and E. Hans Freund. New York: Harper & Row, 1959.

———. *On the Way to Language*. Trans. Peter D. Hertz. New York: Harper & Row, 1971.

Heine, Steven. *Dōgen and the Kōan Tradition: A Tale of Two Shōbōgenzō Texts*. Albany: State University of New York Press, 1994.

Herman, Judith B. "The Poet as Editor: Wordsworth's Edition of 1815." *The Wordsworth Circle* 9 (1978): 82–87.

Hilliard, Kevin. "German Philosophy and Criticism." In *A Handbook to English Romanticism*, ed. Jean Raimond and J. R. Watson, 115–18. New York: St. Martin's Press, 1992.

Hisamatsu Shin'ichi. *Zen and the Fine Arts*. Trans. Gishin Tokiwa. Tokyo: Kodansha International, 1971.

Hodgson, John A. *Wordsworth's Philosophical Poetry, 1797–1814*. Lincoln: University of Nebraska Press, 1980.

Holmes, Stewart W., and Chimyo Horioka. *Zen Art for Meditation*. Tokyo, and Rutland, VT: Tuttle, 1973.

Horseman, E. A. "The Design of Wordsworth's *Prelude*." In *Wordsworth's Mind and Art*, comp. and ed. A. W. Thomson, 95–109. Edinburgh: Oliver and Boyd, 1969.

Huang Po. *The Zen Teaching of Huang Po on the Transmission of Mind.* Trans. John Blofeld. New York: Grove Press, 1958.

Hui Neng. *The Sutra of Hui Neng.* In *The Diamond Sutra and The Sutra of Hui Neng*, trans. A. F. Price and Wong Mou-Lam, 1–112. Boston: Shambhala, 1985.

Humphreys, Christmas. *Studies in the Middle Way: Being Thoughts on Buddhism Applied.* London: Curzon Press; Wheaton, IL: Theosophical Publishing House, 1984.

Huxley, Aldous. *The Devils of Loudun.* London: Folio Society, 1986.

Inada, Kenneth K. "The American Involvement with Śūnyatā: Prospects." In *Buddhism and American Thinkers*, ed. Kenneth K. Inada and Nolan Pliny Jacobson, 70–88. Albany: State University of New York Press, 1984.

———, trans. and ed. *Nāgārjuna: A Translation of his Mūlamadhyamakakārikā with an Introductory Essay.* Tokyo: Hokuseido Press, 1970.

Jacobson, Nolan Pliny. *Buddhism and the Contemporary World: Change and Self-Correction.* Carbondale: Southern Illinois University Press, 1983.

———. *Buddhism: The Religion of Analysis.* Carbondale: Southern Illinois University Press, 1966.

———. *The Heart of Buddhist Philosophy.* Carbondale: Southern Illinois University Press, 1988.

———. *Understanding Buddhism.* Carbondale: Southern Illinois University Press, 1986.

Johnston, Kenneth R. "The Idiom of Vision." In *New Perspectives on Coleridge and Wordsworth: Selected Papers from the English Institute*, ed. with a foreword by Geoffrey H. Hartman, 1–39. New York: Columbia University Press, 1972.

Johnston, William. *The Still Point: Reflections on Zen and Christian Mysticism.* New York: Fordham University Press, 1970.

Jones, John. *The Egotistical Sublime: A History of Wordsworth's Imagination.* London: Chatto and Windus, 1970.

Joshu Sasaki. *Buddha is the Center of Gravity.* Trans. Fusako Akinu. San Cristobal, NM: Lama Foundation, 1974.

Kapleau, Philip. *The Three Pillars of Zen: Teaching, Practice, and Enlightenment.* Rev. ed. New York: Doubleday/Anchor Books, 1980.

Kasulis, T. P. *Zen Action/Zen Person*. Honolulu: University of Hawaii Press, 1981.

Katagiri Dainin. *Returning to Silence: Zen Practice in Daily Life*. Ed. Yūkō Conniff and Willa Hathaway. Boston: Shambhala, 1988.

Kenji Miyazawa. "November 3rd." In *From the Country of the Eight Islands: An Anthology of Japanese Poetry*, trans. and ed. Hiroaki Sato and Burton Watson, 505–6. Seattle: University of Washington Press, 1981.

Kroeber, Karl. *William Wordsworth*. In *The English Romantic Poets: A Review of Research and Criticism*, 4th ed., ed. Frank Jordan, 255–339. New York: Modern Language Association of America, 1985.

Kubose, Gyomay M. *The Center Within*. Union City, CA: Heian International, 1986.

Kusan Sunim. *The Way of Korean Zen*. Trans. Martine Fages. Ed. Stephen Batchelor. New York: Weatherhill, 1985.

Lainoff, Seymour. "Wordsworth's Final Phase: Glimpses of Eternity." *SEL* 1 (autumn 1961): 63–79.

Lao Tzu. *Tao Te Ching*. Trans. Stephen Addiss and Stanley Lombardo. Indianapolis: Hackett Publishing, 1993.

Levinson, Marjorie. *Wordsworth's Great Period Poems: Four Essays*. Cambridge: Cambridge University Press, 1986.

Lin-chi. *The Zen Teachings of Master Lin-chi*. Trans. Burton Watson. Boston: Shambhala, 1993.

Linssen, Robert. *Living Zen*. Trans. Diana Abrahams-Curiel. New York: Grove Press, 1958.

Low, Albert. The *Butterfly's Dream: In Search of the Roots of Zen*. Boston: Tuttle, 1993.

Masunaga Reiho. *The Sōtō Approach to Zen*. Tokyo: Layman Buddhist Society Press, 1958.

McFarland, Thomas. "The Wordsworthian Rigidity." In *William Wordsworth: Modern Critical Views*, ed. Harold Bloom, 151–71. New York: Chelsea House, 1985.

McGann, Jerome. *The Romantic Ideology: A Critical Investigation*. Chicago: University of Chicago Press, 1983.

Meisenhelder, Susan Edwards. *Wordsworth's Informed Reader: Structures of Experience in His Poetry*. Nashville: Vanderbilt University Press, 1988.

Merton, Thomas. *Mystics and Zen Masters*. New York: Farrar, Straus and Giroux, 1961.

———. *Zen and the Birds of Appetite*. New York: New Directions, 1968.

Merzel, Dennis Genpo. *The Eye Never Sleeps: Striking to the Heart of Zen*. Ed. Stephen Muho Proskauer. Boston: Shambhala, 1991.

Miller, J. Hillis. *The Linguistic Moment: From Wordsworth to Stevens*. Princeton: Princeton University Press, 1985.

Milton, John. *Complete Poems and Major Prose*. Ed. Merrit Y. Hughes. Indianapolis: Odyssey Press, 1957.

Mitchell, Donald. *Spirituality and Emptiness: The Dynamics of Spiritual Life in Buddhism and Christianity*. New York: Paulist Press, 1991.

Moorman, Mary. *William Wordsworth, A Biography: The Early Years, 1770–1803*. Oxford: Clarendon Press, 1957.

Morris, Stephen. "Beyond Christianity: Transcendentalism and Zen." *The Eastern Buddhist* 24 (autumn 1991): 33–68.

Mu Soeng Sunim. *Heart Sutra: Ancient Buddhist Wisdom in the Light of Quantum Reality*. Cumberland, RI: Primary Point Press, 1991.

Nicholson, Mervyn. "The New Cosmology in Romantic Poetry." *The Wordsworth Circle* 20 (1989): 123–31.

Nishida Kitarō. *Fundamental Problems of Philosophy: The World of Action and the Dialectical World*. Trans. David A. Dilworth. Tokyo: Sophia University Press, 1970.

———. *An Inquiry into the Good*. Trans. Masao Abe and Christopher Ives. New Haven: Yale University Press, 1990.

———. *Last Writings: Nothingness and the Religious Worldview*. Trans. David A. Dilworth. Honolulu: University of Hawaii Press, 1987.

———. *A Study of Good*. Trans. V. H. Viglielmo. New York: Greenwood Press, 1988.

Nishitani Keiji. *Religion and Nothingness*. With a foreword by Winston L. King. Trans. Jan Van Bragt. Berkeley and Los Angeles: University of California Press, 1982.

Odin, Steve. *Process Metaphysics and Hua-yen Buddhism: A Critical Study of Cumulative Penetration vs. Interpenetration*. Albany: State University of New York Press, 1982.

Perkins, David. *The Quest for Permanence: The Symbolism of Wordsworth, Shelley, and Keats*. Cambridge: Harvard University Press, 1959.

Pinion, F. B. *A Wordsworth Companion: Survey and Assessment*. New York: Macmillan, 1984.

Pollack, David, trans. and ed. *Zen Poems of the Five Mountains*. New York: Crossroad Publishing and Scholars Press, 1985.

Radcliff, Benjamin, and Amy Radcliff. *Understanding Zen*. Boston: Tuttle, 1993.

Rahula, Walpola. *What the Buddha Taught*. Rev. ed. New York: Grove Press, 1974.

Rajan, Tilottama. *Dark Interpreter: The Discourse of Romanticism*. Ithaca: Cornell University Press, 1980.

Richie, Donald. *Zen Inklings: Some Stories, Fables, Parables, and Sermons*. New York: Weatherhill, 1982.

Robinson, Jeffrey C. "The Structure of Wordsworth's *Memorials of a Tour in Scotland, 1803*." *PLL* 13 (1977): 54–70.

Ross, Nancy Wilson. *Three Ways of Asian Wisdom: Hinduism, Buddhism, Zen and Their Significance for the West*. New York: Simon and Schuster, 1966.

Rudy, John G. "Beyond Vocation and Ego: Self-displacement in Wordsworth's 1803 *Memorials*." *SEL* 29 (1989): 637–53.

———. "Wordsworth and the Zen Void." *Thought: A Review of Culture and Idea* 65 (1990): 127–42.

Ruoff, Gene W. "Critical Implications of Wordsworth's 1815 Categorization, with Some Animadversions on Binaristic Commentary." *The Wordsworth Circle* 9 (1978): 75–82.

Rzepka, Charles J. *The Self as Mind: Vision and Identity in Wordsworth, Coleridge, and Keats*. Cambridge: Harvard University Press, 1986.

Sayama, Mike K. *Samadhi: Self-Development in Zen, Swordsmanship, and Psychotherapy*. Albany: State University of New York Press, 1986.

Schapiro, Barbara. "Wordsworth's Visionary Imagination: A New Critical Context." *The Wordsworth Circle* 18 (1987): 137–43.

Schiller, Friedrich. *On the Aesthetic Education of Man: In a Series of Letters*. Trans. Reginald Snell. New York: Frederick Ungar, 1965.

Schloegl, Irmgard. *The Wisdom of the Zen Masters*. New York: New Directions, 1975.

Scoggins, James. *Imagination and Fancy: Complementary Modes in the Poetry of Wordsworth*. Lincoln: University of Nebraska Press, 1966.

Sekida Katsuki. *Zen Training: Methods and Philosophy*. Ed. A. V. Grimstone. New York: Weatherhill, 1975.

Senzaki Nyogen and Ruth Strout McCandless, comps., trans., and eds. *Buddhism and Zen*. New York: Wisdom Library, 1953.

Sessan Amakuki. "Hakuin's 'Song of Meditation.'" In *A First Zen Reader*, comp. and trans. Trevor Leggett, 65–199. Rutland, VT: Tuttle, 1960.

Shaku Soyen. *Zen for Americans*. Trans. Daisetz Teitaro Suzuki. La Salle, IL: Open Court, 1974.

Sheng-yen. *The Sword of Wisdom: Lectures on the Song of Enlightenment*. Ed. Christopher Marano. Elmhurst, NY: Dharma Drum Publications, 1990.

————, trans. and ed. *The Poetry of Enlightenment: Poems by Ancient Ch'an Masters*. Elmhurst, NY: Dharma Drum Publications, 1987.

Shibayama Zenkei. *A Flower Does Not Talk: Zen Essays*. Trans. Sumiko Kudo. Rutland, VT: Tuttle, 1970.

————. *Zen Comments on the* Mumonkan. Trans. Sumiko Kudo. San Francisco: Harper & Row, 1974.

Simpson, David. *Wordsworth and the Figurings of the Real*. Atlantic Highlands, NJ: Humanities Press, 1982.

————. *Wordsworth's Historical Imagination: The Poetry of Displacement*. New York and London: Methuen, 1987.

Soho Takuan. *Immovable Wisdom: The Art of Zen Strategy; The Teachings of Takuan Soho*. Comp. and trans. Nobuko Hirose. Shaftesbury, Dorset, and Rockport, MA: Element Books, 1992.

Sokei-an. *The Zen Eye: A Collection of Zen Talks by Sokei-an*. Ed. Mary Farkas. Tokyo and New York: Weatherhill, 1993.

Sperry, W. L. *Wordsworth's Anti-Climax*. Cambridge: Harvard University Press, 1935. Reprint, New York: Russell & Russell, 1966.

Spiegelman, Willard. *Wordsworth's Heroes*. Berkeley and Los Angeles: University of California Press, 1985.

Stambaugh, Joan. *Impermanence Is Buddha-Nature: Dōgen's Understanding of Temporality*. Honolulu: Hawaii University Press, 1990.

Stelzig, Eugene L. "Mutability, Ageing, and Permanence in Wordsworth's Later Poetry." *SEL* 19 (1979): 623–44.

Stryk, Lucien. *Encounter with Zen: Writings on Poetry and Zen*. Athens: Ohio University Press/Swallow Press, 1981.

Stryk, Lucien, and Takashi Ikemoto, trans. and eds. *The Penguin Book of Zen Poetry*. London: Penguin Books, 1981.

————, trans. and comps. *Zen Poems of China and Japan: The Crane's Bill*. With a foreword by Taigan Takayama. New York: Grove Weidenfeld, 1973.

————, trans. and eds. *Zen: Poems, Prayers, Sermons, Anecdotes, Interviews*. 2d ed. Athens: Ohio University Press/Swallow Press, 1981.

Suzuki Daisetz Teitaro. *Manual of Zen Buddhism*. New York: Grove Press, 1960.

————. "The Morning Glory." *The Way* 2 (November 1950): 1–4.

————. "Self the Unattainable." In *The Buddha Eye: An Anthology of the Kyoto School*, ed. Frederick Franck, 15–21. New York: Crossroad, 1991.

————. *Zen and Japanese Culture*. Princeton: Princeton University Press, 1970.

———. *The Zen Doctrine of No-Mind: The Significance of the Sūtra of Hui-neng (Wei-lang)*. Ed. Christmas Humphreys. London: Rider, 1983.

Ta Hui. *Swampland Flowers: Letters and Lectures of Zen Master Ta Hui*. Trans. Christopher Cleary. New York: Grove Press, 1977.

Takahashi Shinkichi. *Triumph of the Sparrow: Zen Poems of Shinkichi Takahashi*. Trans. Lucien Stryk and Takashi Ikemoto. Urbana: University of Illinois Press, 1986.

Thomas, Keith G. *Wordsworth and Philosophy: Empiricism and Transcendentalism in the Poetry*. Ann Arbor, MI: UMI Research Press, 1989.

Tokiwa Gishin. "Chan (Zen) View of Suffering." *Buddhist-Christian Studies* 5 (1985): 103–29.

Trickett, Rachael. "The Language of Wordsworth's Later Poems." *The Wordsworth Circle* 21 (1990): 46–51.

Trilling, Lionel. "Wordsworth and the Rabbis." In *The Opposing Self: Nine Essays in Criticism*, 104–32. New York: Harcourt Brace Jovanovich, 1978.

Twitchell, James B. "Romanticism and Cosmic Consciousness." *The Centennial Review* 19 (1975): 287–307.

Uchiyama Kōshō. *Opening the Hand of Thought: Approach to Zen*. Trans. Shōhaku Okumura and Tom Wright. Ed. Jishō Cary Warner. New York: Penguin/Arkana, 1993.

Watts, Alan W. *The Way of Zen*. New York: Vintage Books, 1957.

Wei, Henry. *The Guiding Light of Lao Tzu: A New Translation and Commentary on the Tao Te Ching*. Wheaton, IL: Theosophical Publishing House, 1982.

Wei Wu Wei. *Open Secret*. Hong Kong: Hong Kong University Press, 1970.

Weiskel, Thomas. *The Romantic Sublime: Studies in the Structure and Psychology of Transcendence*. Baltimore: Johns Hopkins University Press, 1986.

Welbon, Guy Richard. *The Buddhist Nirvana and Its Western Interpreters*. Chicago: University of Chicago Press, 1968.

Wen-shu Upāsaka (Richard Hunn), ed. Introduction to *Empty Cloud: The Autobiography of the Chinese Zen Master Xu-Yun*, trans. Charles Luk. Longmead: Element Books, 1988.

Wilbur, Ken. *The Spectrum of Consciousness*. Wheaton, IL: Theosophical Publishing House, 1977.

Wlecke, Albert O. *Wordsworth and the Sublime*. Berkeley and Los Angeles: University of California Press, 1973.

Wolfson, Susan J. *The Questioning Presence: Wordsworth, Keats, and the Interrogative Mode in Romantic Poetry*. Ithaca: Cornell University Press, 1986.

Wordsworth, Jonathan. "The Mind as Lord and Master: Wordsworth and Wallace Stevens." *The Wordsworth Circle* 14 (1983): 183–91.

Wordsworth, William. *Literary Criticism of William Wordsworth*. Ed. Paul M. Zall. Lincoln: University of Nebraska Press, 1966.

———. *The Poetical Works of William Wordsworth*. 5 vols. Ed. Ernest de Selincourt. 2d ed., rev. Helen Darbishire. Oxford: Clarendon Press, 1952–59.

———. *The Prelude: A Parallel Text*. Ed. J. C. Maxwell. New Haven: Yale University Press, 1971.

———. "The Ruined Cottage." In *The Ruined Cottage and The Pedlar*, ed. James Butler, MS.D, 43–75. Ithaca: Cornell University Press, 1979.

Wordsworth, William, and Dorothy Wordsworth. *The Letters of William and Dorothy Wordsworth: The Early Years, 1787–1805*. Ed. Ernest de Selincourt, rev. Chester L. Shaver. Oxford: Clarendon Press, 1967.

Wu, Qian-Zhi. "The Wordsworthian Imagination: Seeing Nature as IT IS— A Taoist Reading of Wordsworth." Ph.D. diss., Columbia University, 1987. Abstract in *Dissertations Abstract International*, 49 (1988): 514A.

Yeh, Michelle. "Beyond Negation: Zen as Deconstruction." In *Zen in American Life and Letters*, ed. Robert S. Ellwood, 17–32. Malibu: Undena Publications, 1987.

Yuanwu. *Zen Letters: Teachings of Yuanwu*. Trans. and ed. J. C. Cleary and Thomas Cleary. Boston: Shambhala, 1994.

Zimmerman, Michael E. *Eclipse of the Self: The Development of Heidegger's Concept of Authenticity*. Athens: Ohio University Press, 1981.

INDEX

Abe Masao, 13, 15, 66, 79, 103, 175, 177, 184; on being and becoming, 27, 34; on change (impermanence), 135, 136; on emptiness emptying itself, 101-102, 106, 116-117, 135, 178, 179, 210; on human expression, 148, 175, 177-178, 234n. 15

Abrams, M. H., 57, 213-214n. 4, 246n. 15; on marriage metaphor in Wordsworth, 10; on reciprocity of mind and nature, 12, 215-216n. 13

the absolute, 14, 91, 147, 148, 180, 183, 191; and intersection with phenomenal, 91

acceptance, 66, 81, 92-93, 107, 114-115, 131, 135, 138, 187, 188-189, 140-141, 209

action intuition (*kōiteki-chokkan*), 178-179

Adam, Michael, 28, 61, 82, 110, 205

aesthetics: of change, 81, 190-191, 194-196; and form, 111, 136-137, 173, 194; and relation of artificial and natural, 141, 142, 191-193; and suffering, 164

Aitken, Robert, 40, 45, 124, 125, 126

Ames, Roger T., 56

analytic mind, 66-67, 69-70, 78, 109-110, 141, 151, 175. *See also* intellect, mind

Andô Shôei, 62-63

anti-intellectualism, 67, 153

App, Urs, 92

Aristotle, 133-134

art: as cosmic expression, 178; as self-emptying process, 173, 181-182, 183, 195-196, 197; and self-preservation, 190; as separate realm, 138, 156; as voice of nature, 191-197

atheism, 214n. 8

autonomy, 114, 205-206

awakening, 79, 91-92, 101-102, 110, 112, 150-154, 173, 176, 185, 190-191; and Zen method of no-method, 92-93. *See also* enlightenment, *satori*

The Awakening of Faith, 90-91

aware (impermanence), ix, 9, 131-148, 149

Bankei, 154-155

Barnstone, Tony, 192, 194

Barnstone, Willis, 192, 194

basho (place of absolute nothingness), 179, 184-185, 190, 193-194; and poetry, 196-197

Bashō, 116-117, 118; "The Goi," 45; "In plum-flower scent," 40; "*Nazuna*," 113; "This Road," 126

beauty, 131-132, 162

being: and becoming, 34; and nonbeing, 60-61, 99-100; as time, 41

Bhikkhu (one who begs for food), 124, 130

Blackstone, Bernard, 223n. 10

Blofeld, John, 37-38

259

PR 5892 .P5 R83 1996
Rudy, John G., 1943-
Wordsworth and the Zen mind

PR 5892 .P5 R83 1996
Rudy, John G., 1943-
Wordsworth and the Zen mind

JAN 27.

DATE	ISSUED TO
FEB 03	Daniel Wright

CONCORDIA UNIVERSITY LIBRARY
2811 NE Holman St.
Portland, OR 97211